The Poetics and Ethics of (Un-) Grievability in Contemporary Anglophone Fiction

The working hypothesis of the book is that, since the 1990s, an increasing number of Anglophone fictions are responding to the new ethical and political demands arising out of the facts of war, exclusion, climate change, contagion, posthumanism and other central issues of our post-trauma age by adapting the conventions of traditional forms of expressing grievability, such as elegy, testimony or (pseudo-)autobiography. Situating themselves in the wake of Judith Butler's work on (un-)grievablability, the essays collected in this volume seek to cast new light on these issues by delving into the socio-cultural constructions of grievability and other types of vulnerabilities, invisibilities and inaudibilities linked with the neglect and/or abuse of non-normative individuals and submerged groups that have been framed as disposable, exploitable and/or unmournable by such determinant factors as sex, gender, ethnic origin, health, thereby refining and displacing the category of subalternity associated with the poetics of postmodernism.

Susana Onega is Emeritus Professor of English Literature at the University of Zaragoza and a member of the *Academia Europaea*. She has written extensively on contemporary British literature, narrative poetics, ethics and trauma. She is currently editing with Jean-Michel Ganteau *The Brill Handbook on Literary Criticism and Theory*.

Jean-Michel Ganteau is Professor of Contemporary British Literature at the University Paul-Valéry Montpellier 3. He is the editor of *Études britanniques contemporaines* and has authored *The Ethics and Aesthetics of Vulnerability in Contemporary British Literature* (Routledge, 2015) and *The Ethics and Aesthetics of Attention in Contemporary British Literature* (Routledge, 2023).

Routledge Studies in Contemporary Literature

54 **Of Love and Loss**
Hardy Yeats Larkin
Tom McAlindon

55 **Real Recognition**
What Literary Texts Reveal About Social Validation and the
Politics of Identity
Marie-Elisabeth Lei Pihl

56 **Connie Willis's Science Fiction**
Doomsday Every Day
Carissa Turner Smith

57 **"All Will Be Swept Away"**
Dimensions of Elegy in the Poetry of Paul Muldoon
Wit Pietrzak

58 **The Poetics and Ethics of (Un-)Grievability in Contemporary
Anglophone Fiction**
Edited by Susana Onega and Jean-Michel Ganteau

59 **Representing Vulnerabilities in Contemporary Literature**
Miriam Fernández-Santiago and Cristina M. Gámez-Fernández

60 **The Poetics and Ethics of Attention in Contemporary British
Narrative**
Jean-Michel Ganteau

For more information about this series, please visit: https://www.
routledge.com/Routledge-Studies-in-Contemporary-Literature/book-
series/RSCL

The Poetics and Ethics of (Un-)Grievability in Contemporary Anglophone Fiction

Edited by
Susana Onega and
Jean-Michel Ganteau

NEW YORK AND LONDON

First published 2023
by Routledge
605 Third Avenue, New York, NY 10158

and by Routledge
4 Park Square, Milton Park, Abingdon, Oxon, OX14 4RN

Routledge is an imprint of the Taylor & Francis Group, an informa business

© 2023 selection and editorial matter, Susana Onega and
Jean-Michel Ganteau individual chapters, the contributors

The right of Susana Onega and Jean-Michel Ganteau to be
identified as the authors of the editorial material, and of the
authors for their individual chapters, has been asserted in
accordance with sections 77 and 78 of the Copyright, Designs
and Patents Act 1988.

All rights reserved. No part of this book may be reprinted
or reproduced or utilised in any form or by any electronic,
mechanical, or other means, now known or hereafter invented,
including photocopying and recording, or in any information
storage or retrieval system, without permission in writing from
the publishers.

Trademark notice: Product or corporate names may be
trademarks or registered trademarks, and are used only for
identification and explanation without intent to infringe.

ISBN: 9781032389752 (hbk)
ISBN: 9781032389769 (pbk)
ISBN: 9781003347811 (ebk)

DOI: 10.4324/9781003347811

Typeset in Sabon
by codeMantra

Contents

List of Contributors	vii
Acknowledgements	xi

Introduction: The Poetics and Ethics of (Un-)Grievability in Contemporary Anglophone Fiction JEAN-MICHEL GANTEAU AND SUSANA ONEGA	1

PART I
The Presence of History — 13

1 Trading Relations, the Evil of Violence and the Ungrievability of the Other in David Mitchell's *The One Thousand Autumns of Jacob de Zoet* SUSANA ONEGA	15
2 Undermining the Hierarchy of Grief in Rachel Seiffert's *A Boy in Winter* PAULA ROMO-MAYOR	36
3 Escaping "Dead Time": The Temporal Ethics of (Un-)Grievability in Ali Smith's *The Accidental* KATIA MARCELLIN	55

PART II
Grieving the Earth — 73

4 "How bold to mix the dreamings": The Ethics and Poetics of Mourning in Alexis Wright's *The Swan Book* BÁRBARA ARIZTI	75

vi *Contents*

5 From Elegy to Apocalypse: Ecological Grief and Human
Grievability in Ben Smith's *Doggerland*   96
ANGELO MONACO

PART III
Outcasts   117

6 Ungrievable Incest: Ecology and Kinship in Michael
Stewart's *Ill Will*   119
MAITE ESCUDERO-ALÍAS

7 (Un-)Grieving Celestial in Toni Morrison's *Love*   135
PAULA MARTÍN-SALVÁN

PART IV
Contamination   151

8 What Remains of (Un-)Grievability in Hollinghurst's and
Tóibín's AIDS Fiction   153
JOSÉ M. YEBRA

9 Overcoming Grief and Salvaging Memory: Rebecca
Makkai's *The Great Believers*   169
GIULIO MILONE

PART V
After the Subject   185

10 Grieving for the Subhuman in *Never Let Me Go* by
Kazuo Ishiguro   187
SYLVIE MAUREL

11 The Grievability of the Non-Human: Ian McEwan's
Machines Like Me   202
JEAN-MICHEL GANTEAU

Index   217

Contributors

Bárbara Arizti is Senior Lecturer in English Literature at the University of Zaragoza and a member of the competitive research team "Contemporary Narrative in English." Since 2021, she works within the University Research Institute for Employment, Digital Society and Sustainability (IEDIS-University of Zaragoza). Arizti is a specialist in contemporary Australian literature, the relationship between ethics and the novel, Trauma Studies, Memory Studies and Transmodernity. One of her most recent publications is the special issue *Beneath the Waves: Feminisms in the Transmodern Era* for *The European Legacy: Toward New Paradigms* (2021), edited together with her colleagues Silvia Pellicer-Ortín and Silvia Martínez-Falquina.

Maite Escudero-Alías is Senior Lecturer in English and Irish Literature at the University of Zaragoza and a member of the "Contemporary Narrative in English" research team and the Research Institute for Employment, Digital Society and Sustainability (IEDIS). Her research focuses on feminism, lesbian criticism, queer theory and animacies, on which she has published articles and book chapters. She is also the author of *Long Live the King: A Genealogy of Performative Genders* (2009) and co-editor of *Traumatic Memory and the Ethical, Political and Transhistorical Functions of Literature* (2017).

Jean-Michel Ganteau is Professor of Contemporary British Literature at the University Paul-Valéry Montpellier 3, and a member of the Academia Europaea. He is the editor of *Études britanniques contemporaines* and the author of four monographs among which are *The Ethics and Aesthetics of Vulnerability in Contemporary British Literature* (2015) and *The Ethics and Aesthetics of Attention in Contemporary British Literature* (2022). He has co-edited fourteen collective books with Christine Reynier and Susana Onega. He has published extensively on contemporary British fiction, with a special interest in the ethics of affects, trauma criticism and theory, the ethics of vulnerability and the ethics of attention.

viii *Contributors*

Katia Marcellin is a postgraduate student at the University Paul Valéry in Montpellier (France), currently writing her thesis under the supervision of Professor Jean-Michel Ganteau. Her research focuses on the representation of trauma in contemporary British literature, in particular the ways in which novels exploring various forms of trauma related to war, gender, sexuality, poverty or precarity develop an ethical approach to trauma based on a metaleptic expression of time and causality. She has published articles on Ali Smith's *Hotel World* and *The Accidental* in *Caliban* and Harry Parker's *Anatomy of a Soldier* in *English: Journal of the English Association.*

Paula Martín-Salván is Professor at the University of Córdoba (Spain) where she teaches English and American Literature. Her research focuses on the representation of communities in modernist and postmodernist fiction, and on contemporary critical theory. She has co-edited the volumes *Community in Twentieth Century Fiction* (Palgrave, 2013) and *New Perspectives on Community and the Modernist Subject* (Routledge, 2017) and is the author of monographs on Graham Greene (Palgrave, 2015) and Don DeLillo (UCOPress, 2009). Her most recent research focuses on secrecy and democracy in Toni Morrison, Colson Whitehead, Don DeLillo and Amy Waldman.

Sylvie Maurel is Senior Lecturer in the Department of English of the University of Toulouse-Jean Jaurès, France. She specializes in twentieth- and twenty-first-century British literature. She is a member of Cultures Anglo-Saxonnes (CAS, EA 801). She has published a monograph (Palgrave Macmillan) and a number of articles on Jean Rhys's novels and short fiction. She has also published articles on contemporary rewritings of fairy tales, Daphne du Maurier, Ian McEwan and A.S. Byatt. Her fields of interest are intertextuality, rewriting, memory and forgetting, precariousness and precarity.

Giulio Milone is a PhD Student in English Literature at the University of Pisa, where he is working on a research project on the forms and mutations of the contemporary British family novel. His academic interests include 21st century Anglo-American literature, trauma theory, life writing and film adaptations.

Angelo Monaco, PhD, from the University of Pisa, is Researcher in English Language and Translation at the University Aldo Moro at Bari, Italy. He has published articles and chapters on contemporary Anglophone fiction, with a special interest in postcolonialism, trauma studies and ecocriticism, in edited volumes (Cambridge Scholars, Routledge, Transcript) or in such journals as *Commonwealth Essays and Studies, Ecozon@, Enthymema, Estudios Irlandeses, Impossibilia, ISLE* and *Postcolonial Text*. He is the author of *Jhumpa Lahiri. Vulnerabilità e resilienza* (ETS Edizioni, 2019).

Susana Onega is Emeritus Professor of English Literature, a member of the Research Institute for Employment, Digital Society and Sustainability (IEDIS) at the University of Zaragoza and a member of the *Academia Europaea*. She was granted the Miguel Servet research award in 2021. She has led numerous competitive research projects and teams and has written extensively on contemporary fiction, narrative theory, ethics and trauma and the transition from postmodernity to transmodernity. She is the author of five monographs and the editor or co-editor of fifteen volumes of collected essays. She is currently editing with Jean-Michel Ganteau *The Brill Handbook on Literary Criticism and Theory*.

Paula Romo-Mayor is Research Fellow in the Department of English and German Philology of the University of Zaragoza, a member of the competitive research team "Contemporary Narrative in English," funded by the Aragonese Government, and a member of the Research Institute for Employment, Digital Society and Sustainability (IEDIS). She is currently enrolled in the Doctoral Programme offered by the University of Zaragoza and is writing her PhD thesis on the work of Rachel Seiffert under the supervision of Prof. Susana Onega and Dr Silvia Pellicer-Ortín. Her main research interests lie in contemporary British fiction and the representation of trauma, memory and ethics, particularly when engaged in the structures of perpetration and complicity.

José M. Yebra is Senior Lecturer in English at the University of Zaragoza (Spain). He has widely published on the fiction of Alan Hollinghurst, Colm Tóibín and Naomi Alderman, among others. He is the author of *The Poetics of Otherness and Transition in Naomi Alderman's Fiction* (Cambridge Scholars Publishing, 2020) and the co-editor, with Jessica Aliaga-Lavrijsen, of *Transmodern Perspectives on Contemporary Literatures in English* (Routledge, 2019). His latest articles explore issues such as gender, sexual orientation, transmodernity, trauma and the crisis of democracy and have appeared in prestigious journals on literary studies. He is part of the Excellence Research Group "Contemporary Narratives in English" in the Department of English and German Philology of the University of Zaragoza.

Acknowledgements

The idea for the present volume originated in a monographic seminar of the same title organised by the editors in the Fifteenth International Conference of the European Society for the Study of English (ESSE) that took place at the University of Lyon (France) in August–September 2021. But the idea of devoting a seminar and a volume of collected essays to this subject should be set in the context of a wider ongoing collaborative research activity carried out by the editors along the last two decades that has materialised in the co-edition of seven volumes: *The Ethical Component in Experimental British Fiction since the 1960s* (Cambridge Scholars Publishing, 2007); *Ethics and Trauma in Contemporary British Fiction* (Rodopi, 2011); *Trauma and Romance in Contemporary British Literature* (Routledge 2013); *Contemporary Trauma Narratives: Liminality and the Ethics of Form* (Routledge, 2014); *Victimhood and Vulnerability in 21st-Century Fiction* (Routledge, 2017); *The Wounded Hero in Contemporary Fiction: A Paradoxical Quest* (Routledge, 2018); and *Transcending the Postmodern: The Singular Response of Literature to the Transmodern Paradigm* (Routledge, 2020).

The co-authorship of the Introduction, the co-editing of the book and the chapter on Ian McEwan by Jean-Michel Ganteau are part of a project funded by the French Ministry of Education through the laboratory to which he belongs (EMMA-EA 741) and a competitive research project in which he participates as external researcher, funded by the Spanish Ministry of Economy, Industry, and Competitiveness (MICINN) (code PID2021-124841NB-I00). The co-authorship of the Introduction, the co-editing of the book and the chapter on David Mitchell by Susana Onega form part of her ongoing research activity as member of the excellency team "Contemporary Narrative in English" (code H03_17R), financed by the Government of Aragón and the European Development Fund (ERDF) and the mentioned competitive research project, funded by the Spanish Ministry of Economy, Industry, and Competitiveness (MICINN) (code PID2021-124841NB-I00). Together with their thanks to the Government of Aragón and the European Development Fund (ERDF), the authors would like to express their gratitude to the French Ministry of Education and the Spanish Ministry of Economy, Industry and Competitiveness, for making the existence of this book possible.

Introduction

The Poetics and Ethics of (Un-) Grievability in Contemporary Anglophone Fiction

Jean-Michel Ganteau and Susana Onega

Emmanuel Levinas's formulation of the notion of absolute alterity in *Totality and Infinity* (1961), and Derrida's response to it in his essay "Violence and Metaphysics" (originally entitled "L'Écriture et la Différance," 1964), lie at the origin of what is now widely known as the "ethical turn" in the related fields of philosophy and critical theory that climaxed in the 1980s. This turn involved a move away from the normative and deontic notions of humanist ethics, based on the primacy of the autonomous subject, and towards a non-deontic, non-cognitive, non-foundational and non-ontological ethics that precluded the possibility of totalising the other in a reductive, essentialist way. As is well known, Levinas refined his theory of alterity in subsequent works, particularly in *Totality and Infinity* (1969), *Humanism of the Other* (1972) and *Otherwise Than Being, or, Beyond Essence* (1974), where he revised his initial position on "the face of the other" in response to Derrida's reading of his work. While, according to Heidegger, the authenticity of my *Dasein* is revealed through my death, according to Levinas the fact that I am beholden to the face, that the face of the other speaks to me, calls to me, makes me realise my own vulnerability. In the rationalist tradition represented by Descartes, Kant and Husserl, this vulnerability would justify the urge of the self to kill or destroy the other, as does Hegel, for instance, in his master-slave dialectic, thus enhancing the sovereignty of the ego. By contrast, Levinas's ethical stance is based on the radical assertion that the face cannot be killed. This ethical prohibition contests the humanist notion of self-identity in that it does not stem from the subject but is rather the product of a relational practice. In the field of literary criticism, this new type of relational ethics, expounded, among others, by thinkers like Andrew Gibson (1999), Robert Eaglestone (1997) or Drucilla Cornell (1992), was so at home with experimentalism that some critics, taking their lead from Zygmunt Bauman (1993), called it a "'postmodern' ethics" (see Ganteau and Onega 2007, 1–9).

Looking back at the devastating critique of the rationalist tradition initiated by Levinas from a present-day perspective, it seems evident that the notion of a non-violent encounter with the face of the other is still dominant in Western thought, even though Levinas's ethics of

DOI: 10.4324/9781003347811-1

2   Jean-Michel Ganteau and Susana Onega

alterity has undergone what Christopher Watkin describes as a process of radical questioning by philosophers with a Marxist background, like Alain Badiou or Slavoj Žižek (Watkin 50–51). As Watkin points out, for Badiou, the whole focus on alterity is dangerously wrong in that it presupposes a reliance on Levinas's God and, what is more, often degrades the other, as "this celebrated 'other' is acceptable only if he is a good other—which is to say what, exactly, if not the same as us?" (Badiou 24, quoted in Watkin 51). According to Badiou, another problem posed by Levinas's ethics is the difficulty of "recognizing the Same, given that 'there are as many differences, say, between the Chinese peasants and a young Norwegian professional as between myself and anybody at all, including myself. As many, but also, then, *neither more nor less*'" (Badiou 26, quoted in Watkin 51; original emphasis). Echoing Badiou, Žižek similarly "argues that 'the tension between the same and the other is secondary with regard to the non-coincidence of the same with itself,' and that 'what Levinas fails to include in the scope of the 'human' is the inhuman itself, a dimension which eludes the face-to-face relationship between humans'" (Žižek 36, 111, quoted in Watkin 51). Badiou's and Žižek's arguments against the ethics of alterity on the grounds that Levinas's definition of the other is not all-inclusive and that his vision of the same fails to account for the irreducible plurality of human and inhuman existence bring to mind what Sheila Benhabib describes as one of the political paradoxes of modernity, synthesised by Hannah Arendt as "the demand that 'the right to have rights' ought to be respected for all humans [coupled with] the deepest awareness that to be a right-bearing individual is to belong to a political commonwealth that defends and upholds our right to have rights" (Benhabib 20). As Benhabib notes, this paradox brings to the fore the need "to do justice to the singular as well as the universal, or in [her] terms, to the standpoint of the concrete as well as the generalized other" (85). As Benhabib further explains in an interview with Shlomo Malka on the Israeli-Palestinian conflict, Levinas defined the other as "the neighbor, who is not necessarily kin, but who can be," but he then went on to admit that "if your neighbor attacks another neighbor or treats him unjustly, [...] then we are faced with the problem of knowing who is right and who is wrong, who is just and who is unjust" (Levinas 1989, 292–93, quoted in Benhabib 88). This admission, which shows Levinas "rather surprisingly oscillating between the language of infinite responsibility and Zionist militancy" (Benhabib 89), reinforces Badiou's and Žižek's outlook on the limited scope of Levinas's definition of the other. Generalising a great deal, it may be stated that the desire to do away with this limitation lies at the heart of Judith Butler's turn to ethics, initiated with *Antigone's Claim. Kinship between Life and Death* (2000) and *Precarious Life. The Powers of Mourning and Violence* (2004), and further developed in her later works, most

Introduction 3

notably in *Frames of War* (2009) and in the more recent *The Force of Non-Violence* (2020).

In *Precarious Life*, Butler starts from the observation of what may be called an ontological vulnerability that she envisages more particularly as a "vulnerability to loss" "that precedes the I" (2004, 19, 31). This leads her to postulate that community is based on exposure to loss, implying that "each of us is constituted politically in part by virtue of the social vulnerability of our bodies—as a site of desire and physical vulnerability, as a site of publicity at once assertive and exposed" (20). By postulating a common vulnerability, the reality of dependence and interdependence among subjects, Butler is situating all types of human beings, including the unjust or evil other, on the same ontological label. Her rejection of the possibility of any individual sovereignty hones out a new category of grievability based on a logic of radical relationality. From this relational perspective, grievability is always already enmeshed in the social and, in Butler's committed writings, in the political.

Written in the global context of violence and warfare triggered by the terrorist attacks in Washington and New York on 9/11, 2001 that brought along the promulgation of the state of exception by the Bush administration as part of the "War on Terror," *Precarious Life* offers a thought-provoking ethical and political reflection on the question of "Who counts as human? Whose lives count as lives?" (Butler 2004, 20). As she observes, the victims of the terrorist attacks were worthy of obituaries in the US press and honoured with emotionally charged private and public acts of mourning, while the deaths of other subjects were declared ungrievable and their lives deprived of all basic human rights. Thus, suspect terrorists were submitted to a regime of "indefinite detention" (50–100) in Guantánamo and Abu-Ghraib, without trial or legal defence, or killed by drones, together with their families, in their own countries. What is more, as Butler points out, not only suspect terrorists were deemed unworthy of mourning or of holding human rights, Muslims in general, no matter whether they were US citizens, and other types of non-normative individuals, such as, for instance, the AIDS victims that had been dying in the previous decades, were considered ungrievable (34–35). Her denunciation of the terrible excesses committed under the banner of the War on Terror brings to mind Giorgio Agamben's contention in *Homo Sacer: Sovereign Power and Bare Life* (1998) that the state of emergency is used by the modern State to deprive certain subjects of their ontological right of citizenship. Agamben equates the bare life created by the modern State to the life of *homo sacer* (sacred man), an "obscure figure of archaic Roman law, in which human life is included in the juridical order [. . .] solely in the form of its exclusion (that is, of its capacity to be killed)" (8). Echoing this definition, Butler contends that the social determination of the ungrievability of certain subjects creates a sense of derealisation that facilitates the perpetuation of violence:

> If violence is done against those who are unreal, then, from the perspective of violence, it fails to injure or negate those lives since those lives are already negated. But they have a strange way of remaining animated and so must be negated again (and again). They cannot be mourned because they are always already lost or, rather, never 'were,' and they must be killed, since they seem to live on, stubbornly, in this state of deadness. Violence renews itself in the face of the apparent inexhaustibility of its object.
>
> (2004, 33–34)

Building on such observations, Butler disclosed what she called "a hierarchy of grief" (32), a notion that she was later to come back to and refine in *Frames of War* into what she designated as a "differential distribution of grievability" (Butler 2009, 24) or, in *The Force of Non-Violence*, into the more explicit "*unequal* distribution of grievability" (Butler 2020, 75; emphasis added). Admittedly, the words mourning, grief and grievability do not exactly bear the same meaning, but they form part of the same complex experience of subjects ruled by biopolitics in the modern State. Therefore, Butler defines grievability as the *capacity* to be grieved or mourned collectively and officially, as is implied by her "Ethico-Political" take on the situation. This is also why, in *The Force of Non-Violence*, she defines grievability through its prospective dimension, as opposed to the retrospective quality of grief or mourning:

> There is a difference between someone's being grieved and that same person's bearing, in their living being, a characteristic of grievability. The second involves the conditional tense: those who are grievable *would* be mourned if their lives *were* lost; the ungrievable are those whose loss would leave no trace, or perhaps barely a trace.
>
> (Butler 2020, 74–75; original emphasis)

A few lines down, in conformity with her political orientation and with her pragmatic insistence on the necessity of an *equality* of grievability, Butler goes on to assess the category in terms of the protection that it affords to the living. In fact, to be grievable implies to be considered, taken care of, so that one's safety becomes an option and may develop into a political objective:

> To say that a life is grievable is to claim that life, even before it is lost, is, or will be, worthy of being grieved on the occasion of its loss; the life has value in relation to mortality. One treats a person differently if one brings the sense of grievability of the other to one's

ethical bearing towards the other. If an other's loss would register as a loss, would be marked and mourned, and if the prospect of loss is feared, and precautions are thus taken to safeguard that life from harm and destruction, then *our* ability to value and safeguard a life depends upon an ongoing sense of its grievability [...].

(75; emphasis added)

In these lines, grievability is synonymous with protection, potential and insurance. And it becomes clear how, as an ethical category (predicated on the taking into account of, and craving for alterity), equal grievability becomes a political proposal, all the more so as the first-person pronoun ("*our* ability to value and safeguard a life") appeals to the reader's (yours and mine) responsibility and action towards the implementation of an equal distribution of grievability.

One of the related issues that are essential to Butler's work involves the norms through which grievability becomes detectable. Such a concern appears as early as *Precarious Life*, when, following in Foucault's wake, she avers that "vulnerability is dependent on various norms of recognition" (Butler 2004, 43). This proposal appears in a context in which Butler works on the examples of obituaries and on the theme of mourning, which suggests that she also means that grievability depends on similar recognition norms. This idea comes to fruition and is given pride of place in *Frames of War*, where the eponymous frames raise the triple issue of the "recognizability," "apprehension" and "intelligibility" of grievability (Butler 2009, 6), thereby soliciting an ethics and a politics of attention to the grievable. Indeed, paying attention to the grievable implies the practice of an ethics of alterity that sets great store by taking into account the officially grievable and those who do not qualify as "normal" according to the frames of perception that are generally accepted, hence used. Such is the argument on which Butler's book relies and that is signposted from the first page: "if lives are not apprehended as such through certain epistemological frames, they are never lived" (1). Her words again echo Agamben's contention that "bare life" is the new kind of inhuman life that modernity necessarily creates within itself and that it simultaneously attempts to eliminate because it can no longer tolerate its presence (Agamben 11). This implies that the (bare) lives of ungrievable others are lost not *after* they have been lived, but from the start, through a radical incapacitation that is also a deprivation. This is re-formulated later, in a pithy aphorism that captures the essence of the conundrum raised by grievability: "there is no life and no death without a relation to some frame" (Butler 2009, 7).

This is tantamount to considering vulnerability, precariousness and grievability as perceptual issues, "since those whose lives are not 'regarded' as potentially grievable, and hence valuable, are made to bear the burden of starvation, underemployment, legal disenfranchisement,

6 *Jean-Michel Ganteau and Susana Onega*

and differential exposure to violence and death" (Butler 2009, 25). Of course, such considerations refer to a specific conception of perception not as a mere quality but as an activity that has to be developed so that we are trained to realise that there are such things as frames and that those could be defined differently or put around other areas of the perceptible. This is what French philosopher Guillaume Le Blanc reminds us of, in his study of social invisibility (*L'invisibilité sociale*), when he contends that perception is not a natural quality but "rather a social activity that introduces into the perceiving subject's environment elements that appear as relevant, worthy to be perceived, and other elements as irrelevant" (Le Blanc 2009, 13; our translation). Le Blanc, who has largely contributed to the dissemination of Butler's ideas in France, redefines perception as a capacity to be exerted and as a lever towards empowerment. Like Butler, Le Blanc never forgets that social invisibility—as both a condition and an effect of exclusion—is not determined by fate and can therefore be reversed and converted into visibility, thereby eroding the social violence to which some categories of subjects are submitted. In other words, learning that there are frames is a condition for taking them into consideration, hence for modifying our perception of who is grievable—which for Butler may extend to *what* is grievable (2020, 76). Needless to say, this awareness of frames also determines the possibility of reacting to the sovereign power of the State that, particularly in times of socio-political crisis, "decid[es] who is grievable" (Butler 2004, 50). A similar idea may be found in Miranda Fricker's work on epistemic injustice. Even if she is not explicitly concerned with grievability, she attends to the ways in which certain categories of people suffer from various forms of epistemic injustice affecting their capacities to testify ("testimonial injustice") and to understand the situation in which they find themselves ("hermeneutic injustice"). She denounces what she calls the "ethical poison of prejudice" (22), which leads to a form of disqualification through "credibility deficit" (17). This makes them passive in front of certain forms of "social power" that disqualifies them not only as witnesses but also as citizens, social power introducing some structural violence against some groups (13). Our contention is that suffering from epistemic injustice in various forms leads to various forms of inaudibility and invisibility that are dependent on the frames of perception and recognition of the groups affected by prejudice. Clearly, this may have immediate bearings on the coefficient of grievability that is attributed to them.

The reference to sovereign State power, in its opposition to a vulnerability that is premised on (inter-)dependence, brings along Agamben's category of "bare life," a notion that, as we have seen, is present throughout *Precarious Life*. As Butler reminds us, to the Italian philosopher "sovereignty re-emerges when the law is suspended" (2004, 60). In the context of the 9/11 crisis that *Precarious Life* is addressing, Butler sees "a resurgence of sovereignty in the context of governmentality" (54) that she considers a source of general and urgent concern as, given our common vulnerability, bare life is a condition that we are all exposed to (67). Of course, Agamben's category is introduced in her discussion of (un-)grievability for the precise reason that being reduced to bare life or *zoē* (animal life) implies being deprived of *bíos*, "a form or way of living particular to an individual or group" (Agamben 1). Agamben sees modern democracy as "constantly trying to transform its own bare life into a way of life and to find, so to speak, the *bios* of *zoē*" (9). As an exception to the democratic situation, some categories of people—like the prisoners of the Nazi death camps, for instance—are deprived of any life form and reduced to bare life. Those who find themselves in such a plight can be "killed without the commission of homicide" (159), which clearly indicates that they cannot be mourned. Bare life is, therefore, tightly connected to ungrievability. To paraphrase Agamben, it may be said that grievability, like bare life, is "included in politics through an exclusion" (11), in this case, the exclusion of the capacity to be mourned, at least officially, and the deprivation of any value that could be attached to the said life.

Such developments clearly raise the issue of disposability, as indicated by Achille Mbembe in *Necropolitics* (2016). In this study, Mbembe returns to the issue of sovereignty, refocusing from a post-colonial perspective (Mbembe 66) the question of biopower raised by Michel Foucault in *The Will to Knowledge* (1976) and later essays, including *The Birth of Biopolitics* (2004). According to Foucault, while in feudal times sovereign power was the power over life and death exerted through a regime of punishment and revenge, the modern State developed what he calls "biopolitics," a system that brought about a profound transformation of the mechanisms of power in the Western world by assuming the regulation and normalisation of power over life through discipline and the optimisation of the subjects' capabilities. This is tantamount to increasing their usefulness, docility and integration into systems of efficient and economic controls (Foucault 1978, 139). Consequently, Foucault sees biopower—the way in which biopolitics is put to work— in positive terms, as the source of the rise of capitalism. By contrast, from Mbembe's post-colonial perspective, "sovereignty fundamentally consists in exerting a power outside the law" (76). Echoing Agamben's state of exception, the Cameroun-born philosopher examines the biopower exerted by the modern State in relation to racism and slavery. To him, in its extreme developments, "sovereignty means the capacity to define who matters and who does not, who is *disposable* and who is not" (80; original emphasis). Mbembe's emphasis on disposability implies a frame of reference that edges away from Foucault's positive analysis of sovereignty as wielded by the modern State towards a mode of post-capitalist economic sovereignty predicated on the violence of

8 *Jean-Michel Ganteau and Susana Onega*

globalised, free-wheeling liberalism. His point of view echoes Athena Athanasiou and Judith Butler's analyses of the "processes of disposability and expendability" that characterise dispossession and precarity (Butler and Athanasiou 27). Indeed, the reification implied by the reference to disposability betrays the loss of value of those lives that may be used and then disposed of, hence deprived of any *valuable* life form, of any "ordinariness"—in Le Blanc's acceptation of the term (2007, 35).

It follows from the above observations that value, the right to lead a valuable life and to be valuable are the issues addressed by grievability and ungrievability. Butler, Mbembe and Le Blanc, following in Agamben's, Levinas's and Foucault's wakes, invite the reader into an ethical consideration of what matters. This implies raising the question of whose lives matter, and hence of who matters, of course. A simple perusal of the fictional works published since the 1990s leaves no doubt that, once again, as they always do, creative writers have intuitively responded to Butler's call to launch on such an ethico-political venture by imagining new literary forms capable of putting these key concerns of our present world into words.

The eleven chapters gathered in this book are original contributions envisaging various modalities of (un-)grievability and observing how it works in various contexts. They are organised around five thematic Parts. The first, entitled "The Presence of History," opens up with Susana Onega's piece on David Mitchell's *The One Thousand Autumns of Jacob de Zoet* (2010). By adopting the prism of an ethics of hospitality, the chapter brings to the fore the various forms of institutionalised cruelty routinely exerted both by the Dutch and the Japanese on their social, racial and/or gender inferiors at a key moment in world history, when Europe is fighting for global commercial control and Japan is immersed in the isolationism of the Edo period. In Chapter 2, Paula Romo-Mayor looks at Rachel Seiffert's *A Boy in Winter* (2017), a novel that evokes the consequences of the Nazi invasion of Ukraine during World War II, relying on the meeting of Jewish, German and Ukrainian characters. It demonstrates how Seiffert's fiction privileges a story of human interdependence so as to show that any human loss is equally grievable. The last chapter in this Part is Katia Marcellin's reading of Ali Smith's *The Accidental* (2005). It examines a series of characters who are stuck in time and thereby enclosed in a state of ungrievability, showing how, through the ethical powers of metalepsis, the novel performs an erasure of the past that precludes grief, reconnects the characters with the past and allows them to acknowledge the figure of the other and come to terms with his or her sense of grievability.

The second Part, "Grieving the Earth," builds up on Butler's encompassing vision of grievability as applying not only to human individuals or groups but also to the world of the living more generally (2020, 74–76). It opens up with Bárbara Arizti's chapter on Alexis Wright's *The Swan*

Book (2013), a "planetary novel" connecting the fates of Indigenous Australians, climate refugees and swans in a dystopian post-apocalyptic scenario. Borrowing from aboriginal philosophy and Western thought—essentially ethics—, the analysis reveals a radically inclusive conception of mourning in which grievability is no longer regarded as the prerogative of humans but extends to the natural world, bringing together climate change fiction and aboriginal realism. In Chapter 5, Angelo Monaco looks at Ben Smith's *Doggerland* (2019), a novel edging towards the generic conventions of eco-dystopia and apocalypse. Although set in the near future, the novel takes the reader back to the time before England drifted apart from continental Europe. It brings together the vision of life on a wind farm in the North Sea, owned by a mysterious corporation, with occasional incursions into a deep geological timescale concerned with the changing nature of Doggerland. The analysis demonstrates that the ethical encounters with eco-precarious manifestations are given pride of place and shows how loss and grievability go beyond the province of the human.

The third Part, "Outcasts," starts with Maite Escudero-Alías's reading of Michael Stewart's *Ill Will. The Untold Story of Heathcliff* (2018), to raise issues of invisibility and ungrievability. Read in the light of Antigone's disruptive work of radical resistance, it exposes the vulnerability of kinship norms even while displaying the outcast's ungrievable body. The outcast is equally at the heart of Toni Morrison's *Love* (2003), here represented by the ghostly, absent figure of Celestial. In Chapter 7, Paula Martín-Salván investigates the ways in which, through the social dynamics of gender and class prejudice, the absent female character in this novel becomes the site of social, epistemic and, more specifically, testimonial injustice as she is a prostitute deprived of any agency both in her lover's circle and as a witness and story-teller. It is the powerful figure of Morrison's ungrieved ghost that appears ultimately, paradoxically rendering the outcast unforgettable, hence somehow grievable.

Part 4, "Contamination," returns to one of the great epidemics that helped shift the contemporary meanings of contagion before the advent of the COVID crisis. José M. Yebra-Pertusa looks at Alan Hollinghurst's *The Line of Beauty* (2004) and Colm Tóibín's *The Blackwater Lightship* (1999), two AIDS fictions evoking the 1980s and the way in which the epidemics made members of disenfranchised groups largely invisible and ungrievable, and essentially purifying in their ungrievability. By paying attention to the literary category of elegy, the chapter shows how fiction allows for the memory and rehabilitation of AIDS victims who were considered sexual dissidents and a menace to the wider, normative, allegedly immune community in the 1980s. In the following chapter, Giorgio Milone analyses US novelist Rebecca Makkai's *The Great Believers* (2018). He pays attention to the ways in which the socio-cultural construction of grievability condemns groups—and more particularly the members of the gay community affected by the AIDS epidemic—to suffer from both testimonial and hermeneutic injustice, which translates into ungrievability. It shows how the trauma of the ungrieved losses is allowed a measure of working through by narrativising the memories of the departed.

The final Part, "After the Subject," brings together two highly visible and acclaimed contemporary British novelists, Kazuo Ishiguro and Ian McEwan, while edging towards the shores of post-human thought and representation. In Chapter 10, Sylvie Maurel looks at Ishiguro's *Never Let Me Go* (2005). She analyses how the narrative demonstrates that the frame of the subhuman is imposed on the clones, so as to commodify, invisibilise and condemn them to ungrievability. She concludes on the novel's elegiac dimension and its restorative use as it transforms the clones into the quintessence of human vulnerability and grievability. In the last chapter, Jean-Michel Ganteau focuses on McEwan's *Machines Like Me. And People Like You* (2019). Starting from the hypothesis that the novel answers Butler's triple question in *Precarious Life*: "Who counts as human? Whose lives count as lives, what makes for a grievable life?" (2004, 20), he demonstrates how, beyond the obvious ungrievability of the android robot at the heart of the narrative, the novel both evinces and performs literature's radical capacity to expose and shift the norms of grievability.

Works Cited

Agamben, Giorgio. *Homo Sacer: Sovereign Power and Bare Life*. 1995. Eds Werner Hamacher and David E. Wellbery. Trans. Daniel Heller-Roazen. Stanford, CA: Stanford UP, 1998.

Badiou, Alain. *Ethics: An Essay on the Understanding of Evil*. London: Verso, 2001.

Bauman, Zygmunt. *Postmodern Ethics*. London: Blackwell, 1993.

Benhabib, Sheila. *Exile, Statelessness, and Migration: Playing Chess with History from Hannah Arendt to Isaiah Berlin*. Princeton, NJ: Princeton UP, 2018.

Butler, Judith. *Antigone's Claim. Kinship between Life and Death*. New York: Columbian UP, 2000.

———. *Precarious Life. The Powers of Mourning and Violence*. London and New York: Verso, 2004.

———. *Frames of War. When Is Life Grievable?* London and New York: Verso, 2009.

———. *The Force of Non-Violence. An Ethico-Political Bind*. 2020. London and New York: Verso, 2021.

Butler, Judith, and Athena Athanasiou. *Dispossession: The Performative in the Political*. Cambridge and Malden, MA: Polity P, 2013.

Cornell, Drucilla. *The Philosophy of the Limit*. London and New York: Routledge, 1992.

Derrida, Jacques. "Violence and Metaphysics: An Essay on the Thought of Emmanuel Levinas." 1967. *Writing and Difference*. Trans. Alan Bass. Chicago, IL: U of Chicago P, 1978. 79–153.

Eaglestone, Robert. *Ethical Criticism: Reading after Levinas*. Edinburgh: Edinburgh UP, 1997.

Foucault, Michel. *The History of Sexuality: The Will to Knowledge*. Vol. 1. 1976. Trans. Robert Hurley. New York: Pantheon Books, 1978.

———. *The Birth of Biopolitics: Lectures at the Collège de France 1978–1979*. 2004. Ed. Michel Senellart. Trans. Graham Burchell. Houndmills, Basingstoke, Hampshire, and New York: Palgrave MacMillan, 2008.

Fricker, Miranda. *Epistemic Injustice. Power and the Ethics of Knowing*. Oxford and New York: OUP, 2007.

Ganteau, Jean-Michel, and Susana Onega. "Introduction". *The Ethical Component in Experimental British Fiction since the 1960s*. Eds Susana Onega and Jean-Michel Ganteau. Newcastle: Cambridge Scholars Publishing, 2007. 1–9.

Gibson, Andrew. *Postmodernity, Ethics and the Novel: From Levinas to Leavis*. London and New York: Routledge, 1999.

Hollinghurst, Alan. *The Line of Beauty*. London: Picador, 2004.

Ishiguro, Kazuo. *Never Let Me Go*. 2005. London: Faber and Faber, 2010.

Levinas, Emmanuel. *Totality and Infinity. An Essay on Exteriority*. 1961. Trans. Alphonso Lingis. The Hague: Martinus Nijhoff, 1969.

———. *Otherwise Than Being, Or, Beyond Essence*. 1974. Trans. Alphonso Lingis. The Hague: Martinus Nijhoff, 1981.

———. *Time and the Other*. 1980. Pittsburgh: Duquesne UP, 1987.

———. "Ethics and Politics." *The Levinas Reader*. Ed. Sean Hand. Oxford and Cambridge, MA: Basil Blackwell, 1989. 289–97.

———. *Humanism of the Other*. 1972. Trans. Nidra Poller. Intro. Richard A. Cohen. Urbana: U of Illinois P, 2006.

Le Blanc, Guillaume. *Vies ordinaires, vies précaires*. Paris: Seuil, 2007.

———. *L'invisibilité sociale*. Paris: Presses Universitaires de France, 2009.

Makkai, Rebecca. *The Great Believers: A Novel*. 2018. New York: Penguin, 2019.

Mbembe, Achille. *Necropolitics*. 2016. Durham and London: Duke UP, 2019.

McEwan, Ian. *Machines Like Me. And People Like You*. London: Cape, 2019.

Mitchell, David. *The One Thousand Autumns of Jacob de Zoet*. 2010. New York: Random House, 2011.

Morrison, Toni. *Love*. New York: Vintage, 2003.

Seiffert, Rachel. *A Boy in Winter*. London: Virago, 2017.

Smith, Ali. *The Accidental*. London: Penguin, 2005.

Smith, Ben. *Doggerland*. London: Fourth Estate, 2019.

Stewart, Michael. *Ill Will. The Untold Story of Heathcliff*. London: Harper Collins, 2018.

Tóibín, Colm. *The Blackwater Lightship*. London: Picador, 1999.

Watkin, Christopher. "A Different Alterity: Jean-Luc Nancy's 'Singular Plural'." *Paragraph* 30.2 (2007): 50–64.

Wright, Alexis. *The Swan Book*. London: Constable, 2013.

Žižek, Slavoj. *The Parallax View*. Cambridge, MA: MIT P, 2006.

Part I

The Presence of History

1 Trading Relations, the Evil of Violence and the Ungrievability of the Other in David Mitchell's *The One Thousand Autumns of Jacob de Zoet*

Susana Onega

Introduction: From the Old Regime to the Commercial Society

Described by David Mitchell as his first attempt to write a historical novel, *The One Thousand Autumns of Jacob de Zoet* (2010) offers a characteristic Mitchellian multiperspectival account of the complex effects of the encounter of European and Japanese cultures at a crucial moment in world history. The action is narrated in the historical present by an external narrator with variable focalisation who alternates the report of events being lived by the eponymous protagonist and other characters on Dejima and Nagasaki, with past events remembered or recounted by the characters themselves, differentiated by the use of italics. This produces a "continuous to and fro movement between two very distinct cultures but also between the past and the present, and between fiction and history" (Larsonneur 145) that is enhanced by the double dating of most chapters according to the Gregorian and the Japanese lunar calendars. The impossibility of establishing exact equivalences between the days of the month, the years and the eras in the two systems produces a sense of temporal relativity and loose correspondence that conveys the incommensurability of the two cultures.

The novel begins in 1799, with Jacob de Zoet's departure from Rotterdam to the trading post on Dejima, a small artificial island in the bay of Nagasaki, and ends with his return in 1817 (Mitchell 2011, 478). This linear chronology suggests the progressiveness of a hero's quest. However, this effect is contradicted by the uneven length of the novel's five parts. The first three, occupying 461 pages out of 479, cover Jacob's first two years in the trading post held on Dejima by the Dutch East India Company (*Vereenigde Oost-Indische Compagnie*, or VOC), from his arrival until the attack of a British warship, the HMS *Phoebus*, in 1800. Part Four (pages 463–71) takes place in 1811, and Part Five (pages 473–79) in 1817. These brief last two parts report the only noteworthy events in Jacob's otherwise anodyne and stagnant life after the development of world history frustrated his plans of returning to Holland as a wealthy man, after fulfilling his five-year contract.

DOI: 10.4324/9781003347811-3

In 1799, Japan was immersed in the peaceful isolationism of the Tokugawa or Edo period (1603–1867). The only contact it had with Europe was the trading post on Dejima. Meanwhile, the European countries were competing for the control of international trading routes and the construction of what Voltaire described as a peaceful new era, constituted by "the European republic of commercial states" (quoted in Vogt 131). The year 1799 is the year of the Anglo-Russian invasion of Holland during the War of the Second Coalition against revolutionary France, when British and Russian troops invaded the North Holland peninsula in the Batavian Republic. By situating the novel on Dejima little before the Dutch fleet was destroyed and Holland annexed by the French, Mitchell is recreating a crucial episode in world history: the transition from the Old Regime to the rise of the commercial society, triggered by the expansion of industrial capitalism.

Enlightenment thinkers, from Voltaire and Montesquieu to members of the Scottish Enlightenment like Adam Ferguson, Adam Smith and John Miller, envisioned the commercial society as the culmination of a long and painful historical evolution from barbarism to civilisation. While, in classical antiquity, the word "barbarian" provided a spatial contrast between the Hellenes living in the *polis* and those living outside, the Enlightenment notion of barbarism, influenced by Christian theology, underwent a shift from spatialisation to temporalisation, so that "barbarians, once the name for a people and later an index for a lack of education, became Heathens—not because they lived in different areas of this world, but because they refuted Jesus Christ" (Vogt 129). By equating barbarians with Heathens, all extra-European societies could be relegated to the past and excluded from world history (136). Thus, while "race" had previously signalled linguistic or religious differences, "in the early or mid-19th century this discourse developed into two directions, one emphasising 'class' (Marx) and one focussing on biology" (Glaser 210–11). While Marxian theory introduced the concept of class struggle, the rise of Social Darwinism, particularly the branch of evolutionary anthropology that sought to adapt Darwin's classification of plants and animals to human beings and societies, provided the "scientific" justification for imperialism: the domination, exploitation and even extinction of "inferior" races became a civilising mission (Glaser 211). Translating this into Judith Butler's terms, it may be stated that class and race now become determining factors in the imperialist states' "differential allocation of grievability that decides what kind of subject is and must be grieved, and which kind of subject must not" (2004, xiv) and is, therefore, "easy to destroy or to expose to forces of destruction" (Butler 2020, 17). To these should be added gender, a secular factor in the differential allocation of grievability rendered invisible in patriarchal states both east and west.

In striking opposition to this, Enlightenment thinkers employed the notion of "barbarous nations" as an idealised intermediate stage between the dispersed clans of savages and the fully developed forms of civilisation and statehood (Möller 141). Thus, Kant argued for a model of global peace and tolerance based on universal hospitality, mutual non-intrusion and respect for cultural differences, choosing precisely as an example Japan's isolationist policy during the Edo period (Möller 144–45). As Kant forcefully argued in his treatise on *Perpetual Peace* (1795), this goal was jeopardised by the inhospitable actions of the European commercial states:

> The injustice which they exhibit on visiting foreign lands and races [...] is such as to fill us with horror. America, the negro countries, the Spice Islands, the Cape etc. were, on being discovered, looked upon as countries which belonged to nobody [...] Oppression of the natives followed, famine, insurrection, perfidy and all the rest of the litany of evils which can afflict mankind.
>
> (Kant 139–40)

To Kant, then, it is the inhabitants of the Old World, not the Heathens of the New, who are barbarous. The position of Kant and other Enlightenment thinkers like Montesquieu foreruns Judith Butler's Levinasian ethics of non-violence based on the perception of a common human vulnerability (2004, 2009, 2020). It also echoes Guillaume Le Blanc's politics of hospitality (2011)—itself a development, among others, of Butler's ethics of ungrievability and Emmanuel Levinas's ethics of hospitality, represented by biblical Rebecca (Genesis 24) (Levinas 33–73)—urging us to recognise our common human fragility and place ourselves in the position of the stranger, as recommended by Matthew (25:43) (Le Blanc 88). From the perspective of our own globalised world of endless warfare and bloody conflicts dictated by biopolitics (Agamben 1998; Nancy 2000)—or, as Achille Mbembe forcefully argues, by "necropolitics": "the ultimate expression of sovereignty largely resid[ing] in the power and capacity to dictate who is able to live and who must die" (67)—it seems evident that the imperialists' equation of barbarians with Heathens initiated the paradigm shift that has led to the current desacralisation and obliteration of the strangers' right of hospitality that Kant saw as a universal and unique civilising force (Le Blanc and Brugère 2017).

Imperialism, Class, Racial and Gender Discrimination, and the Western Trope of Cannibalism

As Mbembe explains, from the sixteenth to the nineteenth century, two forms of colonialism simultaneously developed: commercial even

18 *Susana Onega*

trading-post colonialism, which was "almost entirely lacking in heavy local investment" and exclusively aimed to increase the metropolis wealth by means of inequitable trade relations (11); and settler colonialism, "conceived as an extension of the nation" (11) that was populated by those deemed superfluous: "the poor viewed as scrounging off society and the vagabonds and delinquents seen as harmful to the nation" (10). In both, "the most useful arms and the most vital energies were those provided by the slave trade" (10). These two forms of colonialism provide the historical background to *The Thousand Autumns of Jacob de Zoet*. The novel begins with the description of the sound of Nagasaki celebrating the arrival of the *Shenandoah* at the trading post on Dejima (Mitchell 2011, 5). This description suggests that the trading relations between the Dutch and the Japanese responded to the mutual friendship and respect for cultural difference of the peaceful commercial society theorised by Enlightenment thinkers. However, the fact that one of its passengers is Jacob de Zoet, a clerk commissioned by the VOC to supervise the accounts and the terms of trade in its headquarters in Japan, sets this impression into question. Jacob soon finds that the Dutch and the Japanese treat each other as untrustworthy and potentially dangerous barbarians. Even Aibagawa Orito, the scientific-minded midwife being trained by the Dejima physician, Dr Lucas Marinus, considers Europe an "enlightened and barbaric realm" (5). Her opinion is corroborated by Jacob's red hair. As Deputy Melchior Van Cleef remarks, noting the curiosity he raises in the stevedores: "a genuine 'red-haired barbarian' is worth a good gawp" (20). The commercial transactions on Dejima take place in an atmosphere of mutual suspicion, mistrust, and also misunderstanding as the Japanese interpreters' Dutch is rather poor and learning Japanese is forbidden to the Dutch. Jacob breaks this rule by exchanging classes of Dutch for Japanese with a young translator, Ogawa Uzaemon (92). A little knowledge of Japanese allows him to expose the dishonesty of Mr Kobayashi, the senior interpreter, when he mistranslates "a *thousand* peacock-feather fans [for] one *hundred*" (96; original emphasis), meaning to keep the remaining 900 fans for his and his friends' benefit. However, the ethicality of the Dutch officers is no better. Soon after Jacob's arrival, Daniel Snitker, the acting chief of the trading station, is tried and found guilty of several offenses, including the charge of setting fire to several warehouses in order to steal the goods stored in them (11). After the trial, Chief Unico Vorstenbosch, the officer who had imprisoned Snitker and promised his position to Jacob, convinces the reluctant clerk to forge and sign a letter supposedly sent by the Governor-General of the Dutch East Indies to Magistrate Shiroyama, threatening with the withdrawal of the Netherlands from the Orient (37–39), unless the Japanese increase the quota of copper they badly need to mint coins (36) to finance the war. The ruse works, but the honest clerk soon realises

Trading Relations, Violence and Ungrievability   19

that he has been the victim of a complex scheme to blackmail him into connivance with their corrupt practices (168).

The greed and corruption of the VOC officers concur with their imperialist ideas about the right of conquest, indoctrination and enslavement or extermination of "inferior" or disposable and ungrievable races. During a meal organised to celebrate the arrival of the *Shenandoah*, its Yankee commander Captain Anselm Lacy boasts about the part he played in abolishing monarchy (52) and establishing democracy in the US (51), using settler colonialism clichés. The interpreters are terribly concerned for their own safety, above all when Lacy adds that, if the president turns out to be a bad choice, he can be voted out (51). However, neither the Japanese nor the Dutch are shocked by his preposterous response to Dr Marinus's question if slaves also vote: "'No, Doctor.' [...] 'Nor do oxen, bees, or women'" (51; original emphasis). His answer echoes both Butler's notion of ungrievability and Giorgio Agamben's definition of "bare life" as the result of a process of dispossession and derealisation of the citizens by the modern State, whereby, instead of being treated as rational beings, citizens are deprived of their political identity and dealt with as mere bodies, reduced to their "very animality" (Agamben 77). Significantly, the conversation then turns from slavery to polygamy as simply an economic question for the Japanese, and a desired state for the traders (53). To both, women are sheer objects of exchange by men. The VOC officers have a brothel at their disposal, the House of Wistaria (Mitchell 2011, 1), and they regularly use their servants to satisfy their sexual needs, so that they often father mixed-race illegitimate children. Van Cleef's story of his Uncle Theo is representative in this respect: he did not recognise any of the children he had fathered with his Javanese maids for racial and economic reasons. He made a point of marrying "'currency' mothers—white skinned, rose-cheeked flowers of Protestant Europe—because Batavia born brides all have orangutans cavorting in the family tree" (347). The wives of colonisers led submissive and precarious lives and often died ungrieved in childbirth or due to tropical diseases. All the wives Uncle Theo took to Java died within months of their arrival (347), except for Aunt Gloria, a beautiful woman, younger than her nephew and "meek as a doe" (348), who would cry so quietly after her husband had intercourse with her that only Melchior could hear her (348). Nephew and aunt inevitably engaged in an affair that ended violently when Uncle Theo caught them lying together (351). The mixture of romantic intrigue and violence in this melodramatic story undermines its historical verisimilitude, pointing to it as a stereotypical cuckold romance.

This is only one among many fanciful stories narrated by the Dutch characters. The story of Dr Marinus's boyhood in Leiden "is a Dickensian tale" (O'Donnell 129), and in Chapter 8, several VOC traders

20   *Susana Onega*

tell Jacob their gruesome life stories while, fittingly, they are cheating him in a game of Knave and Devil (Mitchell 2011, 100) with notched cards (110). Arie Grote tells how, after running away from his violent, rum-drinking father (100), he accepted a job that turned out to be a form of enslavement as he was taken in irons to serve in a ship belonging to the VOC (101–13). Evo Oost, a mixed-race natural son (104), tells the dreadful story of his childhood at an orphanage in Batavia. Pier Baert explains how an alluring tavern girl in Dunkirk made him drink so much that he lost consciousness (106). When he awoke, he found himself on a French ship in the Channel, sailing west to participate in the Third Battle of Ushant (107). Another "volunteer" who complained that his religion forbade him to kill was cast overboard by the Captain (107). When a British ship sunk their vessel, Baert saved his life by clinging to a cheese barrel (108), an episode that parodies Ismael's survival of the sinking of *The Pequod* by holding onto Queequeg's empty coffin in *Moby Dick*. These stories are sailors' yarns, a genre that developed alongside the expansion of international commerce. Though their excessiveness challenges the readers' willing suspension of disbelief, they provide an emotionally charged impression of the invisibility and ungrievability of those subjects that, according to Mbembe, were deemed superfluous and therefore employed in the colonial enterprise (see above). As Ivo puts it, referring to the working conditions of children above twelve at the orphanage, they were "[c]heaper than servants [...] cheaper than slaves" (104).

But perhaps the most excessive and stereotyped of all the yarns narrated by VOC traders is that told by Peter Fischer on cannibals. As Gerd Bayer notes, after Columbus' discovery of America, the European trope of cannibalism spread from anthropology, journalism and political speeches, running wild through repetition to other realms, including literature and art, from Daniel Defoe's *Robinson Crusoe* to Charles Dickens, Herman Melville and William Hogarth (104–105). The most widespread and influential types of cannibal narratives were shipboard journalistic accounts and sailors' yarns (Obeyesekere 2002, 169–70). Although often taken for truthful reports, these accounts were in fact the product of "the reveries and yarns" that sailors gifted as *raconteurs* told their comrades after a long day's work, "about the manners and customs of the natives, and especially of their cannibalism" (2002, 170). Echoing this, Fischer presents his story as an autobiographical adventure in Surinam. During an expedition to exterminate runaway slaves (Mitchell 2011, 136), they were attacked and massacred by hundreds of rebels. The cannibals took the survivors to their camp and treated them with bestial ferocity: they carved out the men's hearts while they were still alive (136), laughing (137). Fischer and a Zeelander called Joosse were left for the next day so the butchers could join the feasting and fornication (137). Fischer, who was impaled to the table with a bayonet

(137), freed himself by working the bayonet blade loose with his teeth (137), and then freed Joosse and helped him survive during the seven days it took them to walk through the jungle, eating only "the maggots breeding in [their] wounds" (137). Captain Lacy believes the truculent tale and salutes Fischer's courage (138), but Dr Marinus dismisses it as "vainglorious piffle" (138). The surgeon's disbelief, attributed by Fischer to his sentimental attitude to savages (138), makes Van Cleef express the general opinion of the VOC traders that, though slavery may seem unjust to some, all empires are founded on it (138). When Marinus answers: "Then may the devil [...] take all empires," Fischer agrees with Lacy that, in a colonial officer, these words are extraordinary, "not to say *Jacobinical*" (138; original emphasis). The discussion ends with Fischer enumerating the perils of abolitionism and Van Cleef justifying slavery with an argument that conflates the ideology of the Empire with Social Darwinism and brings to the fore the stark ungrievability and disposability of those who do not enter the frames of perception of the period, which the novel is striving to provide: "In the animal kingdom, [...] the vanquished are eaten by those more favoured by Nature. Slavery is merciful by comparison, the lesser races keep their lives in exchange for their labour" (138).

Together with Gerritszoon, Fischer had just given Sjako an atrocious beating and left him for dead (132). Arie Grote's only comment was that Chief Van Cleef would not approve of this handling of company property, and Captain Lacy concurred with him (133). When Dr Marinus explained that the slave's misbehaviour was motivated by a nervous collapse (134), Captain Lacy choked with laughter: "A 'nervous collapse?' What next? A mule too melancholic to pull? A hen too lachrymose to lay?" (134). While the traders' animalisation of Sjako conforms to Agamben's contention that bare life is the inhuman life that modernity necessarily creates and simultaneously attempts to eliminate because it can no longer tolerate its presence (11), the brutality and impunity with which Gerritszoon and Fischer mistreated him confirm Mbembe's assertion that the slave condition results from a triple loss—"loss of a 'home,' loss of rights over one's body, and loss of political status"—that is identical with absolute domination, natal alienation, and social death (expulsion from humanity altogether)" (74–75). The traders' refusal to make, like Dr Marinus, the ethical move to the position of the stranger and assume the politics of hospitality demanded by Enlightenment thinkers echoes Butler's remark that "[o]ur fear of understanding a point of view belies a deeper fear that we shall be taken up by it, find it is contagious, become infected in a morally perilous way by the thinking of the presumed enemy" (2004, 8). Indeed, the legal violence employed with slaves situates them beyond the bounds of humanity, grievability, and mourning in a social system ruled by the unbridled sovereignty of the Empire (Butler 2009, 20, xii–xiii). The most fortunate slave on Dejima

22 *Susana Onega*

is Eelattu, a young man from Ceylon that Dr Marinus had found in Jaffna, beaten and left for dead by a gang of Portuguese whalers, and whom he had freed and trained as his assistant at the hospital (Mitchell 2011, 26). Captain Lacy's response to Dr Marinus's hospitality by invoking the biblical condemnation of Africans—"God shall enlarge Japheth, and Canaan shall be his servant" (139)—is met by Jacob's disagreement: "those particular verses are problematical" (139).

While the views on race of the VOC officers represent the official doctrine of the centralised powers to justify the ideology of the Empire, Jacob's outlook on race is, like that of Dr Marinus, representative of Enlightenment ethics. As Peter Vogt explains, "the *summum malum* for many writers or thinkers of the eighteenth century was not sin, but cruelty, cruelty in an evidently physical sense" (137). As Montesquieu argued in *The Spirit of the Laws*:

> *What does matter is who is cruel. Cannibals eat the flesh of dead people and we recoil in horror, but it is we who torture and persecute the living [...] arrogance and cruelty mark Europeans, not those whom they disdain as barbarians.*
>
> (quoted in Vogt 137; original emphasis)

Jacob's family belonged to the Dutch Reformed Church, the largest Christian denomination in the Netherlands before the demise of the Batavian Republic. As such, he received a strict religious education and moral sense, particularly from his uncle, the parson of Domburg. Before embarking for Dejima, he gave Jacob the old and tattered family Psalter, with the command to protect it with his life (Mitchel 2011, 14–15). This Psalter had a fabulous history of miracles worked on members of the family along successive generations. Taking Christian texts to Japan was strictly forbidden, so that, by hiding the Psalter in his travelling chest, Jacob was setting his life at risk. Ironically, he overcomes this danger thanks to his interest in the Scottish Enlightenment as, when Interpreter Ogawa inspects the chest and finds the Psalter beneath a copy of *The Wealth of Nations* (28), he decides to keep the secret so he can borrow Adam Smith's book and finish the translation he had started with another loaned copy. Jacob's acquaintance with Smith's doctrine adds a clear enlightened stance on his training, pointing to him as the paragon of the civilised European seeking to contribute to the creation of a worldwide friendly and peaceful commercial society. However, as the meaning of the word "Zoet" suggests (Keene n.p.), Jacob also has a "sweet" side. He has an artistic temperament and a romantic strain, expressed in a talent for drawing and a tendency to fall in love with women beyond his reach, which compromises his unflinching dedication to eradicate corruption and widen the frames of invisibility, exclusion and ungrievability of the racial, social and gender others.

The Trope of the Oriental Woman, Consubstantial Cannibalism and Ethical Responses to Ungrievability

Before departing from Rotterdam, Jacob promised Anna to make a fortune and return from Dejima within six years (Mitchell 2011, 478). However, the bankruptcy of the Dutch East India Company and the disappearance of the Dutch Republic due to the Napoleonic wars left Jacob stranded on Dejima. As Mitchell explained in an interview: "I think in about 1805, 1806, the French annexed the Netherlands and turned it literally into a department of France. So, for a while through a fact of diplomatic sleight of hand the Netherlands was Dejima" (Keene n.p.). The first lesson Jacob learnt was, then, that there were political and social forces out of his control determining the course of his life. But even history bent to the strength his faith, as it saved his and Dr Marinus's lives when the HMS *Phoebus* entered the bay under a Dutch flag and attacked Dejima. After a first carronade shattered the watchtower that Jacob stubbornly refused to abandon, a young member of the crew, Michael Tozen, was caught by the recoil of the cannon and lost a leg (Mitchel 2011, 435–36), a common accident that reminded Captain Penhaligon of his beloved red-haired son, Tristram, killed in a naval battle at Cape St Vincent (332). When Jacob removed his hat to say a last prayer, Penhaligon saw Tristram, instead of Jacob, waiting for death (437), and changed his orders to aim the second carronade at the flag. Jacob's staunch faith was unable, however, to protect him from his own feelings and emotions, as his encounter with Aibagawa Orito totally disrupted the ardent promise of eternal love and faithfulness he had made to Anna at the quay of Rotterdam.

The first time Jacob met Orito, she was pursuing William Pitt, Dr Marinus's monkey, who had just stolen an amputated leg from the operating theatre (49). Knowing that the only women who had access to Dejima were servants, prostitutes and so-called "wives" of the better-paid officers, Jacob first mistakes Orito for a prostitute (48) and then becomes besotted with her. The way she laughs reminds him of Anna (49) and, aware that she is untouchable (57), he starts fantasising about developing a sisterly "friendship" with her (59). According to Marco de Waard, this aspect of his personality contributes to characterise Jacob as "a typical Mitchell hero: unknowing without being naïve, perceptive but unable to see the situation as a whole" (115). Though accurate, this description misses the crucial point, made by Dr Marinus, that Jacob is falling into the "going native" trap:

> It is not even Miss Aibagawa after who you lust, in truth. It is the genus 'The Oriental Woman' who so infatuates you. [...]. How many hundreds of you besotted white men have I seen mired in the same syrupy hole?
>
> (Mitchell 2011, 61)

24   *Susana Onega*

Dr Marinus's warning functions as a realism-undermining mechanism alerting readers that he is repeating the behaviour of the purblind protagonists of colonial narratives like those of Rudyard Kipling, Somerset Maugham, Joseph Conrad, or Charlotte and Emily Brontë (see Glaser 214–21). This stereotyped going-native plot is rounded off when Jacob discovers that Orito and Uzaemon are living an impossible love romance. Although Orito is an educated samurai daughter, Uzaemon's ardent desire to marry her is frustrated by his adoptive father for economic reasons (208) and because she has a burn on her face (4). Uzaemon's expected role was to marry a socially appropriate wife and father sons to ensure the continuation of the family name. In that rigidly stratified Japanese world, the enforcers of women's discrimination were older women, usually mothers-in-law wishing to exert power on their son's wives (85), or also widowed stepmothers, as is the case of Orito. After her father's death, Orito is sold by her father's second wife to Lord Abbott Enomoto and forced to become a nun at Mount Shiranui Shrine. The importance of beauty, rank and family protection in determining the marriageability and, therefore, the social visibility and grievability even of educated Japanese women leaves no doubt about their objectification. This limitation does not affect men. Chamberlain Tomine is the Nagasaki Magistrate's right hand, although he has a smashed nose (7).

After saving the lives of the Magistrate's concubine and unborn child (4–9), Orito's frame of visibility and subjecthood improves: she is granted permission to attend Dr Marinus's classes for male medical students on Dejima. The young midwife, whose goal in life is to help women in labour through scientific knowledge (69), is unperturbed by blood, faeces or amputated members, and she uses words like "vagina" (67) that Jacob had never heard spoken aloud. Her rationalism and courage produce in Jacob the same fascination Oriental women provoke in European travellers in colonial narratives, whose agency strikingly contrasts with the passivity and submissiveness of European women (Glaser 217). Orito's rational stance is representative of the process of secularisation that climaxed in the Edo period thanks to the improvement of commercial and communication networks and the creation of a national Japanese economy (Reider 2001, 86). This evolution is also reflected in the striking difference between progressive Japanese characters like Orito, Uzaemon, Chamberlain Tomine and Magistrate Shiroyama, who live in Nagasaki, at the heart of the commercial society, and the ancestral mores of Lord Abbott Enomoto, the ruler of the Kyôga Domain, a remote mountainous region presided over by a Shintô Shrine devoted to the Goddess of Shiranui (194). Shintô ("the way of the gods") is the oldest indigenous faith of the Japanese. The Supreme Shintô Deity is Amaterasu Ômikami (the Sun Goddess), also known as the Queen of Kami. Theoretically, the function of the Goddess of Shiranui is to ensure the fertility and prosperity of the Kyôga Domain and to protect Lord

Enomoto and his clan. In fact, however, this Shrine represents a sinister type of religious dissidence, as Abbott Enomoto and his acolytes prolong their lives by devouring the souls of the babies they father with the nuns. Though equally fantastic, their cannibalistic practices differ from those attributed to cannibals by Western colonisers in that theirs is a form of sacrificial anthropophagy practised by a "consubstantial community," that is, a community eating of a consecrated substance literally thought to have the same essential nature (Obeyesekere 2005, xvi). This ritual aspect of their cannibalism confers on Lord Abbot Enomoto and his acolytes the awe-inspiring spirituality of religious fanaticism, as the Nagasaki Magistrate does not fail to realise: "*The purest believers* [...] *are the truest monsters*" (Mitchell 2011, 460; original emphasis). To the Magistrate, their existence represents a formidable danger of regression from the ongoing process of secularisation and modernisation.

A salient cultural effect of this process was the transformation of ancient myths into folklore. Orally transmitted tales, such as the *Kaidan-shū*—a collection of supernatural tales of the strange and mysterious often depicting the horrific and gruesome (Reider 2001, 79–99)—were printed during the Edo period. The uncanny supernatural atmosphere of these ancient tales pervades the Kyôga Domain, adding to it a metafictional element comparable to that of the traders' and sailors' yarns. The secrecy enveloping the convent had bred all types of rumours about its evil supernatural status: while the son of a blacksmith claimed that the monks were assassins (Mitchell 2011, 181), a hunter swore having seen "winged monster women dressed as nuns flying around Bare Peak at the summit of Shiranui" (181). Before becoming a nun, Orito had visited Otane, the wise old herbalist of Kurozane, a village in the Kyôga Domain, in search of remedies for women's illnesses. Otane had an ancient medicine cabinet (178) and the image of "Maria-*sama*, the mother of Iesus-*sama*" (182), given to her grandfather's grandfather "from a holy saint named Xavier, who sailed to Japan from paradise on a magical flying boat pulled by golden swans" (182). As the allusion to Saint Francis Xavier suggests, Otane kept alive the Christian faith introduced in various Asiatic countries by Spanish Jesuits in the mid-sixteenth century and banned from Japan in the Edo period. Outlawed Christians like Otane's family created statues of the Virgin Mary disguised as the Buddhist Kannon deity (Goddess of Mercy). These images, called Maria Kannon, represent the virtues of compassion, gentleness, purity of heart and motherhood. Her syncretic Buddhist–Christian faith and her knowledge of herbal remedies point to Otane as a healer with the ancestral wisdom provided by Mother Earth, the supporter and nurturer of Buddha. The Kami Goddess worshipped in the House of Sisters of the Shintô Shrine is also a Mother Goddess, represented as a pregnant woman with breasts full of milk and a navelless belly swollen with a female pregnant foetus containing another smaller pregnant foetus, and so on *ad infinitum*

(213). When Orito escapes through the forbidden area of the Shrine with the help of Otane's cat (239, 247), she enters the caves under Bare Peak that originated the Shrine (268) and finds in succession three altars with evermore awesome images of the Goddess. The first looks young and smiling (267); the second is older and unsmiling, and her paint is peeling (267). The third is rotting and, to Orito's medically trained eye, her face looks syphilitic (268). The progressive state of disrepair of the images and their respective altar rooms evoke the striking inequalities between the wealthy mercantile class, common people and prostitutes, the most abject type of ungrievable other in Japanese society. Eventually, Orito finds a domed chamber with a huge kneeling effigy of the Goddess, dressed in red, with cupped hands, covetous eyes and a wide open, predatory mouth (268). The figure, chiselled from a huge black stone flecked with bright grains, seems to Orito as old as the earth itself (268). When she touches it, she is astonished to find that the stone is warm (268). She then realises that the ancient ideograms inscribed on the circular wall represent Buddhist sins (268), thus adding an element of syncretism to the Shintô deity. According to Buddhist symbolism, her red dress signifies love and compassion; her kneeling position indicates respect and devotion to a higher being; the cupping together of her hands, a common gesture of Japanese Kannon goddesses, represents the *Anjali Mudra*, or Mudra of Offering. But there is an awe-inspiring incongruence between these Buddhist symbols and the Goddess's hungry wide open mouth and covetous eyes, which suggest that she is prey to *Taṇhā* (thirst, greed, craving), the principal cause in the arising of *dukkha* (suffering, pain, unsatisfactoriness) and *saṃsāra* (the cycle of existence). These contradictory traits, consonant with the cosmic duality of yin and yang, evoke the complementariness, interconnectedness and interdependence of good and evil, a central Shintô dogma. This cosmic duality, common to many gods and goddesses, is also attributed to Mother Earth in Western culture. Her grotesque body in Carnival imagery is "an element that devours, swallows up (the grave, the womb) and at the same time is an element of birth, of renaissance (the maternal breasts)" (Bakhtin 21).

Like Orito, all the nuns in the House of Sisters have some kind of blemish or defect that disqualifies them for the matrimonial market and would condemn them to live as freaks or prostitutes (Mitchell 2011, 181). However, while Orito's burn in the face was the result of a childhood accident, the nuns were born with a peculiar physical trait that associates them with a Shintôist animal. Asagao has a cleft lip, like rabbits (192). Sadaie's misshapen skull gives her head a feline shape (192). Yayoi has fox's ears (190) like Kitsune (the Fox), a popular Shintô spirit or deity associated with fertility, agriculture and prosperity. Her life story reads like a supernatural tale of the strange and mysterious in the *Kaidan-shū* tradition. When she was born with fox's ears, the local Buddhist priest said that her mother had been impregnated by a demon (222), and urged her parents to abandon her. Her father readily took her to the circle of pointed rocks in the wood where unwanted daughters were left for wild animals to devour them (223). That night, however, a white fox led a traveller, Yôben the Seer, to the family hut. He told them that the fox's ears were a blessing from Lady Kannon (223), and that they must rescue the baby. On their way to the wood, they heard the dead babies wailing and wolves howling (224). But when they entered the circle of pointed rocks, they found the white fox and Lady Kannon breast-feeding Yayoi (224). After her rescue, Yayoi's father took her to the filthiest inns and sickrooms to make money by letting incurable people hold her ears, until she became old enough to be sold to a brothel in Osaka (224). While Yayoi's sober narration of her father's atrocious behaviour indicates her assumption of the absolute ungrievability of baby girls in agricultural communities, the story itself is one among many Buddhist stories of motherly love, compassion and purity of heart.

Orito's unconditional love for women in need, particularly prostitutes and beggars, stems from the same Buddhist ethics of compassion. Otane's syncretic faith may be said to conflate this ethics with its Christian equivalent, agape (charity), the selfless and unconditional love that serves regardless of changing circumstances (Lewis 183–84). Both prefigure Butler's and Mbembe's pleas to recognise our common human fragility and vulnerability, Nancy's injunction to abandon biopolitics and realise that "Being cannot *be* anything but being-with-one-another" (3) and Le Blanc and Brugère's demand that we recover the politics of hospitality recommended by Enlightenment philosophers and theorised by Levinas.

The virtue of charity is also perceptible in Jacob's concern for the suffering of invisible and ungrievable others. During his first palanquin ride to Nagasaki, his attention is caught by "gnarled old women, pocked monks, unmarried girls with blackened teeth [… and] a girl [… whose] body cannot be ten years old, but her eyes belong to a much older woman" (40). Their common abhorrence of cruelty situates Orito and Jacob in line with Dr Marinus's enlightened ethics of hospitality. However, unlike Marinus, they are purblind characters with limited knowledge of the world. Therefore, their parallel life quests may be said to represent the evolution of their respective cultures in contact.

The Supernatural Counternarrative

In the Acknowledgements, David Mitchell provides a wealth of references to the historical sources employed in the novel. He explains that his characterisation of Jacob de Zoet is based on Hendrik Doeff's memoir, *Recollections of Japan* (Mitchel 2011, 481). As Larsonneur and Machinal note, Hendrik Doeff "acted as Dutch Chief Officer of Dejima between 1799 and 1817" (2). Similarly, Dr Marinus's figure is indebted

28 *Susana Onega*

to Dr Siebold, "a physician attached to the Dutch community in Dejima between 1823 and 1828" (Larsonneur 138). Like Marinus, Siebold created a botanical garden, became a reputed Japanese ethnographer and "had a daughter, Oine (1827–1903), from a Japanese concubine, who became the first female Japanese doctor and may have inspired the character of Orito" (Larsonneur 137–38). These and other historical hypertexts function as realism-enhancing mechanisms. However, this *effect de reel* is constantly undermined either by the secondary characters' stories with grotesque, fantastic and supernatural or, in Mitchell's own terms, "science fiction" traits (Harris-Birtill 180), or by the supernatural nature of Abbott Enomoto and Lucas Marinus. In Part Four, Dr Marinus jokingly compares his impending death to "a grass snake, shedding one skin" (466) and while he is with Jacob on the watchtower braving the carronades of the HMS *Phoebus*, he reassures the worried clerk that he is "indestructible, like a serial Wandering Jew. I'll wake up tomorrow—after a few months—and start all over again" (Mitchell 2011, 440). These comments point to Dr Marinus as an "Atemporal," an immortal soul with the capacity to reincarnate, usually by taking the body of a dying child whose soul has just departed. In Mitchell's fictional macronovel, there are two types of Atemporals: "Returnees" and "Sojourners." The souls of Sojourners leave their body upon death and move directly to another body. Returnees stay for some time in "the dusk, that twilight space between death and rebirth" (Harris-Birtill 180), before entering a new host body. Marinus's remark that "after a few months" he will "start all over again" points to him as a Returnee. While transmigration is dictated by the desire of a bodiless soul to stay in this world, the reincarnation of Atemporals takes place without their willingness or intervention. According to Mitchell, Atemporals differ from religious figures of compassion, like *bodhisattvas* or Messianic figures, in that their role is "to understand the darkness of the human heart to be able to let the light in" (Harris-Birtill 190, 193). More concretely, Atemporals like Dr Marinus are engaged in a never-ending struggle against evil Carnivores like Lord Abbot Enomoto. The voracity of Carnivores aligns them with the *oni*, evil spirits with many gruesome attributes, including cannibalism (Reider 2010, 15). Like their predecessors, the Indian *yasha* and *rasetsu*, Buddhist *oni* inspire not only fear but also respect and the desire to propitiate them through prayer. Their female counterparts, *yakṣa* and *yakshis*, represent fertility and abundance (11). Echoing this, the role of the Goddess of Shiranui, "Fountainhead of Life and Mother of Gifts" (Mitchell 2011, 194), is to ensure "the fertility of Kyôga's streams and rice-fields" (181), in exchange for "the fruits of [the nuns'] wombs" (194). The *oni* usually "live on the periphery of mainstream society" and are "seen as a threat to imperial control" (Reider 2010, 18). Thus, they may be said to represent the marginal and dark others of Japanese normative society. A prototypical example is the story of Shuten Dōji, the chief

Trading Relations, Violence and Ungrievability 29

of an *oni* band that lived on Mt Ōe during Emperor Ichijō's rule (980–1011). The band used to "abduct people, particularly maidens, enslaving them and eventually feasting on their flesh and drinking their blood" until the Emperor sent the warrior hero Minamoto no Raikō and his men to defeat them (2010, 20). This tale provides a neat hypotext for the Enomoto plot. Like Shuten Dōji, Abbott Enomoto is the Lord of a mountainous region, the Kyôga Domain, outside the shogun's control. The spiritual, political and economic power gathered by the Abbott along his more than 600 years of life (316) is so formidable that Lord Shiroyama, the Nagasaki Magistrate, is ready to die in order to poison him (Mitchell 2011, 458). Enomoto is an expert in poisons. Without the daily dose of antidote the nuns and acolytes unwittily drink every day, they would die in a couple of days. This is what happens to Jiritsu, an acolyte who escapes from the convent with a copy of the secret Twelve Creeds ruling the convent, meaning to denounce its cannibalistic practices (184), but he barely has time to give the scroll to Otane before dying. The herbalist also dies after walking all the way to Nagasaki to give Uzaemon the Creeds. Distracted by the news, Uzaemon asks his bosom friend and sword master Shuzai to hire some mercenaries to accompany him to the convent to rescue Orito. Like Minamoto no Raikō, he disguises himself as a pilgrim (291). However, unlike the hero's loyal men, Shuzai and his mercenaries are impoverished samurais, ready to betray Uzaemon for money. Their betrayal evinces the desperate condition of the samurai class, brought about, like that of the landed aristocracy represented by the Magistrate (357), by the rise of the mercantile society.

In striking contrast to them, Orito, after escaping from the convent, wins her true liberty by listening to the dictates of her compassionate heart. Following the Buddha's recommendation to make the right choice, no matter what happens to oneself, she decides to return to the Shrine in time to help Yayoi give birth to twins, on the reflection that her freedom is less important than their lives (271). Showing the unconditional respect for terrible people recommended by the Buddha, Orito then voluntarily assumes the role of midwife in the convent, although she knows that the souls of the babies she is helping to be born will be distilled into Oil of soul (460), and that the nuns will be killed and buried in anonymous graves after their twenty-year period of service. Meanwhile, the threat to Nagasaki represented by Lord Abbott Enomoto becomes tangible. The failure of the Dutch ship to arrive at its appointed time due to the course of the Napoleonic wars reduces Lord Shiroyama's income so drastically that he has to ask the Abbot for a huge loan. When the British warship attacks Dejima and Lord Enomoto proposes to bring to Nagasaki his own armed men (382) to defeat the foreigners (381), Lord Shiroyama accepts the proposal, knowing that he must preserve the family honour by committing seppuku (382). He then devises an elaborate plan to lure the cunny abbot into sharing a poisoned sake with him and

30 *Susana Onega*

Chamberlain Tomine (458). The Magistrate dies convinced that Enomoto is dead, and justice served (460). However, at the moment of the Abbott's death, a black butterfly lands on the white stone of the go game they had been playing before drinking the poisoned sake and unfolds its wings (461). Moths and butterflies are archetypal symbols of transformation, usually associated with the soul and spiritually. Therefore, the appearance of the huge black moth suggests that Enomoto's evil black soul has left his corpse and is attempting to transmigrate to another sentient being, as he cannot reincarnate. In *Utopia Avenue*, Lucas Marinus confirms this interpretation when he tells Jacob's great-great-great grandson, Jasper de Zoet, that the Abbot's soul had lodged itself inside Jacob's head and had stayed there dormant, passing down from father to son, generation after generation, until it reached Jasper himself (Mitchell 2020, 473).

Once readers realise that the black moth is Abbott Enomoto's soul, the birth of Lord Shiroyama's son in Chapter 1 acquires a supernatural dimension as well. While, at the beginning of the novel, the city of Nagasaki is welcoming the arrival of the *Shenandoah*, Dr Marinus and Orito are helping Miss Kawasemi, the Magistrate's concubine, to give birth to a foetus stuck with a prolapse of the arm, already thought to be dead (Mitchell 2011, 4). Orito manages to extract the foetus without dismembering it by mentally rehearsing a similar case she had read in a text written by a Scottish gynaecologist, William Smellier (3). After extracting the tiny body with the forceps, she slaps him, bathes him and places him in the crib, although she "has no hope of coaxing out a miracle" (8). However, just as the doctor draws the curtain, "[a] moth the size of a bird enters and blunders into Orito's face," making her knock the forceps, its clatter onto a pan lid, waking the baby into life (9). While the awakening to life of the stillborn child cannot be explained scientifically, from a Buddhist perspective it is a simple case of reincarnation. In Indic religions, "[t]he fundamental idea of reincarnation is that at death an ancestor or close kin is reborn in the human world whether or not there has been an intermediate sojourn in another sphere of existence or afterworld" (Obeyesekere 2002, 15). The fact that the stillborn baby is the Magistrate's only son and inheritor confirms the survival of the Shiroyama clan, thus granting significance and transcendence to his willing sacrifice. Thus, a new cosmic cycle of struggle between the supernatural forces of good and evil begins, as is suggested by the Magistrate's orders before committing seppuku that the child, fittingly called Naozumi ("Honesty and Innocence"), be taught to play the *go* game (454).

The attraction moths and butterflies feel for Orito points to the compassionate midwife as an agent of transformation and rebirth, her unflinching ethics of care even after the baby's death pointing to the importance she gives to grievability. A few days after the birth of Naozumi, when she was telling Jacob that her goal in life was to prevent

Trading Relations, Violence and Ungrievability 31

women from dying out of ignorance, a white butterfly landed on her hand (69). On another, Jacob associates Orito's eyes with a "pretty little butterfly" (347). Significantly, Jacob also attracts beneficial insects. When he was picking slugs from the cabbages in Dr Marinus's garden, a ladybird landed on his right hand (126). As he made a bridge for it with his left hand, he wondered whether he was also being made to cross an endless sequence of bridges by some superior entity. This is the nearest the staunch Protestant is of considering the Buddhist doctrine of fate and reincarnation. When Lord Abbot Enomoto visited Jacob with the aim of buying the mercury he had brought from Holland (78), he asked him if he believed that the soul can be taken, and Jacob responded that it can be taken by the devil (76). His answer and his red hair convinced the Abbott that Jacob had a spiritual affinity with him (80). So, he invited him to come to his shrine to learn this philosophy in his next reincarnation (77). This supposed affinity would explain why Enomoto's soul decided to transmigrate to Jacob's head. During the same meeting, the Abbott killed a snake ready to bite him by simply making a pressing motion with his flat hand (77). As Interpreter Yonekizu reassures the astonished Jacob, this was neither trick nor magic but Chinese philosophy, the mastery of the force of *ki* (77). *Ki*, or *chi* in Chinese, is the life force that animates everything. In Western culture, its nearest equivalent would be the *spiritus mundi*, God's creative spark existing in all things. In the Renaissance, Hermetic alchemists like Paracelsus and Giordano Bruno tried to bring about the "chemical wedding" of opposites (light/darkness; spirit/matter; God/Goddess), by means of *amor vulgaris*, procreative sexual love (see Yates), the same type of love practised at the Shiranui Mountain Shrine. According to alchemy, mercury is the symbol of the cosmic womb being incubated by the cross of the four elements of creation—earth, air, fire and water. This fact adds an esoteric element to the Abbott's keen interest in mercury beyond its common value as the best cure for syphilis (Mitchel 2011, 79), which opens up a wider perspective on his cannibalism. While the farming of babies was meant to prolong his life and that of his clan *ad infinitum*, the final aim of the Abbot's supernatural practices was, like that of the alchemists, to gain mastery over the life force as a means to exert control over the entire world. At the same time, his belief that "Survival Is Nature's Law" and that Adam Smith would understand the sacrifice of babies as "a messy requisite" for his clan's use and "to purchase the favours of an elite few" (316) equates his predatory practices and domineering goal with those of the advocates of imperialism.

Conclusion

When Jacob de Zoet accepted his clerical post at the trading post on Dejima, he shared the Enlightenment thinkers' view that the role of

32 Susana Onega

international commerce was to establish mutually profitable and friendly relations with other civilised nations, thus contributing to eradicate barbarism. However, his idealised conception of international trading relations was soon dispelled by the cruelty and violence routinely exerted by the "civilised" VOC officers on their social, racial and gender inferiors. Their atrocity, based on Social Darwinist tenets and the biblical mandate to populate the earth and subdue it, provided Western nations with moral justification for colonial and imperial expansion. However, from the perspective of Jacob's agapeic faith, informed by enlightened rationalism and Matthew's recommendation that we take the position of the stranger, the true barbarians on Dejima are neither the cannibals in the VOC officers' truculent yarns nor their slaves. Reduced to the animal condition of bare life through a systematic process of dispossession, derealisation and animalisation, these slaves are the invisible and ungrievable others of the Empire. But gratuitous cruelty and violence are also routinely exerted, both by Europeans and Japanese, on same-race social and gender inferiors, particularly women, who are objectified and condemned to lead submissive lives determined by family protection, class and physical aspect, their only alternative to an enforced marriage being prostitution, beggary or nunnery. At the bottom of the European and Japanese only-male scale of subjectivisation, we find a common conscience of the vulnerability, precariousness and ungrievability of women, the poor, the orphans and illegitimate mixed-race children, like Jacob the Zoet's son, Yûan, who is denied the right to bear his father's name and nationality or inherit his fortune, and must live at the margin of Japanese society as well: "*He is too Japanese to leave [...] but not Japanese enough to belong*" (477; original italics).

When Jacob returns to Batavia, eighteen years after his departure, his expectations and dreams unfulfilled, he finds that Anna had married a socially adequate suitor and died in childbirth (478). He then conforms to the same social norm by marrying the staunch daughter of an associate (478–9), whose youth is considered an adequate compensation for his money (479). Jacob then starts writing his memoirs (479) and bequeaths the miraculous family Psalter to his eldest Dutch son, an honest youth with no curiosity for ultramarine adventures (479). This drab ending seems to confirm the impression that Jacob's struggle against the imperialist forces of evil and greed has failed. However, at the very end of the novel, when he is lying in his deathbed, Jacob is visited by Orito's phantom:

> She places her cool palms on Jacob's fever-glazed face
> [...].
> Her lips touch the place between his eyebrows.
> A well-waxed paper door slides open.

(479)

William Stephenson interprets Orito's kiss "as an inversion of Ogawa's death" (114), shot in the head by Lord Abbott Enomoto, and he explains the metaphor of the Japanese paper door as evidence that "a trace of oriental otherness remains in Jacob's mind despite his return to the Netherlands" (114). We know, however, that Enomoto's soul is lodged inside Jacob's head and that his imminent death will force the Abbott to transmigrate to Jacob's son. This means that Jacob is free at last to overcome the spiritual stagnation caused by his uncanny parasite. Orito arrives at this crucial moment and kisses him between the eyebrows, thus helping him open his brow chakra or third eye, the gate that leads to the inner realms and spaces of higher consciousness. Thus, the novel ends with Orito, a true agent of transformation, performing a final ethical act of care, compassion and grieving, helping Jacob reach the enlightened state he needs to transcend to a higher plane of being, or, in Christian terms, helping him round off his quest for individuation and transcendence. By so doing, Orito shows Jacob, and the readers, that the best way to mitigate the vulnerability, precariousness and ungrievability of the human condition is through the practice of an ethics of care and a politics of hospitality informed by agapeic love and compassion.

Acknowledgements

Research for this chapter was funded by the Spanish Ministry of Science and Innovation (MICINN) (code PID2021-124841NB-I00) and by the Government of Aragón and the European Social Fund (ESF) (code H03_20R).

Works Cited

Agamben, Giorgio. *Homo Sacer: Sovereign Power and Bare Life*. 1995. Eds Werner Hamacher and David E. Wellbery. Trans. Daniel Heller-Roazen. Stanford, CA: Stanford UP, 1998.

Bakhtin, Mikhail. *Rabelais and His World*. 1965. Trans. Helen Iswolsky. Bloomington: Indiana UP, 1984.

Bayer, Gerd. "Cannibalising the Other: David Mitchell's *The Thousand Autumns of Jacob de Zoet* and the Incorporation of 'Exotic' Pasts." *Exoticizing the Past in Neo-Historical Fiction*. Ed. Elodie Rousselot. Houndmills, Basingstoke, Hampshire and New York: Palgrave Macmillan, 2014. 103–19.

Butler, Judith. *Precarious Life: The Powers of Mourning and Violence*. London and New York: Verso, 2004.

———. *Frames of War: When Is Life Grievable?* London and New York: Verso, 2009.

———. *The Force of Non-Violence*. London and New York: Verso, 2020.

de Waard, Marco. "Dutch Decline Redux: Remembering New Amsterdam in the Global and Cosmopolitan Novel." *Imagining Global Amsterdam: History, Culture, and Geography in a World City*. Ed. Marco de Waard. Amsterdam: Amsterdam UP, 2012. 101–22.

34 *Susana Onega*

Glaser, Brigitte. "Crossing Borders: Interracial Relationships in English Colonial Fiction." *Racism, Slavery, and Literature.* Eds Wolfgang Zach and Ulrich Pallua. Frankfurt am Main: Peter Lang, 2010. 209–23.

Harris-Birtill, Rose. *David Mitchell's Post-Secular World: Buddhism, Belief and the Urgency of Compassion.* London and New York: Bloomsbury Academic, 2019.

Kant, Immanuel. *Perpetual Peace: A Philosophical Essay.* Trans., Intro., and Notes by M. Campbell Smith M.A. Preface by Professor Latta. London: John Allen & Unwin Ltd/New York: The MacMillan Company, 1795. Project Gutenberg e-book accessed on 23/07/2020 at: https://www.gutenberg.org/files/50922/50922-h/50922-h.htm/.

Keene, Tom. "Author David Mitchell Talks Economic History on Bloomberg Radio." *Bloomberg News.* CEO Wire. CQ Roll: Waltham 13 July 2010. Accessed on 17/07/2020 at: https://search.proquest.com/docview/609389842?accountid= 14795/.

Larsonneur, Claire. "Revisiting Dejima (Japan): From Recollections to Fiction in David Mitchell's *The Thousand Autumns of Jacob de Zoet* (2010)." *SubStance* 44.1 (2015): 136–47.

Larsonneur, Claire, and Hélène Machinal. "Mediations: Science and Translation in *The Thousand Autumns of Jacob de Zoet* by David Mitchell." *Études britanniques contemporaines* 45 (2013). DOI: https://doi.org/10.4000/ebc.957. Accessed on 12/11/2019 at: http://journals.openedition.org/ebc/957/.

Le Blanc, Guillaume. "Politiques de l'hospitalité." *Cités* 46 (2011): 87–97.

Le Blanc, Guillaume, and Fabienne Brugère. *La Fin de l'hospitalitè. Lampedusa, Lesbos, Calais… jusqu'où irons nous?* Paris: Flammarion, 2017.

Levinas, Emmanuel. "Judaism and the Feminine Element." *Judaism* 18.1 (1969): 33–73.

Lewis, C. S. *The Four Loves.* 1960. New York: Harcourt, Brace, 1988.

Mbembe, Achille. *Necropolitics.* 2016. Trans. Steven Corcoran. Durham and London: Duke UP, 2019.

Mitchell, David. *The One Thousand Autumns of Jacob de Zoet.* 2010. New York: Random House, 2011.

———. *Utopia Avenue.* London: Sceptre, 2020.

Möller, Richard M. "Sublime Barbarism?: Affinities between the Barbarian and the Sublime in Eighteenth-Century Aesthetics." *Barbarism Revisited: New Perspectives on an Old Concept.* Eds Maria Boletsi and Christian Moser. Leiden and Boston, MA: Brill/Rodopi, 2015. 139–54.

Nancy, Jean-Luc. *Being Singular Plural.* 1996. Trans. Robert B. Richardson and Ann E. O'Byrne. Stanford, CA: Stanford UP, 2000.

Obeyesekere, Gananath. *Imagining Karma: Ethical Transformations in Amerindian, Buddhist, and Greek Rebirth.* Berkeley, Los Angeles, London: U of California P, 2002.

———. *Cannibal Talk: The Man-Eating Myth and Human Sacrifice in the South Seas.* Berkeley, Los Angeles, London: U of California P, 2005.

O'Donnell, Patrick. *A Temporary Future: The Fiction of David Mitchell.* London: Bloomsbury, 2015.

Reider, Noriko T. "The Emergence of 'Kaidan-shū' The Collection of Tales of the Strange and Mysterious in the Edo Period." *Asian Folklore*

Studies 60.1 (2001): 79–99. Accessed on 20/07/2020 at: http://www.jstor.com/stable/1178699/.

———. *Japanese Demon Lore: Oni from Ancient Times to the Present.* UP of Colorado; Utah State UP, 2010. Accessed on 20/07/2020 at: http://www.jstor.com/stable/j.ctt4cgpqc.7/.

Stephenson, William. "History, Globalization and the Human Subject in *The Thousand Autumns of Jacob de Zoet.*" *David Mitchell.* Eds Wendy Knepper and Courtney Hopf. London: Bloomsbury Academic, 2019. 101–16.

Vogt, Peter. "The Conceptual History of Barbarism: What Can We Learn from Koselleck and Pocock?" *Barbarism Revisited: New Perspectives on an Old Concept.* Eds Maria Boletsi and Christian Moser. Leiden and Boston, MA: Brill/Rodopi, 2015. 125–38.

Yates, Frances A. *Giordano Bruno and the Hermetic Tradition.* 1964. London: Routledge and Kegan Paul; Chicago, IL: The U of Chicago P, 1977.

2 Undermining the Hierarchy of Grief in Rachel Seiffert's *A Boy in Winter*

Paula Romo-Mayor

Introduction

The traumatic landscapes that characterise the twenty-first century—from waves of terrorism and irregular warfare, through environmental disasters and the effects of global capitalism creating an increasing refugee crisis, to the ongoing COVID-19 pandemic—have brought to the fore human vulnerability as an inescapable existential predicament. Accordingly, throughout the last decades, this notion has surfaced as a necessary conceptual tool in academia, especially in the fields of feminism, gender studies, memory and trauma studies, postcolonialism and, more recently, ecocriticism, international relations and health care. As Susana Onega and Jean-Michel Ganteau argue in the "Introduction" to *Victimhood and Vulnerability in 21st-Century Fiction* (2017), the trauma paradigm originating in the 1990s in the fields of literary criticism and moral philosophy has evolved into a "vulnerability paradigm very much indebted to the ethics of alterity, the ethics of care, precariousness studies, and the ethics of vulnerability" (7). The definitional aspect of this turn to vulnerability expresses a major concern with the universal injurability of the human condition; that is, it conveys the idea that vulnerability is not only attributable to but also inherent in every individual. This is precisely one of Judith Butler's main arguments in *Precarious Life: The Power of Mourning and Violence* (2004). By employing the term "precariousness" as a synonym for the ontological and existential vulnerability of every human life, Butler implies that we are vulnerable not only because of our own mortality but because we are social beings who depend on others to survive. The consolidation of the term "vulnerability" takes place in the 1980s, coinciding with the acknowledgement of PTSD in the medical field and with the turn to ethics in the humanities, influenced, among others, by Emmanuel Levinas's ethics of alterity. One of his main contentions is that the vulnerability of the other has the capacity to invite the self to engage in ethical behaviour. Another, that the non-violent relation to the other entails an epiphanic experience whereby our consciousness is overwhelmed by the face of the other, whose extreme wretchedness summons our responsibility to respond to

DOI: 10.4324/9781003347811-4

it (Levinas 1986, 353). However, when this demand is manipulated by representational regimes and institutions and turned against the other, the ethical mission of the self is severely affected. Butler describes this as a serious problem of our time. Drawing on Giorgio Agamben's concept of "bare life" in modern politics (1998), she contends that vulnerability is not equally distributed around the globe and that we are not just exposed to the violence of others but also to one that depends on our own socio-economic conditions. This type of vulnerability is what she calls "precarity" (Butler 2009, 3). She highlights how dehumanising representations in official and mass media discourses can contribute to shaping people's ability to recognise the life of others and, subsequently, to delimit their domain of grievability. From this Butler goes on to denounce the establishment by those in power of a "hierarchy of grief" (2004, 34) that determines whose lives matter and are worthy of being grieved and whose lives are not mournable and can be easily disposed of. This stratification of life entails the exclusion of alterity from the very notion of humankind and relegates the other to a spectral liminality between life and death (Butler, 33–34). Indeed, the devaluation and negation of their existence not only divests the other of the right to be grieved but also legitimises the use of violence against them, thus generating an unending cycle of hostility. This is why Butler urges the humanities to return to the human in its vulnerability and grievability and engage in the critical task of identifying and transgressing the dehumanising discourses of power (151).

In connection with this, Silvia Pellicer-Ortín has highlighted the strong relationship between trauma, ethics and literature and the potential of literature to voice and mitigate traumatic and vulnerability-inducing experiences (37). Indeed, one of the most important qualities of literature is its capacity to articulate life in its uttermost complexity and, by so doing, shed light on the various forms of devaluating and oppressing outlooks on otherness. In this context, the novels of Rachel Seiffert are particularly enriching analytical objects. Her own burden as the granddaughter of Nazis on her mother's side stimulated an interest in the behaviour of individuals caught in exceptionally violent historical circumstances and in the effects of their actions on their humanness, regardless of their status as victims, perpetrators or in-betweeners.

These ideas have become overarching motifs in her literary fictions. In her debut novel, *The Dark Room* (2001), Seiffert explores the behaviour of three ordinary Germans belonging to different generations who become willingly or unwillingly involved in the Holocaust, and how they deal with ethical responsibility. Her second novel, *Afterwards* (2007), revolves around the lives of two mentally wounded British soldiers after their participation in military actions. The older one had served in the RAF during a counterinsurgency war in colonial Kenya in the 1950s and 1960s, the younger one as a British infantryman during the Troubles of

38   *Paula Romo-Mayor*

Northern Ireland in the 1990s. The third novel, *The Walk Home* (2014), recounts the story of a Protestant family that was violently evicted from its home during the Partition of Ireland (1922) and has been haunted by a problematic fanaticism ever since. Her latest book to date, *A Boy in Winter* (2017), returns to the distress and suffering of the Second World War and the Holocaust. This time, however, Seiffert addresses the Nazi invasion of Ukraine in late 1941 through a multiperspectival narrative structure, giving voice to the reactions of antagonistic characters—Jews, Germans and Ukrainians—in the course of three days. Seiffert's tendency towards formal experimentation and her concern with the behaviour of individuals in armed conflicts or their aftermath aligns her with those contemporary writers who, according to Ganteau, treat fiction as "one of the privileged loci of vulnerability," favouring "a concentration of vulnerable thought and feeling that is both represented and performed textually" (25).

A *Boy in Winter* is set during the Third Reich (1933–45), a period in history characterised by the display of state power and the restriction of the grievability of the other through systematic dehumanisation. In this socio-political context, the Nazis divided humankind into *die Übermenschen*, the members of the biologically and intellectually superior Aryan race, and *die Untermenschen*, conformed by eternally flawed and/or depraved beings such as Jews, Roma and Sinti, the mentally and physically disabled, homosexuals and political opponents to the Nazi regime. This hierarchy of humans, that subsequently allowed the Third Reich to delimit the recognisability of life as such, can be analysed through the prism of Butler's notion of "epistemological frame" (2009, 1). Butler uses this expression to refer to the set of overt or covert rules that regulate the lens through which we perceive reality, distributing and retracting the allotment of life value, and determining which ones can be acknowledged and which ones cannot. Hitler and his henchmen's megalomaniacal project of building a perfect, peaceful and prosperous world legitimised the denial of full humanness to those who did not meet with social, political or ethnic approval. This was the primal manifestation of the dehumanising tendency of Nazism and the most dangerous one, since it paved the way for its most radical expression: organised mass extermination (Bauman 102). Between the Nazis' rise to power in 1933 and the first deportations to concentration camps in 1941 lay a long-term process whereby the so-called enemies, especially the Jews, were gradually and forcefully excluded from life. Among its most significant milestones should be mentioned the enforcement of the Nuremberg Laws (1935), which basically criminalised any kind of relation between Jews and non-Jews; the November Pogrom or *Kristallnacht* (1938), during which both civilians and the paramilitary forces of the *Sturmabteilung* (SA) destroyed Jewish-owned businesses and synagogues throughout Nazi Germany; or *Aktion T4* (1939–41), a programme consisting in the application of large-scale killing methods on disabled individuals for the sake of biological purity. Racism, ableism and ideological discrimination were further enforced by a powerful propaganda campaign that authorised the discrimination and persecution of the so-called enemies of the Reich through systematic degradation and dehumanisation. What is more, the perpetrators justified murderous acts in perfectly reasonable terms. By way of illustration, the *SS* newspaper *Das Schwarze Korps* published in 1937 an article stating the following: "When someone says that man does not have the right to kill, let us reply to him that man has even less right to ruin the work of nature and to keep a being alive that was not born to live" (quoted in Chapoutot 148). As can be inferred from this quotation, the Nazi state confronted rationality and ethics and bet on the former, giving rise to a system where humanity was the main casualty (Bauman 206). These ideas have been grippingly evoked by Martin Amis in *Time's Arrow* (1991) where, as María Jesús Martínez-Alfaro powerfully analyses, reverse narrative and unreliable narration are fundamental to confer some ethical significance to the Nazi project (2011, 134). The necessity for their own subjectivisation led the Nazis to annihilate the subjectivity of the other, establishing a pervasive system of differences characterised by violence, general indifference and profound disaffection (Onega 94), ruled by what Jean Baudrillard called in *The Perfect Crime* (1996) a "'phobic relationship with an artificial other, idealized by hatred' (132)" (quoted in Onega 94). As we know, this phobic relationship, which, according to Baudrillard, constituted the corollary of the technological society, was eventually endorsed by the majority of Germans. Although most Germans were unwilling to implement openly the mandates of the Nazi government, they decided not to interfere and unquestioningly accepted them, so that the population ended up being infected by ethical stagnation and a general indifference to the suffering of the other.

Sixty years after the end of the Second World War, Dagmar Barnouw claimed that the Allies' imposition on the German population of collective guilt for the Nazi crimes and the exclusion from public memory of the atrocities perpetrated against German civilians prevented the defeated survivors from mourning their losses (x). Therefore, this German scholar, who had become a refugee as a child after the bombing of Dresden in 1945, called for a more nuanced and multifaceted view of history. Taking her demand into consideration, this chapter proposes an analysis of *A Boy in Winter* from the perspectives of Holocaust literature and ethics, aimed to demonstrate, firstly, that the interplay of the different voices in the novel erases the possibility of imposing the Nazi discourse of power, thus undermining its intended hierarchy of grief; and secondly, that the encounter between antagonistic characters leads to epiphanic moments where the precariousness of the human condition is recognised in the life of the other. More generally, it attempts to

40 *Paula Romo-Mayor*

demonstrate that Seiffert's narrative opens up a site wherein the acceptance of human life as a set of interdependencies and the grievability of every human loss is possible.

Polyphony as a Challenge to the Monopoly on Truth Exerted by the Discourse of Power

According to the records of the United States Holocaust Memorial Museum (2020), the delimitation of the domain of grievability during the Nazi regime enabled the destruction of 17 million people, including Jews, civilian population in occupied territories, Soviet POWs, disabled persons, Romani, Jehovah's Witnesses, criminal offenders, German political opponents and homosexuals (Anon. n.p.). This colossal human tragedy brought about a crisis of representation that was memorably summarised in Theodor Adorno's dictum "to write poetry after Auschwitz is barbaric" (34). With these words, Adorno was not simply referring to the writing of poetry, but rather to the tension between ethics and aesthetics that would necessarily characterise Western culture from then onwards. As he argued, any work of art, be it in the service of or in opposition to the horrors of the Holocaust, would unavoidably become complicit with the genocide merely because this art arose from the cultural values of the society that enabled it. Coupled with this was the commonly held assumption that the ethical collapse and traumatic impact of the Holocaust and the crimes committed during the Third Reich made them unsignifiable. Writing about the Holocaust thus became an ethical problem, compelling authors to ponder on "what can or should be represented of that event, and how" (Lang x). As Martínez-Alfaro puts it, such a practice amounted—and still amounts—to embarking on a quest for meaning and using it as a vehicle to confront the unspeakability and unrepresentability of the Holocaust (2020, 39). This would explain why Holocaust narratives tend to favour formal experimentation. In her critical work, *Holocaust Fiction* (2000), Sue Vice borrows Russian Formalist ideas to comment on the inextricable link between form and content in Holocaust literature. As she points out, this type of literary texts represents historical facts whose outcome is already determined. Consequently, such novelistic devices as suspense, unpredictable endings or the possibility of undoing evil are out of the question. Nevertheless, the relationship between form and content offers a myriad of possibilities for transcending the limits of history and trauma and for telling a story with ethical potential. This is precisely the case of *A Boy in Winter*, a Holocaust fiction that is described in the back-cover blurb as "[a] story of hope when all is lost, and of mercy when the times have none" (Seiffert 2017) or, as Vice would put it, a story that bears "a crumb of comfort in universal destruction" (2000, 3).

Seiffert's novel is set during the mass shootings undertaken by the *Einsatzgruppen* (the German Special Task Forces) as they moved through Eastern Europe, or, as Patrick Desbois calls it, as they performed "the Holocaust by Bullets" (2008). This episode of the Second World War has been powerfully evoked in D.M. Thomas's *The White Hotel* (1981) and more recently in Tara Lynn Masih's *My Real Name Is Hanna* (2018). Nevertheless, it still remains underexplored in Holocaust literature. The scarcity of literary representations of these crimes, as Vice argues, is caused by the tendency to place them within the broader context of the Holocaust, relegating them to function as "the prelude to the establishment of camps in which mechanized mass murder was to be committed" rather than as the main narrative events (2018, 89). Moreover, the very nature of these murders—immediate, brutal and massive—drastically reduced the victims' chances of survival and, with them, the writing of potential testimonial works about them. The disempowerment of the Holocaust victim, one that has been abused but cannot recount such abusive acts, precisely illustrates Jean-François Lyotard's notion of the "differend," a situation of conflict where the exchange between the participants is not plausible because the victim has been dispossessed of all available channels of communication (1988, 9). This inequality of opportunity to consider each of the testimonies is legitimised by the norms established within the epistemological frames where the wrong is committed and stems from the belief that the life of the other by virtue of its otherness is less grievable and also less credible. Ultimately, it generates a collective and structural form of epistemic discrimination that Miranda Fricker calls "epistemic injustice" (2007), whereby relations of power limit and deny the dominated individuals' ability to make sense of their experience, their right to bear witness to it and therefore their capacity to be mourned in the public sphere. The uneven distribution of credibility and grievability during the Third Reich also explains why the most popular fictional works dealing with mass shootings in occupied Soviet territory tend to revolve around the experiences of perpetrators rather than those of victims (Vice 2018, 97). *A Boy in Winter*, however, avoids the use of a single perspective and delves into the Holocaust by Bullets on a more encompassing scale. In a fashion that recalls Adam Thorpe's exploration of the last weeks of the war in Berlin in *The Rules of Perspective* (2005), Seiffert opts for a third-person narrator with limited omniscience that describes the experiences of a variety of characters through a combination of variable and multiple internal focalisation. A well-known literary technique in contemporary literature in general and in Holocaust literature in particular is fragmentation, a device "aimed at reflecting formally the disruptions inherent in any traumatic experience" (Martínez-Alfaro 2020, 39). In this line, Seiffert's use of fragmentation concerns the substitution of the external narrator's own point of view for the perspectives of a number of characters that belong

42   *Paula Romo-Mayor*

to antagonistic sides of the conflict. This dissolution of the narrator's omniscience echoes the postmodernist deconstruction of "the unitary and totalising truth[s]" imposed by the master narratives of the dominant culture (Lyotard 1984, 12). Among the most prevalent focalisers on the Jewish side, we encounter Ephraim, a town optician who, along with his wife Miryam, his daughter Rosa and other local Jews, packed up for resettlement as instructed by the Nazis, and is awaiting execution in a brick factory in the story's present. At the same time, readers are also granted the perspective of his teenage son, Yankel, the "boy in winter" of the title, who has taken to the road with his little brother Momik in an attempt to avoid the dreadful fate of their community by evading the Nazi soldiers that routinely patrol the streets armed with handguns. On the Ukrainian side, one of the focalisers is Yasia, a young woman suffering from both the oppression of the German newcomers—who have imposed curfews, the wearing of armbands and restrictions on social gatherings—and the absence of her beloved Mykola. Mykola's story is representative of those Ukrainian soldiers who deserted the Red Army and joined the Nazi auxiliary police force, in Mykola's case, on the grounds that he could help rebuild local farms and bring his family and girlfriend food and goods with the wages paid by the Germans. On the German side the main focaliser is Otto Pohl, a middle-aged engineer who has travelled to Ukraine in order to build a thoroughfare across the newly occupied territory but also, and more importantly, to avoid serving in the *Wehrmacht*.[1] At the end of the novel, readers are granted the perspective of another type of German, *Sturmbannführer* Arnold, an ambitious *SS* officer who, after behaving as a loyal servant to the Reich, becomes aware of his own insignificance in the cruel Nazi enterprise.

The novel begins with the extradiegetic-heterodiegetic narrator setting the story on the first fog of morning in an anonymous Ukrainian town and describing Yankel, whose identity is not yet revealed, running hastily along the streets of the town with his younger brother Momik bundled on to his shoulders. Immediately after this description, the narrator assumes Yankel's perspective and reports his thoughts in indirect interior monologue. Thus, we learn that he hears no movement despite his alertness and that the cold has started to penetrate his body and that of his brother, who keeps shivering on his back. Then, the narrative perspective shifts to Otto Pohl, as he is woken up by a door slam and Ukrainians and Germans shouting. These changes in focalisation keep happening throughout the narrative, only announced by a blank space on the page. For example, they allow us to discover without the need of an explanation on the part of the narrator that the background noises that disrupt Pohl's sleep come from a house nearby. A group of *SS* men are throwing out of it a Jewish schoolmaster who regrets not having followed their instructions the previous night. At the same time, in another part of the town, Yasia is startled by the howling of sirens and the splutter of a loudhailer. Since the scenes are focalised through one character at a time, the narrator has a limited field of vision. This effect of limitation becomes more evident when the action is not reported from the perspective of several characters because not all of them are always in the same place and time, and it is intensified by the fact that the novel is narrated in the present. For example, when Ephraim hears rumours about the fate of the Jews in the brick house and becomes anxious, the narrator simply records the character's own reflection: "He wants to know what awaits them as much as anyone, but all these whispers are unsettling; any noise makes him nervous" (Seiffert 2017, 43). Since the story is based on historical events, the reader has a general idea about what the Nazis intend to do to the Jews, but there is no clue as to what the future holds for this particular group of Jewish people, especially for Ephraim. Like him, readers wonder whether he will ever see Yankel and Momik again. Therefore, the overall impression is that the narrator, the telling figure, is at the same level as the characters, the seeing figures, without manipulating, filtering or evaluating their experience of reality, that is, the narration is carried out from a position of internal focalisation. However, this type of focalisation is far from limiting; on the contrary, it offers the readers access to the workings of the characters' minds, including their memories and the possibility of contemplating and judging the events taking place as the characters perceive them. Thus, Pohl's recollection of the moment he arrived in the district months before reveals traces of the ongoing tragedy in the Eastern Front. He had observed with consternation the abandoned battlefields with their scarred and silent soils and how the roadside ditches near the river Bug were strewn with Red Army corpses. While Pohl's reminiscences provide a horrifying panorama of Ukraine after the arrival of the *Wehrmacht*, Yasia, in one of her flashbacks, offers an equally atrocious vision of the Holodomor under Stalin's rule, when millions of Soviet citizens starved to death. Yasia's memories also show that individuals of the same community do not agree with one another on the right thing to do in such afflicting circumstances. Her own father, Fedir, who is satisfied with his life situation now that the Soviets are gone believes that, if helping the Nazis will allow them to move on with their lives, then this is what they must do. Mykola's grandfather, on the contrary, wants no more intruders; he finds Fedir's attitude humiliating and contends that the Ukrainians should fight for their own side. This debate unfolds in the context of Mykola's decision to collaborate with the Nazis. In a private conversation before joining the Ukrainian auxiliary police, the young man had let it out to his girlfriend that he disagreed with both men: the former, because of his selfishness; the latter, because of his excess of pride. Later on in the novel, his train of thought reveals that Mykola thinks of Soviets and Nazis in equal terms: "neither had any care for the wrong and the right of things [...] and Mykola dreaded each

44   *Paula Romo-Mayor*

as much as he loathed them" (147–48). His reason for complying with the invaders is to survive: "no one wants to die at the hands of another" (148). The climactic scene of the mass shooting of Ephraim and the local Jews is too appalling to be told from any viewpoint. However, Seiffert uses multiple focalisation to illustrate how the fatal noise of the gunshots of the massacre penetrates the perceptual angle of more than one character and shrouds their surroundings with silence. It startles Yasia in the streets and leaves her immobile and curled up in a ball; it drives her friend Osip to crowd in a corner of his kitchen and feel how the echoes inundate the rest of the rooms in his house; and it shocks Pohl, who ruminates on the possibility that the Nazis might also start killing those who disobeyed them and tried to help Jews. These examples are illustrative of how the use of variable and multiple internal focalisation in *A Boy in Winter* opens different windows through which to observe and apprehend the diversity and complexity of the reactions of various individuals and groups to the Nazi invasion of Ukraine.

Significantly, Seiffert expresses the refusal of the Nazi characters to share the narrative space with their so-called enemies and inferiors through a very subtle detail: the *Waffen-SS* officers and *Wehrmacht* soldiers that range over the Ukrainian village frequently resort to loud-hailers to make themselves heard. The blare of the megaphones in the streets trying to impose German norms and ways of perceiving the world contrasts sharply with the whispers of both the Jewish and non-Jewish Ukrainians locked up in their houses awaiting catastrophe. In this context of compulsory silence, Seiffert's use of an external narrator with the capacity to enter the minds of the characters and report their innermost secret thoughts effectively dismantles the Nazis' monopoly on truth conveyed by the discourse of power. *A Boy in Winter* can thus be considered an example of what Mikhail Bakhtin calls the polyphonic novel, where "a *plurality of consciousnesses, with equal rights and each with its own world*, combine but are not merged in the unity of the event" (6; original emphasis). This polyphony renders the relationships among the various factions involved in the conflict dialogic, that is, based on interdependence and nuancing, thus subverting the obliteration and erasure of the other and the epistemic injustice perpetuated by the monologic discourse of power. Therefore, we can argue that the poetics of the novel precludes the formation of Butler's epistemological frame and, consequently, the establishment of a hierarchy of lives. Each version of the events as perceived by the characters becomes essential for the understanding of the overall meaning of the story. It reminds readers of the permeability and relativity of truth as well as of the necessity to take into consideration the accounts of manifold subjects, even if inconsistent and irreconcilable, to adopt ethically informed responses to cases of violence and injustice. As we have seen, Seiffert gives voice not only to Jews, the target of the systematic killing of the Holocaust, but also to characters belonging to less explored collectives, such as ordinary Germans and the Ukrainians living in the occupied territory. The precarity of Jews under the Nazi regime is highlighted in the sense that the novel is entitled after Yankel, a Jewish boy whose voice opens the narrative. However, the suffering of Ukrainians is foregrounded as well, since the closing perspective is granted to Yasia. Still, this does not overshadow the situations of danger and the vulnerability in this context of exceptional violence of some ordinary Germans like Otto Pohl, or Ukrainian collaborators like Mykola, thus making the novel sensitive to the pain of characters representing various communal, sociocultural and ethical positions. By giving voice to the silenced discourses of the repressed, the neglected and the troubled by moral scruples, this polyphonic narration may be said to respond to Levinas's demand for a solidary and generous move towards an individual other that would be otherwise bound to the totalising discourse of the self. The ultimate consequence of Seiffert's way of framing the Holocaust by Bullets is, therefore, to foreground and embrace the plural human condition in all its vulnerability and grievability. As I will attempt to show in the following section, her choice of narrative technique allows Seiffert to transmit to readers the ethical message that asks us to appreciate and preserve the dignity of all human lives and oppose power structures and dynamics that consider some of them valueless.

Taking an Ethical Stance on Systematic Violence

Besides undermining the hierarchy of grief imposed by the Nazis, the multiplicity and variety of perspectives and the absence of an authorial voice allow Seiffert to display the individual traits of her characters from their own perspectives, as they think, observe reality, hesitate and, most crucially, meet each other in all their fragility. Instead of giving way to extremely good or inherently evil protagonists, variable and multiple internal focalisation casts light on unexplored subject positions within the wide spectrum of violence, in particular, within the different shades of bystanding. Like real human beings, Seiffert's characters have a complex and individual behaviour that does not exactly fit into the theoretical categories of bystanders—beneficiaries, accomplices, passive witnesses or helpers. Thus, Seiffert challenges the traditional fictional modes of representing warfare in oppositional binary terms and shows that things often differ from what they appear to be from an external perspective. As we have seen, in *A Boy in Winter*, there are bystanders that choose to collaborate with the Nazis, as is the case of Mykola, who joins the Ukrainian auxiliary police and witnesses the murder of innocent victims without intervening; but so too are there bystanders that tilt towards resistance, such as Otto Pohl and Yasia. As a close reading of their behaviour will show, the positionality of these characters turns out to be rather ambivalent and multi-layered. However, the eventual

46   *Paula Romo-Mayor*

decision of some of them to help and rescue others when confronted with their weakness and vulnerability suggests that their ethical stance is strong even in life-endangering situations of unmitigated oppression and violence.

Otto Pohl, the German engineer, has left his wife Dorle back in Münster in order to direct the construction of a road in Ukraine, thus avoiding, as we have seen, his enrolment in the army to serve in a war he does not believe in. An ordinary German, Pohl abhors Hitler's plans, as can be appreciated at the very beginning of the novel when he cautiously addresses his thoughts to his absent wife, rather than tell her in his letters. However, his apparently neutral, technical job does not spare him from becoming involved in Nazi violence both against Jewish and non-Jewish Ukrainians. Although he is aware of this fact, he tries to justify his collaboration by convincing himself that he is creating "*a road for when the war is over* [...] *for when Hitler loses* [...]. *Fit for civilization, not some thousand-year abomination*" (Seiffert 2017, 22–23; original emphasis). This act of self-justification points to Otto Pohl as representative of what Michael Rothberg calls "implicated subjects," beneficiaries of a system that generates dispersed and uneven experiences of trauma and wellbeing simultaneously (1). In the long run, however, the mistreatment of the local Jews he witnesses at a close distance destabilises the consolatory justification he has built around his project, leading him to disobey his superiors. This happens in a scene in the factory where the Jews are locked up before extermination. When he is asked to select the fittest Jewish men to work in the construction of the road in what he deems to be terrible conditions, Pohl not only openly refuses to do so but also calls a halt to his own work. At this moment, he does not know what the Nazis have in store for the Jews, but what he has seen makes him firmly believe that "*[t]hey do not think on a human scale. They do not think they deal with humans*" (Seiffert, 128; original emphasis). His supervisor, *Sturmbannführer* Arnold, had justified the abuse and even the murder of the Jews as a necessary evil for the building of a mighty and powerful Nazi empire by saying that "[w]here the light shines strongest, there is always shadow" (129). However, after his act of rebellion, Pohl reflects that the exploitation of Jewish labourers had to stop, and that he has done something right by refusing to select the Jewish workers and to continue the building of the road: "Nothing [is] worth the shadows they [the Nazis] are casting" (132). At the same time, however, Pohl cannot help but feel guilty for transgressing the norms imposed by his superiors, and he is perfectly aware that his insubordination will have negative consequences for him. Thus, after the gunshots of the *Einsatzgruppen* massacring the Jews are heard across the entire village, he reaches the conclusion that he is an expendable pawn in an industry of evil where "[t]here is no law or truth or trust, no sense of reason; there is no one he can turn to either" (182).

At this point, Pohl understands that his life is in danger and feels that he is being watched and followed by the police and the Gestapo. These circumstances drive him to burn the cathartic but incriminating letter about his terrible experience in Ukraine that he had written to Dorle the night before, and flee from the town. The fact that his perspective is not offered from then onwards suggests that Pohl has been caught and punished. This terrible possibility is confirmed by the end of the novel when *Sturmbannführer* Arnold ponders on Pohl's arrest and imagines the official letter to his wife: "*died whilst trying to escape; died at his own hand*, or some other such bleak Gestapo fiction" (230; original emphasis). From the moment he decides not to bend to their will, Pohl's life loses value for the Nazis in general and for Arnold in particular. As the quotation illustrates, it becomes an ungrievable life, to the point that it no longer matters how he dies or whether the official version of his death matches the actual turn of events. His existence, made significant for the Nazis by his role in the construction of the road, becomes replaceable when Pohl's obligation to select the enforced Jewish workers is fulfilled by dutiful and law-abiding Arnold. However, the loss of Pohl's life, although imperceptible and ungrievable for the Nazis, is very much perceived and grieved by the readers, who, allowed to follow Pohl's gaze from the beginning of the novel, suddenly feel deprived of his viewpoint and his storyline.

Pohl's case illustrates that acts of resistance during the Third Reich did not necessarily come from extraordinary heroes. Most of them originated in common people who, although naturally compliant and prudent, disobeyed the corrupting authorities in order to preserve their ethical principles. While still in Germany, Pohl had already given signs of these principles by refusing to fulfil his duty to serve in the *Wehrmacht* and by feeling uneasy about wearing the Party badge on his lapel when petitioning for a job. Back then, his brother-in-law had tried to appease him by saying that he could wear the Nazi pin and still preserve his moral sense in a tone that implied that it was a stupidity to think otherwise. This exemplifies Zygmunt Bauman's contention that, in such situations, the Germans' "moral conscience" became "their own personal attribute and possession—unlike immorality, which had to be socially produced" (168). This would explain why, in order to transgress the dehumanising practices performed by the Nazis, Pohl has to separate himself from the community where he belonged. In similar circumstances but on another side of the conflict, Yasia, the young peasant girl from the village, ends up becoming the rescuer of Yankel and Momik, the Jewish children that had averted the roundup. She finds them one morning in the streets and the way the elder carries his little brother bundled to his shoulders reminds her of her own younger brothers. After realising that they are looking for shelter and identifying frightened glares in their faces, Yasia decides to hide them in the rafters of Osip's

48   Paula Romo-Mayor

workshop. The rest of Ukrainians in the town are too much afraid to get into trouble with the Nazis, so they opt for ignoring the Jews' fate. Their act of denial is doubly reassuring to them as, by so doing, they are also denying their own vulnerability, the possibility that, just like the Jews, they might be victimised by the Nazis. As Yasia observes, it is easier for them to talk about the Jews and how they are inexplicably taken away than about who will be next. Although she does not approve of their attitude, Yasia is not immune to it. When she finally discovers Yankel and Momik's Jewish identity, she is overwhelmed by the readiness of her community to naturalise the legendary hatred for the Jews on which the Nazi construction of them as phobic others is based. The difference with the other Ukrainians is that Yasia is aware of the fact. As she recognises, "[she] knows little of Jews; nothing to speak of. [...] All she's learned has been *from folk tales, or overheard from townsfolk* — [. . .] why would the Germans come after them?" (Seiffert 2017, 53; emphasis added). The fact that she decides to help Yankel and Momik before knowing that they are Jewish brings to mind Levinas's contention that care and tenderness towards others emerge as a response to their frailty and in a "dis-individualising" stage of recognition that takes place "[p]rior to the manifestation of attributes" (1979, 256). When, after the shooting, Osip discovers that Yasia has been hiding the Jewish boys in his workshop, he starts shouting at her in a mixture of fear and anger. Her decision to help the children and the fear that the rumours that they are disobeying the Germans may spread lead Osip to dismiss them and to suggest that she go to her Uncle's village, which remains uninvaded because it is situated in the marshes beyond the forests. In this sense, just like Pohl, Yasia needs to detach herself from her community to stay loyal to her ethical principles.

Neither Yasia nor Otto Pohl prevent the massive killing of local Jews from happening, but their actions spare some of them, in Pohl's case from further suffering and in Yasia's case from death. The individual decisions taken by these characters call the Nazi structure into question and foreground the capacity for "emphatic unsettlement" (LaCapra 41) and resilience of common human beings. Their ethical stance makes them capable of recognising strangers as fellow human beings regardless of their origins and cultural beliefs, and become solidary with them. After all, "[i]t is only humans that may be objects of ethical propositions" (Bauman 103). Towards the end of the novel, there is a thrilling scene where the Jewish boys, the marsh girl and the German engineer unexpectedly meet in the streets of the town. The encounter takes place at night after the curfew, at a moment in the story when all of them feel particularly vulnerable and frightened. Yasia, Yankel and Momik have just been sent away by Osip with a horse-drawn cart, and Pohl is sneaking out of the boarding house where he was staying with the aim of leaving the district, coinciding with his very last appearance in the novel. When they bump into each other, every single one of them realises that their lives are in the others' hands. The children think that because Pohl is German he might call the Nazi officers and arrest them. Pohl is in a state of paranoia, the perception of his own vulnerability making him suspect that anyone might inform his Nazi superiors about his whereabouts. Nevertheless, nothing as such happens. During their unexpected encounter, they look at each other in the face and decide against violence. Since it is Pohl's perspective that is privileged during this particular incident, we follow his process of realisation and understanding of the precariousness of human life transmitted by the three children, whom he wrongly, but also significantly, perceives as siblings and not necessarily as Jews. He covers them up when a group of drunk Ukrainian policemen, probably returning from the execution in the outskirts of town, suddenly appear. Pohl could have turned the children in to clean his name and maybe save his life but, despite feeling guilty for not having collaborated with the Nazis, he still decides to protect the young strangers. He looks at them and all he can perceive is their destitution, their tattered clothes and their extreme vulnerability. Nevertheless, the reputation of his compatriots precedes him, making it difficult for the children to trust the potentially dangerous stranger. The harsh sounds of his German telling them to escape and his curt manners, a side effect of his own fear and despair, are misinterpreted as violence. Although the children cannot understand it at that moment, his insistence that they remain together when he sees Yasia encouraging the boys to take a different direction reveals that his preoccupation for their wellbeing is genuine. At this stage, the girl becomes aware of her responsibility not only for her own life but also for the lives of the Jewish boys, which makes her unable to leave them behind. This can be clearly appreciated after their chance encounter with Pohl, when, during their arduous trek throughout the inhospitable Ukrainian swamps, she observes how Yankel "shields his young brother from the worst of wet" and "expects her to take him somewhere safer [...] to know the way" (Seiffert 2017, 199). So far, Yankel has revealed himself as rather mistrustful and unfriendly with everyone, even with Yasia, who has helped him and his brother from the moment they met. Yet, as they travel together to reach her Uncle's community, he changes his attitude slightly and thinks how grateful he is to have her by their side. When their journey is interrupted by Momik's illness and Yasia's own exhaustion, it is Yankel who is pierced by the ethical demand of the Levinasian face. His realisation that Yasia's and his brother's lives depend on the people inhabiting the marshland leaves him no chance but to cast aside his insolent attitude, approach a couple of strangers and ask them for help. Yankel's action is eventually rewarded with the refuge provided by Yasia's Uncle. The feeble and ailing state of the newcomers and the fact that it is still snowing, which buys the locals some time before the Nazis' arrival, allow Uncle to postpone the

50   *Paula Romo-Mayor*

neighbours' inquiries concerning the two outsiders. In the meantime, he feeds them and looks after them:

> [Uncle] was unused to children, but Yasia saw his rough care for them, especially the younger one. […]. [He] found him an over-shirt from another village child, cutting it down to size, pulling it over his head so the boy would be warmer; and he tried to glean the small one's name from his timid murmurings […].
>
> (Seiffert 2017, 215–16)

This passage, narrated in the preterit to reproduce the dazed perspective of Yasia while she returns to health, suggests that it is the boys'—especially Momik's—precariousness that inspires these kind gestures in Uncle. After her recovery, Yasia notices that the younger brother has grown healthier and stronger since they arrived; she notices his first shy smiles and realises how the people in the community acknowledge him when he passes by. Momik's socialisation with the villagers contrasts with Yankel's detachment and silence, as he seems wholly immersed in his own thoughts. Yasia cannot guess what he is thinking, but she supposes that, just as she cannot avoid ruminating on Mykola and the other soldiers, he is still processing what they have gone through the past days. At this stage, Yankel seems to be attracted to the idea of retribution from and vengeance on the Germans. During one of the frequent assaults to the village by a group of partisans demanding food, clothes and blankets in exchange for fighting the Nazis, the teenage boy looks at them with admiration. Uncle, who cares for his wellbeing, warns Yankel that not everyone is as tolerant with his Jewishness as him: just like Yankel, the partisans want to oust the Germans from their lands, but that does not mean that they would welcome him with open arms. However, Uncle's protective attitude with the children is eventually adopted by the rest of the marsh community. This is reflected in the epilogue of the novel, which is set in early 1942, at a time when the snow is starting to melt and the families living in the swamps have gathered around the river to welcome their new-borns to the community through baptism. This ceremony is extended to Yankel and Momik, who are given the Ukrainian names of Yevhen and Mirek, respectively. The marsh people's hospitality and integration of the Jewish boys as new members of their society is yet another example of *excendance*, the movement away from the subject position towards the inscrutable face of the other demanded by Levinasian ethics (Levinas 2003, 54–55). The hospitality of the marsh community contrasts with the hostility or indifference of the communities we have seen so far, in the sense that, whereas their ethical stance emerges from the collectivity, Otto Pohl's and Yasia's ethical decisions can only be made as individuals, after detaching themselves from their communities and freeing themselves from the phobic relationship with the other

Undermining the Hierarchy of Grief 51

that governs them. While the Nazis' behaviour responds, as already argued, to Baudrillard's notion of the technological society, the reluctance of common Germans, like Otto Pohl, or Ukrainians like Yasia's neighbours, to make a clear move towards the suffering other points to them as members of what Jean-Luc Nancy has termed the "inoperative community," a community resulting from the horrors of the two World Wars, ruled by mutual suspicion and indifference, at once claustrophobically close and without intimacy, where death has no longer meaning or value (13). By contrast, the behaviour of Uncle's community agrees with the organising forms of thought existing in primitive cultures, where the "irreducible singularity" of otherness was respected (Baudrillard 1996, 115). In agreement with this, the christening ceremony may be said to obey the logic of "symbolic exchange" characteristic of premodern social models, whereby the gift exchanged between different communities is not based on use value but on the fostering of incommensurable and solidary reciprocal relations between individuals (Baudrillard 2017). Yankel had saved the life of Yasia when she could no longer continue the journey and, now, her people are willing to save his life and that of his little brother. This interpretation can be inferred from the final words in the novel, corresponding to Yasia's thoughts about the baptism, which run: "*So*, if anyone should come asking, the two of them are marsh boys" (Seiffert 2017, 237; emphasis added). The introductory adverb implies that the new names and their inclusion in the village population census are a mere formality meant to protect Yankel and Momik when winter ends and the Nazis are no longer held back by the snow.

Conclusion

The representation of the Holocaust in Rachel Seiffert's *A Boy in Winter* engages with vulnerability formally and thematically and, by so doing, creates an ethical space wherein the acceptance of human life as a set of interdependencies and the grievability of every human loss is possible. The polyphony produced by variable and multiple internal narration counteracts the monologic discourse of Nazi ideology with a constructive dialogue, where "oppositional voices are not feared, degraded or dismissed, but valued for the instigation to a sensate democracy they occasionally perform" (Butler 2004, 151). The presentation of the same events from different perceptual angles takes the readers beyond the oppressing ideological frames of the Nazi discourse to reveal that both humankind and truth are permeable and impossible to totalise. In agreement with its poetics and ethics of representation, the novel offers a complex characterisation of Jewish and non-Jewish characters whose thoughts and behaviour disclose not only the difficulty but also the possibility of valuing the life of the others and of grieving their deaths through the recognition of the precariousness of the common

52 Paula Romo-Mayor

human condition. Thus, while the Nazi position is representative of the derealisation of society and the waning of affects brought about by the technological revolution, the nuanced positions of Otto Pohl and Yasia are representative of those members of inoperative societies unwillingly involved in systematic violence who, despite their sociocultural background, and even though threatened by retaliation from their own communities, end up contributing to saving totally strange others. The alternative to the disintegration of ethics and the subsequent collective and individual traumas caused by the Nazis lies, therefore, in the return to the ancestral values of the premodern society. Although set in the 1940s, Rachel Seiffert's novel speaks to our contemporary times in the sense that it addresses pressing ongoing sociocultural and ethical issues such as the marginalisation and legitimation of violence against certain groups, debased to the category of ungrievable bare lives because they do not meet the biopolitical expectations of the dominant culture. By so doing, it provides a better, because more complex and nuanced, understanding of life in our post-capitalist, technological society that can empower readers to challenge the existence of totalising epistemological frames and put an end to institutionalised violence.

Acknowledgements

Research for this chapter was funded by the Spanish Ministry of Science and Innovation (MICINN) (code PID2021-124841NB-I00) in collaboration with the European Regional Development Fund (DGI/ERDF); and by the Government of Aragón and the European Social Fund (ESF) (code H03_20R).

Note

1 In contrast to the *Waffen-SS*, mostly conformed by volunteers, the *Wehrmacht*—the regular German armed forces constituted by the *Heer* (the land force), the *Kriegsmarine* (the naval force) and the *Luftwaffe* (the air force)—was regulated through conscription throughout the Third Reich. The voluntarism of *SS* officers tended to render them more motivated and determined to participate in the Nazi atrocities than the *Wehrmacht* soldiers. However, historians agree that both forces were equally involved in the regime's genocidal programme.

Works Cited

Adorno, Theodor. *Prisms*. 1981. Trans. Samuel Weber and Shierry Weber. Cambridge: MIT P, 1997.
Agamben, Giorgio. *Homo Sacer: Sovereign Power and Bare Life*. Eds Werner Hamacher and David E. Wellbery. Trans. Daniel Heller-Roazen. Stanford, CA: Stanford UP, 1998.

Amis, Martin. *Time's Arrow*. 1991. London: Vintage, 2003.

Anonymous. "Documenting Numbers of Victims of the Holocaust and Nazi Persecution." *United States Holocaust Memorial Museum*. 8 December 2020. Accessed on 20/07/2021 at: https://encyclopedia.ushmm.org/content/en/article/documenting-numbers-of-victims-of-the-holocaust-and-nazi-persecution/.

Bakhtin, Mikhail. *Problems of Dostoevsky's Poetics*. 1963. Trans. Caryl Emerson. Minneapolis: U of Minnesota P, 1984.

Barnouw, Dagmar. *The War in the Empty Air: Victims, Perpetrators, and Postwar Germans*. Bloomington: Indiana UP, 2005.

Baudrillard, Jean. *The Perfect Crime*. 1995. Trans. Chris Turner. London and New York: Verso Books, 1996.

———. *Symbolic Exchange and Death*. 1976. Trans. Ian Hamilton Grant. London: Sage Publications Ltd, 2017.

Bauman, Zygmunt. *Modernity and the Holocaust*. 1989. Oxford: Polity P, 2008.

Butler, Judith. *Precarious Life: The Powers of Mourning and Violence*. London and New York: Verso Books, 2004.

———. *Frames of War: When Is Life Grievable?* London and New York: Verso Books, 2009.

Chapoutot Johann. *The Law of Blood: Thinking and Acting as a Nazi*. 2014. Trans. Miranda Richmond Mouillot. Cambridge and London: The Belknap P of Harvard UP, 2018.

Desbois, Patrick. *The Holocaust by Bullets: A Priest's Journey to Uncover the Truth behind the Murder of 1.5 Million Jews*. Basingstoke: Palgrave Macmillan, 2008.

Fricker, Miranda. *Epistemic Injustice: Power and the Ethics of Knowing*. Oxford: Oxford UP, 2007.

Ganteau, Jean-Michel. *The Ethics and Aesthetics of Vulnerability in Contemporary British Fiction*. New York and London: Routledge, 2015.

LaCapra, Dominick. *Writing History: Writing Trauma*. 2001. Baltimore, MD: Johns Hopkins UP, 2014.

Lang, Berel. *Holocaust Representation: Art within the Limits of History and Ethics*. Baltimore, MD and London: The Johns Hopkins UP, 2000.

Levinas, Emmanuel. *Totality and Infinity: An Essay on Exteriority*. 1969. Trans. Alphonso Lingis. The Hague, Boston, MA and London: Martinus Nijhoff Publishers, 1979.

———. "The Trace of the Other." *Deconstruction in Context: Literature and Philosophy*. Ed. Mark C. Taylor. Chicago, IL and London: Chicago UP, 1986. 345–59.

———. *On Escape: De l'évasion*. 1935. Trans. Bettina Bergo. Stanford, CA: Stanford UP, 2003.

Lyotard, Jean-François. *The Postmodern Condition: A Report on Knowledge*. 1979. Trans. Geoff Bennington and Brian Massumi. Minneapolis: U of Minnesota P, 1984.

———. *The Differend: Phases in Dispute*. 1983. Trans. Georges Van Den Abbeele. Minneapolis: U. of Minnesota P, 1988.

Martínez-Alfaro, María Jesús. "Where Madness Lies: Holocaust Representation and the Ethics of Form in Martin Amis' *Time's Arrow*." *Ethics and*

Trauma in Contemporary British Fiction. Eds Susana Onega and Jean-Michel Ganteau. Leiden: Rodopi, 2011. 127–54.

———. "The Estrangement Effect in Three Holocaust Narratives: Defamiliarising Victims, Perpetrators and the Fairy-Tale Genre." *Atlantis: Journal of the Spanish Association for Anglo-American Studies* 42.1 (2020): 37–56.

Masih, Mara Lynn. *My Real Name is Hanna*. Simbsury, CT: Mandel Vilar P, 2018.

Nancy, Jean-Luc. *The Inoperative Community*. 1986. Ed. Peter Connor. Trans. Lisa Garbus, Michael Holland and Simona Sawney. With a Foreword by Christopher Fynsk. Minneapolis: U of Minnesota P, 1991.

Onega, Susana. "Victimhood." *The Routledge Companion to Literature and Trauma*. Eds Colin Davis and Hanna Meretoja. London: Routledge, 2020. 91–99.

Onega, Susana, and Jean Michel Ganteau. "Introduction." *Victimhood and Vulnerability in 21st Century Fiction*. Eds Jean-Michel Ganteau and Susana Onega. New York and London: Routledge, 2017. 1–18.

Pellicer-Ortín, Silvia. "The Ethical Clock of Trauma in Eva Figes' *Winter Journey*." *Ethics and Trauma in Contemporary British Fiction*. Eds Susana Onega and Jean-Michel Ganteau, Amsterdam and New York: Rodopi, 2011. 37–60.

Rothberg, Michael. *The Implicated Subject: Beyond Victims and Perpetrators*. Stanford, CA: Stanford UP, 2019.

Seiffert, Rachel. *The Dark Room*. 2001. London: Vintage, 2002.

———. *Afterwards*. London: Vintage, 2007.

———. *The Walk Home*. London: Virago, 2014.

———. *A Boy in Winter*. London: Virago, 2017.

Thomas, D.M. *The White Hotel*. 1981. London: Weidenfeld & Nicolson, 2004.

Thorpe, Adam. *The Rules of Perspective*. London: Jonathan Cape, 2005.

Vice, Sue. "'Beyond Words': Representing the 'Holocaust by Bullets.'" *Holocaust Studies* 25.1–2 (2018): 88–100.

———. *Holocaust Fiction*. London and New York: Routledge, 2000.

3 Escaping "Dead Time"

The Temporal Ethics of (Un-) Grievability in Ali Smith's *The Accidental*

Katia Marcellin

Introduction

How does one grieve when time does not pass? This question is directly concerned with trauma, which is specifically characterised by its belonging to "a time that does not pass" (Davoine and Gaudillière 163), where the patient is, as noted by Sigmund Freud, "obliged to *repeat* the repressed material as a contemporary experience instead of, as the physician would prefer to see, *remembering* it as something belonging to the past" (2015, 12; original emphasis). If mourning is a temporary psychical state, a process that will be, once again according to Freud, "overcome after a certain lapse of time" (1971, 244), then we must ask ourselves how, in the case of a trauma caused by loss, the passage of time can have any healing properties since it is precisely *not* perceived as passing, the subject remaining enclosed in an everlasting present. One of the main answers offered by psychoanalysis to trauma was formulated by Pierre Janet (1901) and, as Anne Whitehead reminds us, consists in "a transformation of traumatic memory into narrative memory, so that the event is integrated into a chronology of the past and into the individual's life history" (140). Such a transformation would, therefore, be a precondition for the grieving process to take place, allowing the subject to re-insert him- or herself within the flow of time. However, in her novel *The Accidental*, which deals with both trauma and loss, Ali Smith puts her characters on quite a different path. The members of the Smart family—the parents and their two children—seem to be caught in a time that does not allow for change or accident to occur. The adults in particular seem to be confined in a bourgeois routine that protects them from any affective intrusion, to such an extent that they remain oblivious to the suicide attempt of one of their children. Yet, the (apparently) accidental arrival of a stranger in their lives will force them to radically alter their conception of time and of the way they relate to it, thus making space for the emergence of grief.

As already noted by Patrick O'Donnell, time in *The Accidental*, and especially the time that the Smart family inhabits, appears as a "dead time," as defined by Giorgio Agamben in *Infancy and History*. My

DOI: 10.4324/9781003347811-5

56 *Katia Marcellin*

contention is that this time, "abstracted from experience" (Agamben 96), precludes grief insofar as it maintains the characters in an artificial and unending present. Ali Smith resorts to a performative metalepsis in order to make us perceive the complex workings of temporality in the novel. This figure of speech, which works as a kind of temporal metonymy (Salvan 74), allows for the substitution of the antecedent for the consequence or of the consequence for the antecedent in a causal relation: the readers must, therefore, reconstruct implicitly the complete chain of events.

Firstly, I would like to show how the characters in the novel are involved in a performative, unethical practice of metalepsis: the figure produces the very effect on which it relies, that is, it erases a part of the succession of events so that the characters maintain themselves in a truncated temporality that does not allow for grief. Secondly, I shall analyse how the normative frames they apply, as defined by Judith Butler, progressively "get out of hand" (2009, 10), thus configuring a different temporality that allows for the recasting of norms of intelligibility and the emergence of a grievable other. Finally, I will see how Amber, the intruder, introduces a different, ethical practice of metalepsis which, while acknowledging both the past and the future, emancipates the characters from the normative power of causality. This ethical approach to time thus contributes to the creation of a vulnerable community united through a shared experience of grief.

Erasing the Past through Metalepsis

In the first section of the novel, the members of the Smart family are enclosed within an everlasting and artificial present, dissociated from past and future, which precludes the expression of grief. This practice of "dead time," that is, a time perceived as "homogeneous, rectilinear and empty" (Agamben 96), is particularly embodied by Eve, the mother, and her partner Michael. Their perception of "the beginning"—the title given to the first part of the novel—relies on a constant quest for novelty, completely abstracted from the past, as shown by Michael's expression of joy when he first sees Amber: "Life never stopped being glorious, a glorious surprise, a glorious renewal all over again" (Smith 57). The repetition of the term "glorious," however, directly betrays the meaning of his words: Michael's pathological need to experience renewals actually consists in a compulsion to repeat, with each new lover or infatuation, a parody of novelty. Indeed, as Butler reminds us, "[w]hat is new, newness itself, is founded upon the loss of original place, and so it is a newness that has within it a sense of belatedness, of coming after, and of being thus fundamentally determined by a past that continues to inform it" (2003, 468). Newness is no such thing for Michael as his version of it refuses the notion of loss in favour of a deliberate destruction of the past.

Each year, he initiates a new affair with a student and erases the previous one from his mind, as shown in the following example: "[He] deleted without reading the seven messages from Emma-Louise Sackville, who [...] was at the needy, tearful stage. [...] After graduation there were no more supervisions" (Smith 73). The radical deleting of the student's emails clearly illustrates the purposeful metaleptic process around which Michael organises his life: graduation, as the last term in the causal relation, erases everything that preceded it. The affair is thus discarded from his life to be immediately replaced by a new one: Michael does not allow any space for grief, either his own or that of the dejected lover.

Michael's time is, paradigmatically, a time that does not pass; it keeps repeating and annihilating itself in its endless iteration. His obsession with novelty, understood as an absolute, precludes the very idea that something, anything may have preceded it. Indeed, the metaleptic erasure performed by Michael attempts to make each lover disappear, at least insofar as, once he has discarded them, they only reappear in his life as trophies or icons. For instance, he remembers fondly "that sweet page-boyed one [...] who still sent a card at Christmas" (70), only through a few significant physical features that make her a type, and through signs of her enduring attachment to him. More specifically, this metaleptic process of effacement works as a means to negate the very notion of temporal perspective. Even as he seems capable of placing his numerous lovers very precisely on a timeline, Michael's perception of time appears as completely severed from the notion of experience. This is particularly striking when he enumerates his affairs as a means to keep track of time and of his own ageing process: "Ten years ago it had been romantic, inspiring, energizing (Harriet, Ilanna [...]). Five years ago it had still been good (for instance, Kirsty Anderson). Now Michael Smart, with twenty-year-old Philippa Knott [...], was worried about his spine" (70). In this passage, the character merely juxtaposes various time periods which he identifies through the names of the young women with whom he has had liaisons. Even though we can observe a progression—more precisely a deterioration—in the quality of his relationships, as they seem to have lost some of their appeal, each lover appears to be a mere replacement of the previous one within the same, continuous and non-evolutive affair. This is emphasised by the use of the singular pronoun "it" in the first two sentences or by the expression "it had still been good" in the second one, the adverb "still" highlighting the notion of continuity: the women are replaceable and interchangeable.

Yet, the degradation that Michael identifies does not seem to be attributed to his own ageing, or even to himself for that matter. The structure of the sentences with "it" as a subject underlines the character's passivity and his refusal to consider his own responsibility in the deterioration of the relationships. Despite the hint at his diminishing physical condition in the last sentence—"worried about his spine"—, his

58 *Katia Marcellin*

focus on the lovers themselves suggests that he holds them responsible for the loss of passion he experiences. As instances of what was "romantic, inspiring" or "good," which ultimately make him "worried about his spine," the young women are clearly objectified and ungrievable, as is particularly visible through what Michael's thoughts reveal about his priorities. His back is the one thing he worries about, and, therefore, the one thing he might consider a sign of his own vulnerability and of a physical degradation for which he holds Philippa responsible, rather than age. Grieving for his potential back pain seems indeed easier to him than to become aware of—and to grieve for—his own mortality. The students are merely presented as beautiful objects that are losing quality and ontological density, each version less satisfying than the previous one, as if the mould from which they were cast had become corroded. Yet, even this realisation does neither occasion grief nor leads to any questioning, on Michael's part, of his consumerist attitude towards women. Instead, they keep being replaced, each one more or less similar to the others, and, above all, they do not age. Thus, the degradation of the model is not perceived as the result of a process—which would imply a notion of duration, of lived time and would, therefore, ground it in experience—but as the effect of an iterative phenomenon. The association of the idea that there is one single relationship—"it"—together with the interchangeability of the young women he is with, offers a perfect illustration of Agamben's "dead time": Michael's refusal of experience encloses him in the illusory wish for a fixed time where youth is eternal but, at the same time, this temporality is grounded on ephemerality. It "derives from the experience of manufacturing work and is sanctioned by modern mechanics, which establishes the primacy of uniform rectilinear motion over circular motion" (Agamben 96). Indeed, Michael's fantasy relies on the systematic erasure and replacement of one woman by another in a constant movement forward that rejects the idea of a building up of experience, so that the fantasy itself is worn out over time like a piece of paper that becomes friable after pencil drawings have been rubbed out too many times. Thus, maintaining the fiction of one single relationship allows him to avoid grief and even to make the very notion of grieving irrelevant: for him, nothing ever ends even as something new is always beginning, and the young women's potential suffering is, consequently, completely negated.

The notion of reproducibility at the core of Michael's affairs with his students is clearly reminiscent of Butler's analysis of the functions of the frame in relation to grievability in *Frames of War* (2009). The frame he has delimited and within which his lovers can be granted recognition is clearly materialised on the page when he describes the seduction routine he uses with them: "He liked to tell the story, how he had admired her in class when she'd said ' '" (Smith 69). The quotation marks that circumscribe the blank space in the sentence delimit the frame within which

Michael's young lovers are allowed to insert themselves. This space not only highlights the repetitive nature of his seduction techniques but also emphasises their mechanistic nature: Michael's discourse is prefabricated, as in an industrial process, and he merely fills in the blanks to adapt it to his audience.

Furthermore, the gap that Smith leaves on the page metaleptically stands in for the young women themselves and for the whole process of erasure and replacement that Michael performs. The quotation marks open up the space that the young women will occupy but also anticipate their departure, the moment when they will have to be wiped out of the frame. Thus, the blank space thereby becomes a figure of the Derridean spectre, in the sense that it is already filled with the presence of the lover that will come, but also figures her upcoming erasure—and that of all the women that preceded or will follow the current one (Derrida xix). As a result, we can consider with Butler that this gap on the page is not merely a sign of the iterative nature of Michael's life and relationships but that it is also already unsettled by spectral presences:

> to call the frame into question is to show that the frame never quite contained the scene it was meant to limn, that something was already outside, which made the very sense of the inside possible, recognizable. The frame never quite determined precisely what it is we see, think, recognize, and apprehend. Something exceeds the frame that troubles our sense of reality; in other words, something occurs that does not conform to our established understanding of things.
>
> (Butler 2009, 9)

Amber is, paradigmatically, the one who exceeds this frame as she appears to be completely immune to Michael's charm. However, the departure from the frame is already perceptible through Michael's affair with Philippa Knot. As we have seen, his disappointment with this new lover is already the sign of a temporal progression, even though he does not seem capable of admitting it. Besides, if this evolution underlines Michael's ageing, thus casting a shadow of irony on his promiscuity— the affairs have been progressively divested of their "romantic" aspects (Smith 70) to retain only the more prosaic ones, such as the lack of comfort that accompanies sexual intercourse in an office—, it especially hints at the erosion of the frame. Even though he takes a new lover each year, his seduction pattern is in itself old and seems to be well-known throughout the university. Thus, Philippa appropriates his routine and turns it against him, making him feel "weak, as if hospitalized" (Smith 70). Michael's predatory attitude towards his students is reversed and he is made to play a passive role in the relationship, which seems to take away all the appeal of the affair. He thus asks himself: "Had he had her or had she had him?" (71). Philippa turns the tables on him and

60   *Katia Marcellin*

reappropriates agency within the relationship by becoming the subject of the verb "have," which highlights the process of objectification that Michael wanted to impose on her. She thus subverts, from inside the frame, the relation of vulnerability that Michael used to rely on in order to take advantage of these young women. Yet, at this point, Michael's grief is only directed towards himself, and the passivity that Philippa has forced him into is not enough for him to recognise her as a grievable subject.

Finally, Amber appears as the last stage in the subversion of the frame: she embodies the "excess" that troubles it, this time from the outside, since Michael cannot make her fit even within his fantasies, in spite of all his efforts. While on the train from London, after the disturbing encounter with Philippa, Michael tries to induce himself into a waking sexual fantasy involving Amber, as if to regain control over his sexual performance. However, the woman escapes him: "all he could picture her doing was sitting there, opposite him" (75). Michael's imagination thus betrays him as he finds himself unable to instrumentalise Amber's image for erotic or sexual purposes. As an embodiment of the very "accidental" that gives its title to the novel, Amber appears indeed as a figure that cannot be contained within fixed frames. She resists objectification but also unsettles the mechanical temporality that organises the lives of the Smart family. Thus, Michael's inability to mentally enact his fantasy is not only the result of Amber's refusal to subject herself to him but also of her emancipation from a rigid temporality.

This hints at an inherent distortion within his conception of novelty that actually relies on predictability: the vulnerability of his prey ensures that they will conform to his wish for constant renewal. As noted by Patrick O'Donnell, "Amber is the stranger without and within who brings both knowledge of self and a knowledge of alterity that opens out spatially onto a planetary reality and *temporally onto a future that seems both certain in its existence and radically indeterminate in its direction*" (99; emphasis added). Embodying the excess that subverts the frame from without, Amber denies the mechanistic nature of the Smarts' "dead time" and thus calls for a reconfiguration of their perception of relationality. Michael is only capable of imagining her "sitting [...] opposite him," that is, face to face and not below him in a posture of submission, as in all his attempted fantasies—for instance, "down on her knees in front of him at the back of a near-empty cinema" (Smith 75). He thus finds himself obliged to acknowledge Amber's otherness, in a Levinasian ethical movement, looking into her face, *exposed*—but not subjected—to him, while he *exposes* himself to her (imagined) gaze in return (Levinas 49). The vulnerability he witnesses through this new kind of fantasy is no longer that of the prey in front of its predator but one that engages his responsibility and forces him to recognise Amber as an intelligible and grievable being. We can, therefore, interpret this moment as one when the mechanical routine of Agamben's dead time—in which "the precise fleeting instant is the only human time" (Agamben 96)—but also Emmanuel Levinas's more "temporalised" time—which relies on "a recuperation of all divergencies, through retention, memory and history" (Levinas 9)—are suddenly interrupted by the emergence of a Levinasian "diachrony refractory to all synchronization" (9).

Michael's wife, Eve, also inhabits a "dead time" but, as a writer who specialises in historical novels, she may also be seen as abiding by a more synthetical and temporalised perception of time—which, Levinas suggests, is also incompatible with the "diachrony" that he identifies as the basis for ethical recognition (93–94). Her attempts to grasp the lives of people who lived during the Second World War and to organise them into a linear, synthetised and straightforward story can indeed be considered as pertaining to a temporality where "nothing is lost, everything is presented or represented, everything is considered and lends itself to inscription [...] without time lost, without time to lose, and where the being of substance comes to pass" (Levinas 9). Such an approach to the past and to the existences of those who lived through it precludes an ethical relation to otherness because it relies on the objectification of these historical characters' lives.

This process of objectification is further compounded by the specific kind of stories that Eve writes, which can be seen as completely anti-ethical. Like Michael with his students, her writing implements a metaleptic erasure of the past that consists in telling the imaginary story of people who died in the Second World War "as if he or she had lived on" (Smith 81). Through this method of writing, Eve paradoxically negates the very historicity of the people she has appropriated as her characters. She denies the historical context with which their lives were necessarily intertwined and places them, specifically, in a "dead time" where only "the precise fleeting instant" (Agamben 96) exists. Indeed, the very narration of Eve's novels refuses to acknowledge temporal perspective since the stories are written in a "Question & Answer format" (Smith 81), which means that the main grammatical tense in her novels coincides with the moment of enunciation, that is, with the present. In doing so, she prevents both the emergence of Levinas's radical diachrony and that of a far simpler and easily accessible "historical or recallable past" (9). Eve thus seems to appropriate history in order to negate it even as she sacralises it. The intermingling of past and present does not serve the purpose of highlighting the continuum between these time periods but, on the contrary, expresses a wish to place the past in the present—and vice-versa—, a nostalgia for a uchronic and therefore ungrievable past, for what *would have happened if ...* that actually has no historical meaning.

In addition, since her novels do not merely place people from the past in a contemporary context but go as far as to erase the deaths of

62 *Katia Marcellin*

war victims, Eve clearly implements a metaleptic negation of the past through the artificial and revisionist prolongation of her characters' lives. This process thus deprives the history of WW2 of its very historical weight: if the consequences of the war, and especially the numerous deaths it caused, are erased, then the war itself is wiped out from history. Furthermore, by imagining "an alternative aftermath" (Smith 81) to her characters' lives, Eve denies her readers the possibility to grieve the untimely deaths of these people: she recasts their lives within a normative chronology that negates the notion of human vulnerability and therefore refuses grief. The Derridean spectres—these anachronic presences that manifest the presence of those who are either "already dead or not yet born" (Derrida xviii)—are, therefore, entirely erased from Eve's uchronic time: the unsettling presence of the WW2 dead, which engages our sense of responsibility, is transformed into a never-ending, posthumous life deprived of its traumatic weight.

Unsettling the Frame

However, after Amber's arrival and departure from their lives both Michael and Eve will experience a reconfiguration of their relation to time. As we have seen, at the end of the first part of the novel, Michael is already experiencing a destabilisation of the framework according to which he organises his life. In his fantasies about Amber, we can observe a first emergence of the Levinasian diachrony: his systematic reiteration of the same pattern of seduction, affair and erasure of young women is countered by the figure of Amber, who introduces a form of radical novelty in his life—which must be differentiated from his own artificial obsession with renewal. In his fantasised face to face with the young woman, Michael is already confronted with a form of intrusion of a being and a time that do not belong to him and that resist subjection.

Yet, his final *recognition*—to use Butler's term—of otherness, and of the vulnerability that this recognition entails, occurs when his frame is completely shattered: the relation of power is brutally overturned when the very student whose emails he had been deleting denounces him (Smith 290). While looking at a picture of Eve in the last part of the novel, Michael recalls her reaction to the announcement of the launching of an investigation into his actions (269). Her full acceptance of it as well as her support appear as miraculous to him. However, what is even more striking in this passage is Michael's renewed understanding of both his wife's awareness of his actions and of her seemingly unconditional loyalty to him. The photograph of his wife in a bookshop is what prompts his renewed realisation which, as he explains, occurs to him every day "as incomprehensibly newly as it would if [...] he couldn't remember anything for longer than twenty-four hours" (269). Eve thus suddenly becomes intelligible to him and his own grief mingles with

Escaping "Dead Time"   63

her newly acknowledged grievability. It is indeed because the realisation occurs to him in a moment of fragility that it seems to open him up to Eve's vulnerability: her deep understanding of the reasons behind his current pain suddenly makes him aware of the grief this knowledge has caused her.

In this passage, Michael's metaleptically induced erasure of the past takes place once again but in a radically new context: instead of using the last causal term in a series of events to erase everything that preceded it—as he used to do after discarding his lovers—, it seems that, in this case, what has been deleted is part of the logical relation that could establish the link between his extra-marital relations and his wife. The frame he has been using and enforcing breaks away from itself and from him through the brutal change of context. As Butler explains,

> [w]hat "gets out of hand" is precisely what breaks from the context that frames the event, the image, the text of war. But if contexts are framed (there is no context without an implicit delimitation of context), and if a frame invariably breaks from itself as it moves through space and time (if it must break from itself in order to move across space and time), then the circulating frame has to break with the context in which it is formed if it is to land or arrive somewhere else. [...] the frame does not hold anything together in one place, but itself becomes a kind of perpetual breakage, subject to a temporal logic by which it moves from place to place.
>
> (2009, 10)

The contextualised frame of Michael's wilful erasure of his students has broken away from itself and the character is forced to experience its now subverted functioning. While it used to render unintelligible every woman he had been with and then forgotten, this very frame—which relies on the deletion of the past—now seems to make Michael unintelligible to himself as it unsettles his perception of himself and of the others. Eve is precisely the only woman he cannot erase, the one who remains with him through the passage of time and therefore makes him acknowledge the intermingling of the notions of impermanence and grief. Michael's affliction—his systematic forgetting—thus takes on an ethical dimension (see Marcellin 109): instead of wiping other beings out of his existence, the metaleptic erasure that takes place here consists in the deleting of his own realisation that there was a temporal and logical link between the official revelation of his sexual indiscretions and his wife's awareness of them. Therefore, the metaleptic suppression of parts of the temporal chain of events is, in this case, what causes the character's vulnerability and opens him up to alterity. While the metaleptic erasure of his lovers was a means to reinforcing his immunity to these objectified young women and to the grief he could cause them, this

64   Katia Marcellin

second kind of metalepsis figures the brutal intrusion of otherness and of a time of the other within his frame of reference.

We can indeed consider that the sudden realisation that Eve "had always known" (Smith 269) is so shattering to Michael not only because it obliges him to face the ethical problem of his infidelities but also because it effectively forces him out of his own time. If we define Michael's time as one that has no historical depth, that keeps repeating itself over and over again, then the notion of Eve having "always known" is registered by him as a violent event insofar as it forces him to insert his timeless temporality within a chronological framework: Eve's knowledge takes him back to a time from which he has already extracted himself, that is radically outside of him. In addition, the knowledge of his wife's awareness of his infidelities also metaleptically implies an anticipation by Eve of what would come to pass. When Michael realises that "they had both been waiting for exactly this message" (269), he is forced to take into account not only the past but also the future he had been setting for himself, and the potential for grief contained within these two moments (Eve's grief, of which he was unaware, and their shared grief resulting from his action). The new temporality he enters is thus bound up with grievability. His wife had indeed already inferred what his behaviour would cause, showing that his own obsession with renewal was actually perverted and doomed to fail: if the said renewal actually relies on predictability and reiteration, then the very notion of novelty appears as unfounded.

Furthermore, it is necessary to note that Michael's realisation occurs again in the passage when he is looking at Eve's photograph. Even if it is mediatised, as in the scene on the train, this confrontation with the face of the other is, for Michael, an instance of Levinasian recognition of the other, especially as the temporal destabilisations he experiences confront him with diachrony. Even though Eve's knowledge of his infidelities can probably be replaced within a historically interpretable chronology, the use of the expression "had always known" and, more importantly, the fact that Michael's knowledge of this constantly intrudes upon him place this realisation outside traditional temporal frameworks. These two elements decisively contribute to the insertion of a time that cannot be subsumed into chronology, "a past more ancient than every representable origin, a pre-original and anarchical *passed*" (Levinas 9; original emphasis). In other words, a time that allows for the recognition of the other and of his or her vulnerability.

Eve, for her part, experiences a writing crisis that leads her to question her relation to time and grief. In the first section of the novel, a reference to the Iraq war highlights the way in which she prioritises grief. She thinks of it as a war about which she "still felt a bit guilty, albeit in a measured way, about not doing more, about not having concentrated on more" (Smith 91). The succession of attenuating qualifiers—"a bit," "albeit," "measured"—underlines the limited extend of Eve's implication in the issue of the war. Furthermore, the epanorthosis ironically highlights the inconsistency of Eve's engagement. What she means by "not doing more" is developed in the next clause as "not having concentrated on more," and the profound discrepancy between these two notions—the first one suggesting concrete action while the other merely refers to an intellectual activity—clearly shows the character's absolute lack of concern with the war: what she feels guilty about is merely *not thinking enough* about the war. Eventually, the text reveals Eve's order of priority, her "worrying" about her next book (and not even the writing itself) being more important than a war, which also implicitly suggests, given the topics of her novels, that a war from the past matters more to her than the one happening right before her.

In a review of the novel published in *The Guardian*, Louise France records Ali Smith's comment that "the backdrop to the story, set in 2003, is Iraq" (n.p.), and that, although readers would not see it immediately, she thinks *The Accidental* is a war novel: "We lived through a war as though we were not at war in this country. We saw it on television but we saw a very different version of it which would be unrecognisable to people from elsewhere" (n.p.). Eve's questioning of the reality of other people's suffering is informed, therefore, by the author's own long-distance witnessing of the Iraq war. The incapacity to grieve for the death of strangers is at the heart of the novel and is perfectly illustrated by Eve in relation to the deaths caused by the Iraq war, as her need to bring back to life the WW2 dead overshadows her awareness of people being killed in the present, whose lives thus appear as ungrievable.

However, the crisis in which she finds herself at the beginning of the novel, compounded by Amber's arrival, leads Eve to re-evaluate this order of priority in what can be seen as an ethical attempt to put her writing at the service of contemporary war victims. The iteration of the frame that she had tried to put in place with the systematic reproduction of the same successful narrative device had already started to crack, as she starts suffering from writer's block, giving the impression that her fictional creations resist her attempts to disavow their deaths. In the middle section of the novel, Eve voices to her publisher not only her need to address more contemporary issues in her writing, such as the deaths of Palestinian children or of people in Iraq, but also the importance of acknowledging death itself. Thus, she wishes to write about someone who "dies, and that's it" (Smith 198). This admission of the finality of death, but also of the necessity to recognise it, brings Eve's writing very close to the questions raised by Butler in *Precarious Life* (2004) regarding grievability: "Is a Muslim life as valuable as legibly First World lives? Are the Palestinians yet accorded the status of 'human' in US [we add: and British] policy and press coverage?" (Butler 2006, 12). A confrontation ensues between Eve and her publisher, whose considerations are primarily economic and who is concerned that the choice of such a topic might drastically "[cut] down the market appeal" (Smith 198). This conversation thus raises not only the issue of the commodification of human life but also that of the function of the obituary as analysed by Butler:

> There are no obituaries for the war casualties that the United States inflicts, and there cannot be. If there were to be an obituary, there would have had to have been a life, a life worth noting, a life worth valuing and preserving, a life that qualifies for recognition.
>
> (2006, 34)

The publisher's comment about the market appeal of Palestinian or Iraqi lives speaks for itself: they have no value even on a merely commercial level.

Eve's desire to write about these lives, to avow death and vulnerability, testifies to a renewed awareness of the power of metalepsis, which she proposes to perform in an ethical way. Unlike her other books, which consisted in a metaleptic erasure of the past through the negation of the characters' deaths, the new format that Eve proposes offers to do precisely the opposite. If we consider with Butler the circularity and self-generating power of grievability—meaning that "'a life has been lived,' is presupposed at the beginning of a life that has only begun to be lived" and that "'this will be a life that will have been lived' is the presupposition of a grievable life" (2009, 15)—it may be stated that what Eve now envisions is a performative practice of obituary writing. As such, it seeks to operate a backwards movement to reintroduce the grievable status of these lives at their very origin, that is, *before* they have been lost in order to make them lives "that will have been lived." By writing about the deaths of those whose lives are deemed ungrievable, she does not only contest the perception—or, more aptly, the non-perception—of these deaths but also metaleptically transforms the lives that preceded them: if her novels grieve for the deaths of these Palestinian and Iraqi citizens, then their lives are made intelligible, they will retroactively have been grievable.

Causality and Grievability

The Smart children, for their part, present an approach to time that differs from that of the adults and which—paradoxically, if we consider their young age—seems to be exclusively turned towards death and the end of time. Unlike the adults who try to recapture and repeat the past or attempt to live in the constant renewal offered by the fleeting instant, Astrid and Magnus seem to live in a teleological time, riddled with an inescapable causality. This is particularly striking in the opening of the first passage devoted to Magnus. For him, "the beginning of this = the end of everything" (Smith 36).

Escaping "Dead Time" 67

The eldest of the Smart children is stuck in the unending present of his perpetrator trauma after he took part in a terrible school prank, when he helped other boys circulate round the school a fake pornographic picture of a classmate, the girl ultimately committing suicide. The shock of this event makes him unable to reconcile his former and current selves, so that he seems to be living in a perpetual trauma time: his former self is stuck in the past while the "real" one is all-encompassing, "massive, unavoidable" (38). He is, in his own way, also caught up in a mechanical "dead time" because his conception of time is rectilinear and cumulative. His suffering comes from the inescapable equation in which he places himself as, driven by an unavoidable repetition compulsion, he keeps acting out the chain of atrocious events that led to the tragedy: "They took her head. They fixed it on the other body. Then they sent it round everybody's email. Then she killed herself" (36). The lapidary and paratactic succession of sentences leaves no room for escape or error. It later becomes metaleptic as Magnus ceases to make full sentences: "First they. They then. Then they. Then she" (38). It is merely thanks to their repetition and their strict succession that these seemingly harmless words express the terrible reality behind the teenager's trauma. The series of actions that led to Catherine Masson's death is repeated throughout the passage, each time with a few variations in its phrasing but always with the same ending: "she killed herself," as if to emphasise the inevitability of Magnus's trauma and guilt: no matter the slight differences between the various paths that can be taken, they all eventually lead to the same inescapable conclusion.

A similarly teleological reflexion can be observed in the case of Astrid in the first pages of the novel. Not unlike Michael, she is obsessed with beginnings but, whereas he systematically erases the past in order to initiate each time something entirely new, Astrid collects beginnings in her quest to identify an ultimate point of origin. Therefore, while Michael is constantly moving forward, his whole life aimed towards what he sees as an open-ended future, Astrid repeatedly turns to the past. So much so that her questions on the beginning of vision take her back to the very formation of the foetus in the womb (8). What is more, these biological considerations lead her to the question of her identity as she seems to have a determinist conception of life. This point is illustrated by her constant hesitation between the last name of her step-father and that of her biological father, which she keeps repeating one after the other like a mantra: "Astrid Smart. Astrid Berenski." The endless repetition of these names underlines the impossible reconciliation of Astrid's cumulative vision of the past and her belief in determinism: she is both Astrid Smart and Berenski but, in the face of the social imperative to choose only one last name, it seems that she cannot decide whether social or biological determinism is more important. Eventually, however, Amber forces her to change her conception of herself and to admit the complexity of her

68   *Katia Marcellin*

identity, first by accepting to grieve for the loss of her father but also by changing her relation to the past and to memory. The destruction of the camera with which Astrid obsessively videotapes everything she sees is a prompt for her to recognise the value of affects rather than the process of archiving the present. The strict causality of events that have been carefully recorded and from which one can infer what was before or comes next does not matter. Astrid progressively becomes aware of this and, in the last section of the novel, she accepts a metaleptic erasure of the past, that is, the fading out or loosening of the links between causes and effects. For instance, she finds out that while she can remember "the sensation of laughing" with Amber, she cannot remember what caused it, but she acknowledges that "[the sensation] is the thing to remember" (226–27). She thus illustrates Sara Ahmed's theory of affects, in particular what she identifies as "impressions" in regard to loss and grief:

> To preserve an attachment is not to make an external other internal, *but to keep one's impressions alive,* as aspects of one's self that are both oneself and more than oneself, as a sign of one's debt to others. One can let go of another as an outsider, but maintain one's attachments, by keeping alive one's impressions of the lost other.
>
> (160; original emphasis)

After Amber has completely emptied the house of the Smart family, Astrid must find ways to maintain the link between herself and the idea of her father other than through the letters she had stolen from her mother. In this last section, she seems to have accepted the complexity of her own identity by refusing to choose between two names. She has retained impressions of her lost father and allowed them to mix with the other aspects of her identity so that all these elements can be transformed within herself. She thus performs a metaleptic blurring of causal links and creates a new name for herself: "Asterid Smart the smart asteroid" (Smith 234). This is an identity whose newness is, as Butler says, "founded upon the loss of original place" (2003, 468), one that acknowledge loss and grief as well as their transformative powers.

The intrusion of Amber in Magnus's life similarly disrupts his conception of time and causality. When he confesses to her, "I broke somebody," she replies "So?," "And?" (149), as if questioning the mathematical conclusion that he reached a few pages before and which was that he had no other choice but to kill himself. The teenager's rigid application of the *lex talionis* is dismissed by Amber. Her short questions echo Butler's contention that we must ask ourselves "whether the experiences of vulnerability and loss have to lead straightaway to military violence and retribution" (2006, xii). Needless to say, the young man's obsession with causality and retribution goes beyond the individual and has much wider political implications, especially if we consider that, in the first section of

Escaping "Dead Time" 69

the novel, Eve remembers her son declaring himself in favour of the Iraq war (91). He thus seems to have applied to himself a political logic that relies on the perpetuation of a cycle of revenge by seeking an equivalent retribution for what he has done.

Yet, to the mathematical "+" and "=" signs that rule over Magnus's life Amber opposes the more flexible "and" of association and transformation, thus introducing him to a different performative power of metalepsis. Metalepsis is a figure that, by making implicit one of the terms of a causal relation, destabilises the very logic of causality. As Geneviève Salvan explains, it actually shifts from one point of view to another while retaining the trace of this journey (80), thus producing anamorphic images. Through her questions, Amber operates such a shift, offering Magnus a different point of view on himself as well as the next step to his mathematical reasoning. While his own equation stopped at the girl's death, as if it marked the end of his own life, Amber opens up a potential future: the word "And?" thus questions the metaleptic link that Magnus had created, suggesting that, if the implicit consequence to the antecedent "I broke somebody" is obvious to him, it is not to her. His calculations are countered by Amber, who encourages him not only to change his point of view on himself—what he has done, even if atrocious, should not determine the rest of his life—but also to accept the change that this event has induced in him. This new approach to temporality thus emancipates him from the mechanistic immediacy of the logic of retribution and situates Magnus in the time of experience and vulnerability, a time where he can finally grieve as he eventually admits that even in maths "[s]ome error is tolerable" (157).

Conclusion

Ali Smith's novel presents characters whose approaches to time are fairly different and yet similar, as each in his or her own way seems to be stuck in a kind of stasis. The adults are obsessed with erasing the past while the children appear paralysed by its weight. However, they all keep repeating the same pattern: Michael renews his affairs every year; Eve keeps using the same successful formula for her novels; Astrid constantly videotapes everything; and Magnus compulsively repeats the events that led to his trauma. These egotistical practices of time allow them to remain impermeable to grief and grievability: they enclose the characters within separate temporalities that asymptotically aim towards alterity but actually foreclose it because they cannot admit a time of the other.

Amber's intrusion in their lives thus appears as the disruptive element that will be the catalyser for their frames' breaking away from themselves. As an other who infringes on the other characters' fixed temporalities, Amber not only intrudes upon them but also highlights the instability of the frames they rely on. By questioning either the iterability

70 Katia Marcellin

or the deterministic nature of these frames, the figure of Amber allows Smith to point out the link between causality and grievability. Only by disrupting strict relations of causality can we acknowledge other forms of grievability and envision different ways of relating to one another. Indeed, as Butler explains in *Precarious Life*,

> Perhaps mourning has to do with agreeing to undergo a transformation (perhaps one should say submitting to a transformation) the full result of which one cannot know in advance. There is losing, as we know, but there is also the transformative effect of loss, and this latter cannot be charted or planned.
>
> (2006, 21)

This transformation is the result of what Butler identifies as our "fundamental dependency on anonymous others" (2006, xii). Magnus becomes aware of this as his newfound fascination with the word "and" makes him conscious of the intricate links that unite him to the rest of the world, as a "living thing" dependent on trees or photosynthesis but also on "all food, fossil, fuels in both the past and the present" (Smith 156–57). His mother comes to a similar conclusion when, after looking at the Abu Ghraib pictures, she acknowledges the necessity to "grieve for the living" (294). The metaleptic reversal that she operates here takes Eve away from the artificial consecration of the past that permeated her novels to consider the living as always-already grievable. Through such a temporal reversal, Ali Smith suggests that the present is always haunted by anachronic presences, if only because the spectre of our own mortality inevitably confronts us with our vulnerability, and asserts that we must have recourse to an ethics of grief that does not seek retribution for violence but, on the contrary, aims to re-cast vulnerability as a shared human condition.

Works Cited

Agamben, Giorgio. *Infancy and History: The Destruction of Experience.* 1978. Trans. Liz Heron. London: Verso, 1993.

Ahmed, Sara. *The Cultural Politics of Emotion.* New York: Routledge, 2004.

Butler, Judith. "Afterword: After Loss, What Then?" *Loss: The Politics of Mourning.* Eds David L. Eng and David Kazanjian. Berkeley: U of California P, 2003. 467–73.

———. *Precarious Life: The Powers of Mourning and Violence.* 2004. London: Verso, 2006.

———. *Frames of War: When Is Life Grievable?* New York: Verso, 2009.

Davoine, Francoise, and Jean-Max Gaudillière. *History Beyond Trauma.* New York: Other P, 2013.

Derrida, Jacques. *Specters of Marx: The State of the Debt, the Work of Mourning, and the New International*. 1993. With an Introduction by Bernd Magnus and Stephen Cullenberg. Trans. Peggy Kamuf. New York: Routledge, 1994.

France, Louise. "Life Stories." *The Guardian*. 22 May 2005. Accessed on 01/01/2022 at: https://www.theguardian.com/books/2005/may/22/fiction.bookerprize2005/.

Freud, Sigmund. "Mourning and Melancholia." 1917. *The Standard Edition of the Complete Psychological Works of Sigmund Freud* Vol. XIV. Trans. Joan Riviere. Ed. James Strachey. London: Hogarth, P., 1971. 243–58.

———. *Beyond the Pleasure Principle*. 1920. Trans. James Strachey. Mineola, NY: Dover Thrift Editions, 2015.

Janet, Pierre. *The Mental State of Hystericals: A Study of Mental Stigmata and Mental Accidents*. With a Preface by J. M. Charcot. Trans. Caroline Rollin Corson. New York and London: G. P. Putnam's Sons, 1901.

Levinas, Emmanuel. *Otherwise Than Being or Beyond Essence*. Dordrecht: Kluwer Academic Publishers, 1991.

Marcellin, Katia. "Materialising Oblivion: The Creative and Poetic Powers of Metalepsis in Ali Smith's *Hotel World* and *The Accidental*." *Caliban. French Journal of English Studies* 60 (2019): 100–13. *La vie de l'oubli dans la littérature britannique des XXe et XXIe siècles: The Life of Forgetting. Oblivion's Enduring Ghosts in British Literature*. Guest eds Adèle Cassigneul and Sylvie Maurel. DOI: 10.4000/caliban.4352.

O'Donnell, Patrick. "'The Space That Wrecks Our Abode': The Stranger in Ali Smith's *Hotel World* and *The Accidental*." *Ali Smith: Contemporary Critical Perspectives*. Eds Monica Germanà and Emily Horton. London: Bloomsbury, 2013. 89–100.

Salvan, Geneviève. "Dire décalé et sélection de point de vue dans la métalepse." *Langue française* 160 (2010): 73–87.

Smith, Ali. *The Accidental*. London: Penguin, 2005.

Whitehead, Anne. *Trauma Fiction*. Edinburgh: Edinburgh U P, 2004.

Part II
Grieving the Earth

4 "How bold to mix the dreamings"

The Ethics and Poetics of Mourning in Alexis Wright's *The Swan Book*

Bárbara Arizti

Introduction

The author of three novels, a short story collection and three works of non-fiction, Alexis Wright is a key figure in Indigenous Australian writing. Her second novel, *Carpentaria* (2006a), won the Miles Franklin award, Australia's most prestigious literary prize, in 2007. The award was established in 1957 under the testament of Stella Miles Franklin, herself a writer, in order to encourage the consolidation of a distinct Australian literature. Significantly enough, Alexis Wright became the first Indigenous novelist to benefit solo from the prize, paving the way for other winners like Melissa Lucashenko (2019) and Tara June Winch (2020). Kim Scott had shared the prize with Thea Astley in the year 2000 and won it again in 2011, this time on his own.

Alexis Wright's long-time activism in favour of Indigenous peoples' rights and self-government nourishes and inspires the whole of her writing career. Wright is a member of the Waanji nation, originally from the Gulf of Carpentaria in Queensland, but driven off their land by the pastoral industry during colonial times (Vernay 119). Her family history provides a dramatic example of the suffering of the rightful inhabitants of Australia under colonial rule. As Wright explained in an interview with Jean-François Vernay:

> My grandmother used to tell the story of her mother and another little girl who were found up in a tree by a pastoralist [...] towards the end of the 19th century, named Frank Hann. Hann kept a diary held in the Western Australia State Library in which he records his thoughts—his distaste for Aboriginal people—and things he did while he occupied our country. We know from various sources that he killed a lot of Aboriginal people. In the case of my great-grandmother and another little girl, they were probably taken as a result of a massacre of their family to be broken in as slaves on Hann's pastoral property. Hann had recorded taking my great-grandmother as a child. This corresponds with my grandmother's story. We also

DOI: 10.4324/9781003347811-7

76 Bárbara Arizti

know that children were also taken for other purposes by these white men who didn't have wives with them.

(Vernay 119)

As it happens, those who had the greatest losses to mourn were deprived of their right to grieve and to be grieved, both by white individuals like Hann and, cardinally, by the colonial authorities. The efforts at turning Australia into a white-man's country involved bloodshed, exclusion and control, as well as the attempt at eradicating Indigenous culture on the grounds that it was primitive. The fact that Aboriginal and Torres Strait Islanders were denied formal citizenship until 1967 (Brennan n.p.) can be read as a further proof of the relevance of Giorgio Agamben's notion of "bare life" set in the context of Australia. As is well known, Agamben reconceptualised Walter Benjamin's concept of "bare life" by equating it to the life of *homo sacer* (sacred man), an obscure figure in Roman law defined solely by its capacity to be killed (Agamben 8). Similarly, the colonial powers stripped the country's original population down to its bare life and set it "outside human jurisdiction" (Agamben 52). The "capacity to be killed" (68) of *homo sacer* was thought to inhere in Indigenous Australians, who were routinely hunted, killed and massacred, without punishment, let alone mourning. Their lives were reduced to *zoē*, pure animal life, at the same time as their *bíos*, "the form or way of living proper to an individual or a group" (Agamben 9), was severely curtailed. The postcolonial scholar Achille Mbembe gets to the root of the matter in "Necropolitics," when, echoing Agamben, he writes that: "the ultimate expression of sovereignty resides, to a large extent, in the power and the capacity to dictate who may live and who must die" (11).

The Swan Book, Wright's third novel published in 2013, exposes the damage inflicted on Indigenous Australians "after two plus centuries of illegal occupation" of their traditional lands (Wright 2013, 10). They have suffered a loss so great that they feel like "strangers walking around in their country" (79), explains the external narrator. The novel also records the authorities' sometimes well-meaning but often misguided attempts at making amends, mostly involving strong doses of dirigisme and paternalism, and showing total ignorance of Indigenous knowledges and perspectives. Although for the most part set in Australia, *The Swan Book* has been saluted by the critics as a planetary novel (Atkinson 40). Events unfold in a dystopian post-apocalyptic scenario in the twenty-second century, featuring a changed world where Mother Nature has transmogrified into "Mother Catastrophe," bringing governments down across the earth (Wright 2013, 6) and leading to massive displacement of peoples. Wright not only foregrounds the plights of Indigenous Australians but offers as well a powerful denunciation of the country's recent history of detention camps and tough refugee policies. In particular, she connects the fates of Indigenous Australians, climate refugees from the Northern Hemisphere and swans. She employs a wide-angle lens to show a complex mesh of unmourned losses brought about by the empire and human mismanagement both in the human and natural world: loss of country and cultural heritage; loss of life, health, freedom and governance capacity; death and loss of home and land due to climate-change-induced disasters; death and habitat loss provoked by war, destruction, degradation and disorientation. The variety of these losses, together with their degree of interconnection, shows the futility of competing for the space of mourning. Rather, the need for mourning in *The Swan Book* can be said to share the multidirectional nature of memory as insightfully described by Michael Rothberg (2009).

This essay argues that the planetary scale of loss in *The Swan Book* calls forth an equally planetary kind of mourning based on the realisation that people and wildlife are structurally vulnerable and thus attributed with grievable lives. In *The Swan Book*, Wright makes a strong case for considering all life worthy of living and grieving as she overturns distinctions between human beings based on race, provenance and social status and extends this equality to animals, wildlife and the land itself. Relatedly, the novel's inclusive, all-embracing ethics is embodied in a poetics that borrows from a wealth of world texts and traditions and takes on an experimental form that combines the fragmentary with the holistic. The analysis of the empathic extension of mourning advocated by Wright draws on and is in dialogue with both Western and Indigenous thinkers. In fact, it intends to trace a conceptual arc between Judith Butler's insights into the need to extend grievability to the global community and the organic nature of Indigenous cultures as explained by the Indigenous Australians Vicki Grieves and David Mowaljarlai, among others. To be sure, this cross-cultural approach is invited by the encompassing regard that underpins the ethics and the poetics of Wright's novel. In my opinion, it is also justified by the planetary and transmodern critical trends gathering momentum in contemporary times, which make a staunch defence of a common cultural understanding at a global scale.

As Butler states, not all lives are endowed with grievability: "those who are grievable *would* be mourned if their lives *were* lost; the ungrievable are those whose loss would leave no trace, or perhaps barely a trace" (2021, 75; original emphasis). While Butler's conception of grievability can, no doubt, help cast light on *The Swan Book*, the philosophical basis underneath Wright's view of reality lies more fully in Aboriginal culture and lore. Grieves explains that this system of beliefs is very much alive today despite thoroughgoing debasement during colonisation (2009a, 4), and that, in fact, it has helped the Indigenous population to endure the hardships of life under colonial rule (25). It cannot be neatly separated from spirituality, understood, as Richard M. Eckersley explains, as "a deeply intuitive, but not always consciously expressed sense of

78 *Bárbara Arizti*

connectedness to the world in which we live" (2007, 54). It thus follows that no distinction is made between the sacred and the profane and that life is revered and celebrated in all its complexity of forms (11). Grieves puts forward the term "wholistic"—"developed from the word 'whole', which describes a matter in its entirety" (2009a, 1)—to refer to the philosophical foundation of Aboriginal and Torres Strait Islander culture. This philosophy, Grieves explains, "establishes the wholistic notion of the interconnectedness of the elements of the earth and the universe, animate and inanimate, whereby people, the plants and animals, landforms and celestial bodies are interrelated" (7). It is ruled by four main principles—respect, complexity, creation and connection (26)—alongside the practice of "sharing and caring," which applies to people beyond family as well as to the wider world (25). In consequence, in this system, any loss, no matter who or what experiences it, has subtle, far-reaching repercussions for the whole and needs to be acknowledged and mourned so as to redress the original balance. The ideas of responsibility and custodianship of all things created are deeply ingrained in Aboriginal philosophy and spirituality (13).

According to Grieves, Indigenous ontologies, epistemologies and axiologies are of "potential value to all peoples" (2009a, v). As a matter of fact, Indigenous Australians' and other non-dominant worldviews like that of Native Americans are eliciting more and more interest in Western circles, among ordinary citizens and scholars alike. This is not totally new, as evident in the practice of appropriation denounced by Indigenous peoples as an unethical form of neocolonial exploitation. However, as I see it, and notwithstanding the fact that there are still cases of blatant appropriation and Indigenous impersonation, the current interest seems to stem from serious and profound reasons rather than from commercial purposes, New-Age folklorism or a superficial crave for the exotic. In Grieves's words: "Contemporary Western thinkers are referencing Aboriginal Spirituality in their quest for meaning and in their critiques of Western materialist notions of progress" (2009a, 28). More importantly, some contemporary Indigenous voices affirm to be happy to share their culture in order to help improve relationships among human beings and contribute to the sustainability and the healing of the earth. Mowaljarlai, senior Lawman of the Ngarinyin people and a recognised artist and philosopher, put it in the following words in his address to a group of white Australians:

> We are really sorry for you people. We cry for you because you haven't got meaning of culture in this country. We have a gift we want to give you. We keep getting blocked from giving you that gift. We get blocked by politics and politicians. We get blocked by media, by process of law. All we want to do is come out from under all of this and give you this gift. And it's the gift of pattern thinking. It's the

The Ethics and Poetics of Mourning 79

culture which is the blood of this country, of Aboriginal groups, of
the ecology, of the land itself.
(quoted in Grieves 2009a, 7; see also Grieves 2009b)[1]

Apart from direct inspiration in Indigenous sources, it can safely be
argued that the ideas of radical relationality, common vulnerability and
the need for respect, attention and care for all creatures are gaining critical mass in current Western thought. Butler's work is only one example
among other scholarly publications that emphasise the interdependence
of life on earth.[2] In keeping with this convergence, I will draw on sources
by Indigenous Australians alongside Western authors in order to analyse
the implications of the inclusive nature of mourning in *The Swan Book*,
both as an ethics and in its literary expression. For the broad picture,
and before carrying out a more detailed analysis of Wright's novel, I will
resort to the concept of planetarity developed by Amy J. Elias and Christian Moraru as well as to the theory of transmodernity, both announc-
ing a change of paradigm.

Planetarity and transmodernity share an interest in investigating the
world that has succeeded the postmodern era, which they basically see as
a reconfiguration of modernity. Some modes of planetarity and transmodernity also share specific insights into the nature of contemporary reality, such us the urgent need to counter the excesses of twenty-first-century
globalisation with an ethical rearmament largely based on Emmanuel
Levinas's ethics of alterity. According to Elias and Moraru, we are witnessing an ongoing planetary turn that they explain as "a paradigmatic
translation of world cultures into a planetary setup in which globalization's homogenizing, one-becoming pulsion is challenged by *relationality*, namely, by an ethicization of the ecumenic process of coming
together or 'worldling'" (xi–xii; original emphasis). Ethics is perceived as
a necessary correction to the detrimental effects of globalisation, which,
in contrast to planetarity, is based on "techno-mercantile connectedness" and benefits only a few with its unequal distribution of economic
gain at the same time that it exploits the earth's resources and accelerates
climate change (xix). According to the emerging discourse of planetarity,
the planet is a living organism (xii) and the current climate crisis a commonality that affects us all (xix). Masao Miyoshi highlights the role of
literature and literary studies in pushing for change: "[They] now have
one basis and goal: to nurture our common bonds to the planet—to
replace the imaginaries of exclusionist familialism, communitarianism,
nationhood, ethnic culture, regionalism, 'globalization,' or even humanism, with the ideal of planetarianism" (295).

According to the Spanish philosopher Rosa María Rodríguez Magda,
transmodernity is characterised by the "Grand Fact" of globalisation,
which has come to replace the grand narratives of modernity after the
postmodern critique levelled at them (2004, 5). In her opinion, neoliberal

80   *Bárbara Arizti*

globalisation is equally totalising and "employs both evident and subtle mechanisms of exclusion" (2019, 26), which need to be uncovered and fought. Rodríguez Magda explains that the prefix "trans" evokes connection as well as transformation, transcendence and transgression (2011, 7; 2019, 29). In her opinion, in order "to create new values, new realities" (2011, 29) and help "preserve that fragile life that we are as a planet and as individuals," we need to construct narratives of the limit (2019, 26, 28), "new hopeful fictions" that resist "the delirious transformation in which we find ourselves" (29). Taking on a different outlook, Enrique Dussel writes back to the Eurocentric, universalising tendencies of modernity and regards transmodernity as

> a task [...] whose point of departure is that which has been [...] devalued and judged useless among global cultures, including colonized or peripheral philosophies. This project involves the development of the potential of those cultures and philosophies that have been ignored, upon the basis of their own resources, in constructive dialogue with European and North American modernity.
>
> (514)

It is in this light that I intend to explore *The Swan Book*'s approach to mourning, that is, by putting in conversation Indigenous philosophy and Western scholarship. It is obvious that the novel confronts readers with some of the effects of modernity's overindulgence: extreme individualism, ruthless exploitation of the earth, unchecked globalisation and epistemological arrogance. In doing so, it partakes of the postmodern critique of the grand narratives of self-sufficiency, unlimited progress, universalism and the civilising mission of the empire. In this sense, Wright's work can be read as a narrative of the limit in Rodríguez Magda's acceptation, since it exposes the unhomeliness of the contemporary moment in all its rawness. At the same time, *The Swan Book* salvages premodern aspects discarded by modernity, namely Indigenous Australian thought-worlds and ancient wisdom. The novel's favourable reception inside and outside Australia accounts for a growing interest in forms of knowledge that have not lost sight of the inextricable pattern of connections that lies underneath life on earth. The planetary scope of mourning in *The Swan Book* revises the distinction between centre and periphery, the local and the global, and—in the midst of widespread unrest—it appeals for an ethics that transcends the human and reaches out to animals and the earth itself.

The Ethics of Mourning

The dedication of Butler's *Precarious Life: The Powers of Mourning and Violence* reads: "For Isaac, who imagines otherwise." There follow five essays on grief and mourning, written after the 9/11 attacks, in which the author laments how the United States missed the chance to reinvent itself in the face of vulnerability and loss "as part of a global community" (2004 xi), and sought instead revenge through military intervention. As the dedication hints, the underlying purpose of Butler's book is, basically, to promote other ways of political mourning that highlight the "inevitable interdependency" of human lives (xii) and deem any life equally worthy of being grieved. Butler's imagining otherwise finds an echo in Wright's comment in an interview with Jane Sullivan on the origin of *The Swan Book*, at the time when John Howard's policies supported a backlash against Indigenous Australians:

> I wanted to write a different sort of book. There were other ways of looking at the world and ideas and the spirit of things and how you can change the world, or at least change what you think. No matter what happens to you, you can maintain your own control about what you believe and who you are.
>
> (Sullivan n.p.)

Just as Wright does in *The Swan Book*, so Butler upholds in *Precarious Life* a comprehensive conception of mourning; denounces that certain populations are more likely to experience arbitrary violence than others (Butler 2004, xii); and exposes the futile efforts of current forms of national sovereignty to overcome vulnerability and violability, when they are in fact "ineradicable dimensions of human dependency and sociality," as she puts it (xiv). Neither the US philosopher nor the Indigenous Australian author offer "grand utopian conclusions" (Butler 2004, xiii). However, it is very significant that both espouse a non-violent ethics "based on an understanding of how easily human life is annulled" (Butler 2004, xvii). Thus, Butler's essay and Wright's novel open up a space for the ethical within the political, in the wake of Levinas's concern for the precarious life of the other (Butler 2004, xvii), an other for which we are always already responsible.

In spite of the fact that Butler and Wright tap into the commonalities of human existence, *The Swan Book* makes it clear that Wright's inclusive mourning stems from Aboriginal epistemology and ontology, especially the concept of "Dreaming" or "Dreamtime," a rough translation from Aboriginal languages (Grieves 2009a, 8). This concept resists definition and defies the rational logic of the Western mind: it can be communicated in the form of a dream but has little to do with dreams; it can be transmitted through narratives but it is much more than simple stories (Ashcroft, Devlin-Glass, and McCredden 208). Dreamtime narratives and laws conform to a radically ecological view of life that does not conceive of humans as separate from each other or the land; regard Country[3] as sentient and sacred; and perceive

82 Bárbara Arizti

differences as generating what Deborah Bird Rose describes as "mutual interdependence" (57). The key word for understanding the Dreaming is interrelationality:

> Dreaming narratives integrate fields that are separate discursive domains in western knowledge—philosophy, religion, economic, ecology, epistemology, kinship, gender behaviour, kinship systems, interpersonal relations, geography and mapping.
> (Ashcroft, Devlin-Glass and McCredden 209)

As Linda Daley notes, Wright's work fictionalises an Indigenous thought-world that escapes "the logic of Western rationalist individualism" and avoids the pitfalls of dualistic thinking (9) already exposed by postmodern and poststructuralist Western thinkers (10), as well as by Braidotti's posthumanist theory.

The Swan Book provides ample evidence of Wright's nod to mourning as a planetary right. Significantly, the author does not exclusively focus on the mourning of Indigenous Australians and their culture, one of the oldest on earth (Wright 2013, 106; Grieves 2009a, 2). In contrast to the notion of the "unequal distribution of grievability," developed by Butler in *The Force of Non-Violence* (2021, 75), the novel is an elegy envisaging loss without distinction. The shift of focus between the individual and the communal, the local and the planetary, the human and wildlife reinforces this thesis. Wright's choice of characters further enhances an all-inclusive regard. Even if the book features a clear protagonist, Oblivia, her role is supplemented by other main characters like Bella Donna and Warren Finch, the first Indigenous president of Australia. Significantly, the work connects the fates of Indigenous Australians and climate refugees through Oblivia—an Aboriginal teenage girl who goes voluntarily mute after a gang rape by a group of impoverished Indigenous boys addicted to sniffing petrol—and Bella Donna, an old woman who has fled her Northern Hemisphere country ravaged by climate catastrophe. After the rape, Oblivia takes refuge inside a giant eucalypt tree for a decade. Bella Donna arrives in Australia guided by a swan and rescues Oblivia from her tree shelter, much to the girl's dismay. They settle at an Aboriginal reservation known as Swan Lake, which was flooded into a swamp by the erratic weather, and is currently controlled by the Army and used as a dump place. Inspired by the old woman's stories about swans, Oblivia befriends and looks after the black swans that start arriving *en masse*. After Bella Donna's death, she ends up in an arranged marriage to Warren Finch—who abducts her from her swamp and orders the destruction of the place—only to become a widow when Finch is assassinated. The epilogue features Oblivia back in Swan Lake, now a droughty, dusty place, caring for the last surviving black swan (Wright 2013, 331).

The Ethics and Poetics of Mourning   83

Singling out Oblivia and Bella Donna as representative of the plights of their communities focuses the reader's attention on the two characters and, in the case of Bella Donna, offers at least a meagre chance to be mourned: "Only the girl felt the sadness of losing the old woman forever" (75). What is more remarkable is the fact that the novel grants space and agency to the destitute masses themselves, who function as collective characters and offer an idea of the daunting scale of loss. Oblivia's neighbours at the Aboriginal reservation, climate migrants sailing the seas "in that world of unwanted people" (220), and the urban homeless described in the chapter entitled "City of Refugees" can be said to constitute the "emergent precariat," in Zygmunt Bauman's phrase (15). These communities of socially excluded people, as Bauman denounces in his work, provoke fear, are subject to stigmatisation, or are met with indifference at best. In my opinion, they serve some related purposes in the novel: to highlight the fragility of human life at the hands of oppression and in the face of overwhelming natural forces; to render visible their stories of loss and condemn society's neglect; and to prove the pointlessness of drawing up borders and erecting walls in a world that is more and more interdependent. Borrowing from Bauman, "whatever choices are resorted to, what we need to keep in mind is that they can't but affect our joint/shared (hopefully long) future" (20). The cure for indifference, Bauman suggests, coincides to a certain extent with the ethical agenda of *The Swan Book*. In Bauman's own words:

> instead of refusing to face up to the realities of the 'one planet, one humanity' challenges of our times, washing our hands and fencing ourselves off from the annoying differences, dissimilarities and self-imposed estrangements, we must seek occasions to come into a close and increasingly intimate contact with them.
>
> (18–19)

Although Wright's regard for the excluded avoids idealisation, she provides them with a dignity that complicates judgement on their situation. Their tough lives are still depicted as worthy of being lived and, at least in the case of the Aborigines of Swan Lake, they persist in their attempts at regaining sovereignty and be respected by the powers that be. The following quotation is representative of the mixture of hopelessness and hope that characterises the novel: "They were the children of the homeless poor people of the city. Well! They were boys and girls of all ages and from all racial backgrounds mingling together like friends when they followed the swans through the city to the lane" (Wright 2013, 247). The racial diversity of the group marks yet another significant departure from received Western notions of race. For a moment, the spotlight is not on their victim status but on the joys of coming together after the swans, their poverty notwithstanding. The interjection serves to hinge the two

84 *Bárbara Arizti*

realities, which are shown to be complementary rather than set in dual opposition. Actually, the narrator explains that "[i]t was miracles these children were after": "And they felt closer to a miracle just from looking up to the sky and seeing the swans as they swarmed through the lane. They started calling the very ordinary lane a sacred site" (247). In the midst of destitution and a soulless cityscape, the transformative power of nature and wildlife becomes evident, as does the sacrality of place, much in line with Indigenous spiritual beliefs.

As noted earlier, the Waanyi author's writing is triggered by the need to denounce "the living hell of the lives of many Aboriginal people" (Wright 2002, 13). The title of her essay *Croire en l'incroyable*, published exclusively in French, points to her desire to assert their right of property over traditional lands (2000, 44). This claim does not obey to purely economic reasons, for the earth is considered sacred and made synonymous with the people (10). The loss of the tribal lands detracts from Aboriginal identity and wellbeing in a very profound way. Wright says it takes courage and determination to change the mentality of the population and picture a new Australia where "Aborigines will no longer be threatened, dominated or rejected" (39; my translation). Despite some advances towards reconciliation and reparation on the part of the federal government, changes have not materialised in a sufficiently concrete way to be credible. Wright demands "a Treaty, now" (30; my translation). In the novel, the Aborigines of Swan Lake have been deprived of sovereignty over their traditional lands. They are described as "the poorest people in a rich land" (Wright 2013, 31) and "the littlest people of Australia" (131). After "wandering around homelessly for years" they decide to return "to their rightful place of belonging, their ancestral domain" (10). There, they discover the irrelevance of the "Native Title," the official recognition of rights over a tribe's lands as long as they can prove uninterrupted occupation: "on the day that they had left their land, their Native Title had been lost irredeemably and disappeared from the face of the planet" (10).

Wright has drawn attention in several essays to the effects of white neglect of Indigenous Australians and interference with their customs and ways: "The good, the bad and the incompetent have created chaos with their myriad solutions that bear little or no relation to one another. They are features of a governance system that still cannot, even to this day, do one simple thing: embrace the Indigenous vision" (Wright 2006b, 107). The Aborigines of Swan Lake have lost the right to raise their children according to their culture, as the following quotation shows: The "Canberra-imposed controller of the Swan Lake Aboriginal Government [...] was supposed to implement white ways of loving children as being better than theirs" (Wright 2013, 136, 137). In this way, the novel lays bare the feeling of superiority of white settlers, who, since the first contacts, regarded the Indigenous society as primitive and "backward,

The Ethics and Poetics of Mourning   85

with nothing to offer the modern, progressive ideals of the colonial project" (Grieves 2009a, 27). There are frequent allusions in *The Swan Book* to the policies of forced assimilation and to the Stolen Generations, the Indigenous children of mixed descent who were taken away from their homes to be educated in religious institutions and white foster families throughout the twentieth century. The Northern Territory Intervention, a more recent attempt at controlling the Indigenous population under the pretext of protecting children from domestic abuse, enforced by the Howard government, is also mentioned in the novel, as well as the desecration of spiritual ancestors and burial grounds by mining companies (Wright 2013, 68), besides many other nefarious activities.

Among the Aboriginal characters, the case of Warren Finch yields relevant insights for the study of grievability. His assassination when in office as the first Indigenous president of Australia offers an opportunity for exploring forms of official mourning in the novel. Paradoxically enough, the life that elicits the most explicit, even excessive, manifestation of public mourning is that of an Indigenous figure. His body is laid in state in the country's biggest cathedral, "kept overflowing with mourners": "The poor from the streets and alleyway communes started elbowing for space with overseas dignitaries, Heads of State of other countries—many with fragile diplomatic relationships with Australia" (Wright 2013, 285). In spite of this display of grieving, Finch's characterisation moves between the ambivalent and the downright evil, as demonstrated by his forcing Oblivia into marriage and by the destruction of Swan Lake, her homeland. His role as a president, despite the fact that he was brought up according to Indigenous culture, stereotypically fits the usual pattern of Western politicians, since he proves unable to fulfil his promises of protecting the environment or closing the gap between Indigenous and non-Indigenous Australians. In truth, he is viewed by other Aborigines as too assimilated: "they were sick of hearing about Warren Finch, the role model for how Aboriginal children could become good Australians" (126). On top of this, the controversy about where he should be buried and according to what rite, and the fact that his body ends up in a *"Fresh Food People* long-haul semitrailer" (296; original emphasis) travelling the roads of the nation, takes down from the solemnity of the official mourning. Besides the farcical scenes, the tongue-in-cheek description of the ceremonies surrounding Finch's death corroborates Wright's wariness of ineffectual Australian politicians and her lack of interest in forms of mourning that, while proving a life worthy of grieving, are empty and insincere.

Following the Indigenous belief in mutual interdependency alongside a respect for difference, in *The Swan Book* Wright extends mourning to climate refugees, the land itself and the vegetal and animal worlds. Oblivia's story is intimately connected to that of Bella Donna, the only survivor of a large group of climate refugees, boat people coming from

86   Bárbara Arizti

the Northern Hemisphere as part of a flux of "twenty-first-century cast-outs ploughing the wilderness of oceans" (34) who are described as "the new gypsies" (23), "the banished people of the world" (31). Oblivia and Bella Donna's different experiences of exile, loss and grieving are made to converge as their common vulnerability and interdependency are highlighted. The Indigenous and the foreign meet in this unlikely pair. The cross-racial relationship, nevertheless, is far from idealised. Readers are made aware of how difficult communication can be between the dumb Aboriginal girl and the cantankerous old European woman. Bella Donna is sometimes described as an angel, "the patroness of World Rejection" (32), and others as an invader (32) who reached Australia by boat, like the colonisers of old. She patronises and controls Oblivia in ways that echo the assimilation policies of the Australian government. Despite this, Bella Donna is instrumental in looking after Oblivia, especially in that it is from her that the girl learns how to talk to swans (69). While Bella Donna feeds Oblivia with stories about swans, the girl, mesmerised, shows signs of affection: "Frequently the girl would interrupt her by laying her hand on the old woman's arm" (73). Until, one day, when she was about to begin what is described as "a new love story," "Aunty Bella Donna of the Champions of the earth, who might have been an angel, died" (73). She does not completely disappear from the narrative, though. Beyond surviving in Oblivia's memories, Bella Donna, as happens to other characters in the book, haunts the girl as a ghost. In accordance with the Indigenous vision, in *The Swan Book* the world of the spirits and the ancestors exists alongside that of the living. Extrapolating from Aileen Moreton-Robinson's description of Aboriginal spirituality and relationality, the different dimensions of existence are perceived as an organic whole "populated by spirits which connect places and people" (quoted in Grieves 2009a, 16).

Furthermore, *The Swan Book* presents the human and the other than human—culture and nature, *zoē* and *bíos*—as spiritually connected and forming part of a continuum. Butler's notion of the common fragility and equal right to grievability of all human beings is expanded by Wright to include the natural world. At the same time, in the novel, knowledge is always embedded and embodied, that is, grounded in the materiality of the earth and the body. The inhabitants of Swan Lake regard the ground as sacred and stick to the earth of their ancestors even if it is not "pure and pristine anymore" (Wright 2013, 11). Some specimens are singled out from the landscape as particularly worthy of attention, like the tree that provided a shelter for Oblivia, which is worshipped as the community's "older living relative for looking after the memories" (79). Unfortunately, when the girl is found, the army destroys the tree "on the premise that this nexus of dangerous beliefs had to be broken, to close the gap between Aboriginal people and white people" (79). The patronising attitude of the army and their disregard for Aboriginal culture and

The Ethics and Poetics of Mourning   87

the natural world is set in opposition to the reverence the Indigenous characters show towards the environment. This is how the sacred eucalypt tree comes to swell the list of Oblivia's losses and, like Bella Donna, becomes the object of her mourning.

Nevertheless, it is the swans that constitute the centrepiece of the novel. Although they are significant on many levels, they cannot be reduced to mere symbols since they are portrayed as sentient beings and they too have their dreamings and stories, in the Indigenous sense. As happens with people and plants, the swans matter as a flock but also individually. Two swans stand out: the white swan that leads Bella Donna to safety in the coast of Australia, and Stranger, the black cygnet Oblivia saves from extinction and takes back to Swan Lake (308). At the beginning of the story, Bella Donna's nostalgia for the white swan that saved her life is met with the arrival at the swamp of a huge flock of black swans. Like the multiracial children of the poor mentioned above, black swans serve to evoke racial diversity and to challenge old Eurocentric views. The novel recounts the first sighting of black swans off the coast of Western Australian by Dutch explorers back in the seventeenth century (81). Prior to it, they were considered mere figments of the imagination by Westerners. Like Bella Donna and Oblivia, the swans have undergone losses and are depicted as exiles (14) and mourners (91). In the epilogue, Stranger finds his solitude unbearable and is "never the same after losing his flock" (332). Swans suffer the ravages of climate change almost to the point of extinction. The narrator refers to them as both signs of hope and "the paragon of anxious premonitions" (14). Such is the ambivalence of the novel that it is difficult to decide on which association bears greater weight. It is true that in the closing sentences the narrator hypothesises with the return of swans to Swan Lake. Nonetheless, the place they would return to, a "ghost place," "like desert!" (334), shows no signs of hopefulness. Perhaps the answer comes extratextually from Wright herself, who states in the interview with Sullivan that swans "bring beauty and make us feel good about ourselves" (Sullivan n.p.). According to Wright, this is in part the purpose of *The Swan Book*: "trying to catch the beauty in the world. To love it a bit and love ourselves and love other people" before it is too late (Sullivan n.p.).

Oblivia's concern for the swans illustrates the empathic extension of mourning that characterises the novel's ethics. Despite the passing of time, she never ceases to be a *"wulumbarra*, teenage girl" (Wright 2013, 334), which stresses the durability and validity of the beliefs and practices she stands for. By the end of *The Swan Book*, the girl appears as the only custodian of the land and wildlife, and as inextricably connected to her country. Her final journey from the city, where she was held captive by Finch, to Swan Lake embodies the Aboriginal wish of "returning to country" (Grieves 2009a, 13). For Indigenous Australians, everything begins with the land (13). As Michael Dodson puts it: "Removed from

88 *Bárbara Arizti*

our lands, we are literally removed from ourselves" (41). This relationship involves accepting responsibility for the environment. The state of Swan Lake resonates with Rose's description of the havoc wreaked by colonisation on Indigenous Australia: "Once a multiplicity of nourishing terrains, there is now a multiplicity of devastations" (81). However, like care for an infirm relative, "the relationship between Indigenous people and country persists; [...] no matter what the damage, people care" (81). This shows a commitment and endurance that also characterise Oblivia throughout *The Swan Book*. Needless to say, it is a *modus operandi* that can help restore relationships and the health of the earth as well.

The Poetics of Mourning

This section is devoted to analysing how the form of *The Swan Book* enacts its inclusive message by breaking down barriers between literary traditions and conventions across the world. I argue that, when writing the novel, Wright seems to have been guided by the four principles of Aboriginal philosophy: respect, complexity, creation and connection. The text is indeed an extraordinarily complex artefact made up of juxtaposed fragments arranged into chapters. They are framed by a prelude narrated by Oblivia—the only time her voice reaches the reader in unmediated form—and an epilogue that presents the ending of her story through an external voice. Each section bears a simple title, several of them revolving around swans. Wright succeeds in creating a unique, original and polyphonic work by connecting a myriad of sources that range from the popular to the erudite, deployed in a variety of styles. For the most part, *The Swan Book* is written in Standard English, but, sporadically, Wright introduces Waanyi words and Aboriginal English, which render Indigenous Australians more visible among the plurality of voices. Like the previous thematic approach, this section seeks to show that the novel's form is best analysed through the synergies between Indigenous and Western critical frameworks. Were I to choose a single category for describing the novel's poetics, I would no doubt settle on "Aboriginal realism," coined but little fleshed out by the author herself (quoted in Leane n.p.). Even so, I believe that broadening the scope of analysis to include other related perspectives does more justice to Wright's multifarious narrative.

Significantly for the ethical stance of the novel, which advocates equal grievability for Aborigines and migrants, Wright's work combines foreign and Indigenous poetics. In broad lines, *The Swan Book* relies on the genre of the novel but supplements prose with narrative techniques that recall orality. The novel is indebted to the rich oral tradition of storytelling in Indigenous Australia, stories recounted to an audience sometimes incorporating poetry, music, dance and other rituals so as to pass on ancient wisdom alongside practical advice. The relationship between

The Ethics and Poetics of Mourning   89

the orator and the audience is thematised in the recurrent picture of Oblivia listening to Bella Donna's stories about swans. Her attentive listening can be read as an instance of *Dadirri*, an Aboriginal quality that consists, according to Miriam-Rose Ungunmerr-Baumann, in "inner deep listening and quiet still awareness" (n.p.). As Ungunmerr-Baumann argues, Indigenous people do not fear silence, but rather relish it because it allows them to adopt a contemplative attitude in life: "We could not live good and useful lives unless we listened" (n.p.). While Oblivia's muteness is basically the defensive reaction of a girl traumatised by rape, her self-imposed silence makes the character particularly sensitive to her environment and keeps her attuned to her own needs and the needs of others, especially the swans.

Formally, the novel has been described by Arnaud Barras as a "transnational collage of allusions" (11), encompassing an array of Western and Eastern myths, poems and quotations—mostly about swans—alongside Indigenous stories of the Dreaming. Wright documented herself thoroughly on the life of swans and read extensively on their representations in literature. Among other examples, Bella Donna declaims a verse on swans by an unnamed Hungarian poet (Wright 2013, 25); recites by heart lines from Yeats's "The Wild Swans at Coole" (28, 29); alludes to Wagner's opera *Lohengrin*, where the knight arrives in a boat drawn by a swan (28–29); quotes Hans Christian Andersen about "a swan sitting on a nest of fledglings that perpetually flew off to populate the world with poetry inspired by their own beauty" (44); and talks of having flown in her imagination among black-beaked Whistling Swans lifting into the Alaskan skies, and of speaking to the descendants of the great Kugui flocks in Japan (41). "Here was this creature that in all the literature I read seems to bring out the best in us," Wright affirms, delving into the idea of the salvific qualities of swans (Sullivan n.p.).

Besides this planetary intertextuality pointed out by Barras, I suggest analysing *The Swan Book*'s overall structure as part of current burgeoning fictional trends. In my opinion, the novel shares two characteristics with a sizeable group of contemporary novels: a poetics of fragmentation, and a narrative structure that, while retaining a background teleology, evokes the form of a global net. In "The Rise of the Fragmented Novel" (2013), Ted Gioia speaks of a new type of fragmentation that far from emphasising "disjunction and dissolution" appears "holistic and coalescent" (n.p.). To be sure, this is the case with *The Swan Book*, which counteracts the apparent disunity of its form by connecting the different strands of mourning through the character of Oblivia. Concomitantly, Aris Mousoutzanis's "Network Fictions and the Global Unhomely" and Caroline Edwards's "The Networked Novel" coincide in identifying a group of works that "interweave multiple interlocking narratives set in different times and spaces around the globe and involve many characters, often in a state of mobility and travel" (Mousoutzanis 2).

90 *Bárbara Arizti*

Mousoutzanis draws on Freud's *Unheimlich* to explain the feeling of unhomeliness and uncanniness these network fictions present, both on a personal and a global level. Edwards quotes Caren Irr, for whom these "world novels" register "the simultaneous and multidirectional movements of the world's population" and deal with "the major issues of our era, including peace, ecological crisis, and nuclear threats" (Edwards 15). Given the thematic overlaps and the interconnected sets of narratives concerning the experience of loss for Indigenous Australians, climate refugees and swans, I believe Wright's work aptly fits the net pattern described by Mousoutzanis and Edwards.

The form of *The Swan Book* can also be analysed by resorting to classical Western terminology. Maria Karen Takolander, for instance, considers the novel an example of magical realism. In her opinion, rather than a postcolonial strategy "embodying a racialized epistemology allegedly inclusive of magic" (95), as some critics would contend, magical realism is for Wright a form of irony that "far from verifying fantasy as evidence of cultural difference [...,] advocate[s] a self-conscious commitment to history as the key to an empowered future" (101). I agree that irony does play a crucial role in *The Swan Book*. Not even the mourning of the Indigenous leader escapes unscathed, as seen before. However, I believe that reading the instances of magic realism exclusively as irony and remarking Wright's commitment to history do not fully elucidate the complex worldview of the novel, which, as the author has made clear, is accretive rather than exclusionary, and insists on cultural difference.

Putting together Western literary theory and Indigenous thought, Linda Daley affirms that Wright

> invents an Aboriginal modernism that eschews the realist conventions of narration (of speaking subject, of the logic of cause and effect, of a single order of reality, and of linear chronology) to express the social and political problems of modernity for her people and how speech acts participate in these problems.
>
> (306)

That *The Swan Book* denounces the pernicious effects of the modern project has already been pointed out. As Daley suggests, the novel's experimental form questions the assumptions that lie behind traditional realism: that the subject is unified, self-sufficient and ultimately apprehensible; that nature is mostly a background on which events unfold; that life can be truthfully and faithfully portrayed through social mimesis; and that there is linear progression in history, with the present succeeding the past to be in due time superseded by the future. Oblivia's impenetrability, the degree of interdependency of human beings, the elevation of nature and wildlife to sentient status through the extension of

The Ethics and Poetics of Mourning 91

the notion of grievability, as well as a diffuse temporality which at times seems to collapse past, present and future clearly depart from classical realism.

Although established categories such as magical realism and modernism, together with more recent coinages like the fragmented novel and networked fiction can help explain Wright's formal choices in *The Swan Book* and its deviation from conventional realism, it is the concept of Aboriginal realism that most accurately and fairly describes the poetics of *The Swan Book*. This is especially true when considered in connection with the novel's inclusive conception of mourning, nourished, as we have seen, by Indigenous Australians' philosophy and spirituality. The term "Aboriginal realism" was employed by the Indigenous writer and scholar Jeanine Leane to describe Wright's poetics in her earlier novel *Carpentaria*, prompted by Wright's rejection of the magical realism label: "Some people call the book magic realism but really in a way it's an Aboriginal realism which carries all sorts of things" (quoted in Leane n.p.). Jane Gleeson-White makes use of the concept in her review of *The Swan Book* and quotes Wright on her view of fiction, inspired by an Indigenous relational ethics firmly rooted in the land:

> The world I [Wright] try to inhabit in my writing is like looking at the ancestral tracks spanning our traditional country which, if I look at the land, combines all stories, all realities from the ancient to the new, and makes it one—like all the strands on a long rope.
> (quoted in Gleeson-White n.p.)

Aboriginal realism escapes the pitfalls of magical realism—a product of Western binary thought. It more faithfully reflects the comprehensive Indigenous worldview, capacious enough to hold together the factual and the apparently fantastic, the ordinary and the numinous, space and time, their coexistence granted by an organic connection to the land. The following quotation from the novel is representative of the conflation between time and space, the generative power of the land and a radical embeddedness in the local environment: "They passed through old times, coming through hillock after hillock covered in spinifex, of Country that had a serious Law story for every place, and of everything belonging to that place life family" (Wright 2013, 191).

Mowaljarlai's "gift of pattern thinking" offers a glimpse of the core of reality as traditionally perceived by Indigenous Australians. Ambelin Kwaymullina summarises Mowaljarlai's thought in words reminiscent of those of Wright quoted above:

> This pattern has many threads of many colours, and every thread is connected to, and has a relationship with, all the others. The individual threads are every shape of life. [...] Human is there too,

92 *Bárbara Arizti*

though it is neither the most or the least important thread—it is one among many; equal with the others. [...] The whole is more than its parts, and the whole is in all its parts.

(quoted in Grieves 2009a, 14)

In *The Swan Book*, the fact that animals and the natural world are as worthy of grieving as humans is reflected in focalisation, since some swans (Wright 2013, 18), Oblivia's eucalypt tree (79), and a monkey called Rigoletto (281) act as focalisers alongside the human characters. When taking a close look at the pattern of the novel, the stories of Oblivia, Bella Donna and the swans stand out as autonomous and important in their own right. When looking at it from a distance, one perceives how interlocked they all are. As a whole, the pattern reveals a deep reverence for all forms of life, be it that of Indigenous Australians, boat people or the natural world.

Conclusion

A novel is always a door to the concerns of its author. In Wright's earlier works, *Plains of Promise* (1997) and *Carpentaria*, the door opened to disclose the stark realities of Aboriginal Australia in the long aftermath of colonisation. With *The Swan Book*, Wright proves that, in this increasingly globalised world, the fate of her people is inescapably connected with that of other deprived human groups as well as with the destiny of animals. What is more, the lives and fortunes of swans, climate migrants and Indigenous Australians are shown to be dependent on the preservation of the earth at large as a habitable place. Wright imagines a catastrophic future, looming only two centuries ahead, the result of human-induced climate change, armed conflicts, the ongoing migratory crisis and the unresolved historical legacy from colonial times.

This chapter has studied how *The Swan Book* takes stock of traumatic loss with a wholistic regard. If mourning involves the recognition of the victim, Wright's novel acknowledges the inherent grievability of any form of life. It does so by advocating an inclusive ethics that addresses human and environmental concerns on an equal footing. This turns out to be crucial in unsettling the rankings of grief and the exceptionalism of the human over other species. The novel's ethics hinges on the character of Oblivia, the young Aboriginal girl, and her relationship with a white woman, Bella Donna, who provides her with the key to the world of swans. In the midst of chaos and suffering, Oblivia never gives up on caring for the black swans and finally succeeds in returning to the land of her ancestors. The allusions to the literary representations of swans across the cultures of the earth create an intertextual net and serve as a unifying thread in a largely fragmentary narrative, where the different stories of loss interlock in an organic whole. Although my approach to

The Ethics and Poetics of Mourning   93

mourning has benefitted from the convergence of Western and Indigenous knowledge systems, ultimately, it is Aboriginal philosophy and spirituality that better explain the ethics of *The Swan Book*. The same happens with the novel's poetics—analysed as an example of Aboriginal realism—which, in accounting for all realities, supports the ethical *desideratum* of Wright's work. By framing the analysis within planetarity and transmodernity what appears is that the novel is not a solitary voice clamouring for change but part of a wider cultural surge that, when facing the challenges of today's world, invites an ethics of care beyond species, nation, social status and race.

Acknowledgements

Research for this chapter was funded by the Spanish Ministry of Science and Innovation (MICINN) (code PID2021-124841NB-I00) and by the Government of Aragón and the European Social Fund (ESF) (code H03_20R).

Notes

1 The Anglo-Celtic Australian author Tim Winton reproduces part of the quotation in his landscape memoir *Island Home* (191).
2 Eco-feminism and posthuman theory, as represented by Stacy Alaimo (2010) and Rosi Braidotti (2013), are equally concerned with a vision of embeddings and interdependences.
3 The word "Country" has special connotations for Indigenous Australians that highlight the cultural connection with their homeland.

Works Cited

Agamben, Giorgio. *Homo Sacer: Sovereign Power and Bare Life*. 1995. Stanford, CA: Stanford UP, 1998.
Alaimo, Stacy. *Bodily Natures: Science, Environment, and the Material Self*. Bloomington: Indiana UP, 2010.
Ashcroft, Bill, Frances Devlin-Glass, and Lyn McCredden. *Intimate Horizons: The Post-Colonial Sacred in Australian Literature*. Adelaide: ATF P, 2009.
Atkinson, Meera. "Alexis Wright's Literary Testimony to Intersecting Traumas." *Animal Studies Journal* 7.1 (2018): 41–58. Accessed on 14/01/2022 at: https://ro.uow.edu.au/asj/vol7/iss1/3/.
Barras, Arnaud. "The Law of Storytelling: The Hermeneutics of Relationality in Alexis Wright's *The Swan Book*." *Journal of the Association for the Study of Australian Literature* 15.3 (2015): 1–12.
Bauman, Zygmunt. *Strangers at Our Door*. Cambridge, Malden, MA: Polity P, 2016.
Braidotti, Rosi. *The Posthuman*. Hoboken, NJ: Wiley & Sons, 2013.
Brennan, Elliot. "On This Day: Indigenous People Get Citizenship." *Australian Geographic*, 7 November 2013. Accessed on 27/12/2021 at: https://

94 *Bárbara Arizti*

www.australiangeographic.com.au/blogs/on-this-day/2013/11/on-this-day-indigenous-people-get-citizenship/.

Butler, Judith. *Precarious Life*: *The Powers of Mourning and Violence*. London and New York: Verso, 2004.

———. *The Force of Non-Violence. An Ethico-Political Bind*. 2020. London and New York: Verso, 2021.

Daley, Linda. "Fabulation: Toward Untimely and Inhuman Life in Alexis Wright's *The Swan Book*." *Australian Feminist Studies* 31.89 (2016): 305–18.

Dodson, Michael. "Land Rights and Social Justice." *Our Land is Our Life: Land Rights—Past, Present and Future*. Ed. Galarrwuy Yunupingu. St Lucia: U of Queensland P, 1997. 39–41.

Dussel, Enrique. "A New Age in the History of Philosophy. The World Dialogue between Philosophical Traditions." *Philosophy & Social Criticism* 35.5 (2009): 499–516.

Eckersley, Richard M. "Culture, Spirituality, Religion and Health: Looking at the Big Picture." *Medical Journal of Australia* 186.10 (2007): 54–56.

Edwards, Caroline. "The Networked Novel." *The Routledge Companion to Twenty-First Century Literary Fiction*. Eds Daniel O'Gorman and Robert Eaglestone. London: Routledge, 2019. 13–24.

Elias, Amy J. and Christian Moraru, eds and intro. *The Planetary Turn: Relationality and Geoaesthetics in the Twenty-First Century*. Evanston, IL: Northwestern UP, 2015.

Gioia, Ted. "The Rise of the Fragmented Novel (An Essay in 26 Fragments)." 2013. Accessed on 3/06/2022 at https://www.modernliterature.org/rise-fragmented-novel-essay-26-fragments-by-ted-gioia/

Gleeson-White, Jane. "Going Viral: *The Swan Book* by Alexis Wright." *Sydney Review of Books* 23 August 2013. Accessed on 27/08/2021 at: https://sydneyreviewofbooks.com/review/going-viral/.

Grieves, Vicki. *Aboriginal Spirituality: Aboriginal Philosophy. The Basis of Aboriginal Social and Emotional Wellbeing*. Casuarina, NT: Cooperative Research Centre for Aboriginal Health, 2009a.

———. "Opening the Dialogue for Indigenous Knowledges: Developments in Australia." A Review of Martin Nakata's *Disciplining the Savages, Savaging the Disciplines*. *Cultural Studies Review* 15.2 (2009b): 199–203.

Irr, Caren. *Toward the Geopolitical Novel: U.S. Fiction in the Twenty-First Century*. New York: Columbia UP, 2014.

Leane, Jeanine. "9. Historyless People." *Long History, Deep Time: Deepening Histories of Place*. Eds Ann McGrath and Mary Anne Jebb. Canberra: ANU P, 2015. Accessed on 3/06/2022 at: https://press-files.anu.edu.au/ downloads/press/p319821/html/ch09.xhtml/.

Mbembe, Achille. "Necropolitics." *Public Culture* 15.1 (2003): 11–40.

Miyoshi, Masao. "Turn to the Planet: Literature, Diversity, and Totality." *Comparative Literature* 53.4 (Autumn, 2001): 283–97.

Mousoutzanis, Aris. "Network Fictions and the Global Unhomely." *C21 Literature: Journal of 21st-Century Writings* 4(1).7 (2016): 1–19.

Rodríguez Magda, Rosa María. *Transmodernidad*. Barcelona: Anthropos, 2004.

———. "Transmodernidad: un nuevo paradigma." *Transmodernity: Journal of Peripheral Cultural Production of the Luso-Hispanic World* 1.1 (2011): 1–13. Accessed on 30/12/2021 at: https://escholarship.org/uc/item/57c8s9gr/.

———. "The Crossroads of Transmodernity." *Transmodern Perspectives on Contemporary Literatures in English.* Eds Jessica Aliaga-Lavrijsen and José María Yebra-Pertusa. New York and London: Routledge, 2019: 21–29.

Rose, Deborah Bird. *Nourishing Terrains: Australian Aboriginal Views of Landscape and Wilderness.* Canberra: Australian Heritage Commission, 1996.

Rothberg, Michael. *Multidirectional Memory: Remembering the Holocaust in the Age of Decolonization.* Stanford, CA: Stanford UP, 2009.

Takolander, Maria Karen. "Theorizing Irony and Trauma in Magical Realism: Junot Díaz's *The Brief Wondrous Life of Oscar Wao* and Alexis Wright's *The Swan Book." Ariel: A Review of International English Literature* 47.3 (2016): 95–122.

Sullivan, Jane. "Interview: Alexis Wright." *The Sydney Morning Herald* 3 August, 2013. Accessed on 3/06/2022 at: https://www.smh.com.au/entertainment/books/interview-alexis-wright-20130801-2r045.html/

Ungunmerr-Baumann, Miriam-Rose. "Dadirri - A Reflection." Accessed on 20/01/2022 at: http://www.dadirri.org.au/wp-content/uploads/2015/03/Dadirri-Inner-Deep-Listening-M-R-Ungunmerr-Bauman-Refl1.pdf/

Vernay, Jean-François. "An Interview with Alexis Wright." *Antipodes* 18.2 (December 2004): 119–22.

Winton, Tim. *Island Home: A Landscape Memoir.* London: Picador, 2015.

Wright, Alexis. *Plains of Promise.* St Lucia: U of Queensland P, 1997.

———. *Croire en l'incroyable.* Arles: Actes Sud, 2000.

———. "The Politics of Writing." *Southerly* 62.2 (Summer 2002): 10–20.

———. *Carpentaria.* Sydney: Giramondo, 2006a.

———. "Embracing the Indigenous Vision." *Meanjin* 65.1 (March 2006b): 104–108.

———. *The Swan Book.* London: Constable, 2013.

5 From Elegy to Apocalypse

Ecological Grief and Human Grievability in Ben Smith's *Doggerland*

Angelo Monaco

Introduction

In his work, English author Ben Smith consistently shows an interest in climate change and the way in which environmental questions can be represented in literary forms. His poetry collection, *Sky Burials* (2014), presents a number of challenges for the reader since the poems address the intricate relationship between human and non-human as "viable, visual and tangible" (Klein n.p.). In his debut novel, *Doggerland* (2019), there is a unique combination of the author's concern with environmental questions—Smith is a lecturer in creative writing at Plymouth University, specialised in environmental literature—and an experimental vein that blends poetry and fiction. In an early review that appeared in *The Guardian*, Alan Warner praises the emotional atmosphere of the novel, claiming that Smith's tale is "an example of how intense and deeply focused the novel can be when examining a closed universe" (n.p.). Likewise, in *The Irish Times*, Sarah Gilmartin describes *Doggerland* as a compelling novel, underlining an "enigmatic quality that can be frustrating" (n.p.). As these comments show, Smith's highly evocative language can be said to conjure up an eerie and claustrophobic environment with strong ethical implications. The ethical value of the novel emerges in its very title. "Doggerland" was once an endless stretch of marshes and valleys that connected the south-east coast of England to continental Europe, specifically to Germany, Jutland and the Netherlands. This area, where settlements, rivers, hills and woods once existed, was flooded with the rise of the North Sea around 8,200 BC owing to huge ice melting. As Nicholas Crane argues in *The Making of the British Landscape*, in the Mesolithic, Doggerland was a rich place "for foraging and hunting" (Crane 23),[1] but the rise of the sea level turned the area into a large watershed that was eventually submerged because of rapid climate change, as happens in J.G. Ballard's hyper-influential novel *The Drowned World* (1962). Thus, as the title suggests, Smith's tale unearths geological secrets, thereby transcending human finitude. Moreover, central to the novel is the discourse of grieving and survival. On the one hand, the humans that populate *Doggerland* seem to be the last survivors

DOI: 10.4324/9781003347811-8

of a post-apocalyptic world. On the other, the theme of environmental devastation is a looming presence. In so doing, *Doggerland* engages with ethical dilemmas between facts and fiction, expressing an environmentally based lament in which both humans and non-humans are vulnerable, thus juxtaposing ecological grief with human grievability.

In *Doggerland*, plastic and rubbish seem to be in rich health, while frailty and loneliness are the only distinctive features of the human condition. Set in a near future, the novel features two male protagonists, an old man and an orphan boy, who live in a wind farm in the North Sea, almost cut off from the rest of the world. The wind farm, with its 6,000 turbines, "stretched away in every direction, the towers spreading out in rows, like the spokes of a wheel" (Smith 2019, 29). The first characteristic that strikes the reader is the dark and forbidding landscape, "where the grey of the sea became the grey of the sky" (2). Thus, early in the novel, the reader is confronted with a harsh landscape dominated by the cold winds of the North, churning water, greasy metals and rusting turbines, while waste and cast-offs are pushed around by sea currents. Human beings, instead, are vaguely characterised. A relevant aspect of the enigmatic atmosphere that surrounds the two protagonists is their very mysterious identity. The extradiegetic heterodiegetic narrator uses their names only on a few occasions, claiming that names are "relative" (2) in this grey, impersonal landscape. Consequently, the reader discovers almost accidentally that the two men have personal names. The boy, Jem, who "was not really a boy" (2), as the narrator explains, is perhaps in his mid-twenties and has inherited his father's position in the offshore rig owing to a binding contract with a mysterious Company. Greil, the old man—though it seems impossible to know "how old the old man actually was" (7)—has been working for this Company for a long time. While Jem grieves his father's death and enquires into the causes of his mysterious disappearance from the farm, the old man collects artefacts from the seabed dating back to the Stone Age. Each day, the automated system tells them what job to do and which turbines to repair. As this description suggests, *Doggerland* revolves around sterility, isolation and mysteries.

In formal terms, the fluctuating nature of human life strikingly contrasts with the detailed portrayal of the environment. The account of the two characters' monotonous lives in the ruined wind farm is constantly interspersed with short chapters that delve into the deep geological timescale of the place, reconstructing in a non-linear way the natural changes of Doggerland, first as marshes converted into dry land and eventually back into sea. In the already mentioned review, Warner sees these two narrative strands as a major flaw, arguing that the short lyrical vignettes "add little to the narrative and clarify less" (n.p.). However, in my view, this dialogism between different narrative perspectives establishes significant connections between humans and non-humans

98   *Angelo Monaco*

by exhibiting a common condition of precariousness, thus intertwining the sterile and austere human atmosphere with the changing natural properties of the place. Therefore, I would contend that the chapters about the geological mutations of the landscape are of some relevance to Jem and Greil's story. Specifically, the dialogic interaction between these two focal perspectives promotes a sense of responsibility towards the other, here understood also as the non-human.[2] In other words, this alternation favours a certain ethical investment in the equal allocation of the conditions of precariousness and grievability to humans and non-humans in the age of the Anthropocene. In its exploration of various manifestations of vulnerability, Smith's novel addresses ideas of wreckage and fragmentation, sliding between the protagonists' forlorn existences and natural disruptions.

Doggerland hence exhibits a fascination for precariousness and grievability, key terms in Judith Butler's philosophy. While the boy still mourns for his father's death, other forms of vulnerability materialise in relation to the old man and the environment. Grief, as Butler argues, demonstrates that we are "in the thrall of our relations with others" (2004, 19), as it exposes our vulnerability to an external dependency for survival. In moments of loss, grief dissolves the border between self and other, human and non-human, reminding us, as Butler explains, that "we are, from the start and by virtue of being a bodily being, already given over, beyond ourselves, implicated in lives that are not our own" (28). In this respect, *Doggerland* privileges the typical tone of elegy by revealing an obsession with the past and thus plunging into loss and unresolved mourning. This addiction to the past is not only suggested by the geological transformations of the landscape, as it also emerges in the protagonists' exposure to grief—particularly Jem who is prey to frequent bouts of melancholia. As David Kennedy argues, grieving and the yearning for the past are "inextricable from our general experience," thus entailing "mood more than formal mode" (2). In a similar way to human fragility, the environmental degradation of Doggerland, which leads to the disappearance of the flora and the fauna of the place, adds a further layer to the representation of grievability and dispossession. In Pramod K. Nayar's words, it discloses an instance of "ecoprecarity," understood as the "intertwined set of discourses of fragility, vulnerability, power relations across species and imminent extinction" (Nayar 2019, 6). This evocation of ecological grief begs readers to envisage a world in decay that stretches "beyond solely human bodies into the sensuous experiences of the more-than-human world(s)" (Cunsolo and Landman 3). This projection into the future can be read, therefore, as the materialisation of an apocalyptic imagination that disorients normative concepts like time, human and non-human, while also allowing for the emergence of a form of relationality between different forms of life. Thus, what appears at first sight to be a melancholic lamentation soon

Ecological Grief and Human Grievability 99

veers towards the genre of eco-dystopia, which implies the "consciousness that we cannot exist outside or beyond the material world" (Hughes and Wheeler 4).

Significantly for my line of argument, the boy and the old man's ontological position points to a condition of exclusion from political and social life as they are exposed to surveillance and control. This dissolution between the ontological dimension and the socio-political order recalls Giorgio Agamben's conceptualisation of the "bare life" of contemporary *homo sacer*.[3] What is bare about the life of the *homo sacer* is that his/her life can be taken by anyone, thus displacing any legal order (Agamben 1998, 71). Bare life then is the consequence of an inclusive-exclusion resulting from a sovereign decision regarding what is distinctively human. In this respect, Smith develops a narrative articulation of human life as sensitive to the exposure to grievability and precariousness that resonates with Agamben's bare life as humans are caught in a space of abandonment, thus becoming the raw material of sovereign power. The same condition of bareness returns in the exploration of the environment, which seems to be sacrificed for human matters. Therefore, the landscape around the farm can be read as an instance of what Canadian sociologist Rob Shields calls "bare nature," a spectral presence that, though being deprived of its semantic form, entails "a form of absence that is nonetheless paradoxically present" (Shields 7).

In this essay, I take the formal dialogue between elegy and dystopia, past and future, human and non-human as the starting point for my analysis of *Doggerland*. I will specifically show how Smith's novel ties in with Butler's categories of "grievability" and "vulnerability," and the related notions of "precariousness" and "dispossession," not only for the exposure of human life to the feeling of anxiety that pervades our post-trauma age but also because it favours an ethical encounter with non-human forms of fragility. In its combination of minimalism and lyrical prose, *Doggerland* can be said to rely on narrative mechanisms that frame the representation of precariousness and grievability beyond human matters. The multi-layered narrative architecture of the story, with its temporal disorientation, provides the reader with various fragments of vulnerability that once patched together can elicit some sort of connectivity. In the following pages, I will first address the materialisations of precariousness and grievability from the perspective of the natural environment, with a specific focus on the elegiac mode and on the intricate temporal structure of the novel. Through the use of a fragmented, non-linear narrative frame, a form of dispossession emerges, generating a paradoxical "present absence" (Shields 13) that favours an ethical encounter with the other and, to a certain extent, also mitigates the negative side of bare life and bare nature. I will then shift the focus from the elegiac tones of the novel to the post-apocalyptic and dystopian imagination it hinges around, in order to demonstrate that *Doggerland*

100 *Angelo Monaco*

engages with relationality as a potential to move away from the obsession with frailty and grief, thereby expanding on Butler's conceptualisation of grievability.

Elegiac Form, Temporality and the Ecological Uncanny

In their original acceptations, "grievability" and "precariousness" were employed by Butler to designate the human condition of loss and fragility. As Drew Walker points out, these concepts entail an ethical grounding in that they "illuminate and contest both these unjust conditions and the persistence of people in spite of these injustices" (162). The term "precariousness," for instance, derives from "precarity," which describes the progressively lower socio-economic levels of security in the field of employment. From Butler's perspective, Walker adds, its meaning extends to cover "oppression or the denial of human rights as inhabiting a space in which they [marginalised humans] are rendered inhuman, invisible, spectral or derealised" (141–42). In *Precarious Life*, Butler discusses precariousness as an existential condition: drawing on Emmanuel Levinas's ethics of alterity, she sees precariousness as related to vulnerability and, therefore, as a means for understanding the other. Precariousness, she writes, means "to be awake to what is precarious in another life or, rather, the precariousness of life itself" (2004, 134). In *Frames of War*, however, Butler moves away from the singularity of individuals, claiming that precariousness "has to be grasped not simply as a feature of *this* or *that* life, but as a generalized condition" (2009, 22; original emphasis), thereby understanding precariousness as a shared, collective condition. Likewise, grievability is concerned with the question of publicly mourning the death of victims of violence and oppression. As the American philosopher herself puts it, grievability "precedes and makes possible the apprehension of the living being as living" (2009, 15). In the wake of 9/11, Butler considers the different ways in which lives are mourned, highlighting how certain cultural frames, like news or photographs, govern the public distribution of grievability and empathy, determining which lives are grievable and which are ungrievable.

Bearing these ideas in mind, I will consider in this section the way in which *Doggerland* addresses some forms of vulnerable manifestations such as precariousness, grievability and dispossession, specifically through the analysis of the elegiac framework of the novel and its temporal disorientation. Formally, *Doggerland* is modelled on a mode that echoes the conventions of the elegy: Jem's melancholic lamentation and interior dialogue with his departed father; Greil's ailing health; the marine environment, whose depth epitomises an "uncanny zone between life and death" (Mills 494) evoking emptiness, death and loss; and Smith's tendency to switch from past to present tenses as a means to convey a sense of eternal vigil, are all main motifs of an elegiac

Ecological Grief and Human Grievability 101

mode that recalls Jean-Michel Ganteau's category of "vulnerable form" because of its openness to "the risk of failure" (1). As he explains, vulnerable forms textually perform and thematise an exposure to loss and frailty, taking "human fragility as their main theme and build[ing] up an urn of language" (95). In Smith's novel, frailties have an impact not only on the human and the non-human but also on the very format of the narrative. This is achieved thanks to some frames through which vulnerability comes to be thematised, namely the dialogic framing structure that incorporates human voices and the sounds of the environment.[4]

The palpable fragility of life is reflected, for instance, in the titles of the chapters. The seven chapters on the geological transformations of Doggerland are entitled after the years when these crucial climatic changes occur, covering a temporal arc that goes from 20,000 BCE to the year 1 CE. By contrast, the remaining twenty chapters have single keywords as titles, such as "Nothing" (Smith 2019, 18, 216), "Cracks" (36, 204), "Junk" (43), "Something" (72), "Bottles" (92) and so on. These single words metaphorically condense the desolate atmosphere in the wind farm where human life has almost evaporated and seems to be dwarfed by objects. Two words, "Nothing" and "Cracks," are used twice as titles. In the chapters entitled "Nothing," the feeling of void is conveyed by the missing components of the turbines that Jem and Greil have to repair (20); by the food shortage (21); by the lack of communication between the two protagonists; and by the fact that "nothing stayed new or resilient for long" (23) in this unwelcoming landscape. Such an association with feelings of disintegration invites the reader to reconstruct the struggles endured by the protagonists and by the environment, conveying a poetics of fragility and fallibility where a sense of ontological breakdown looms large. *Doggerland* thus addresses an ethics of attention to grievability, engaging readers emotionally by making them perceive the elegiac and mournful mood of the narrative punctuated with a huge sense of void affecting both human and non-human as the holes in the heart of the broken towers of the turbines demonstrate (230).

In such a post-apocalyptic scenario, objects are so agentive that they seem to acquire an anthropomorphic nature. This is suggested, for instance, in the first chapter entitled "Cracks," where the wind puffs of the North Sea break the silence of the farm, rasping and stuttering (40) like an old man or an infant. Further instances of grievability are evoked in the vibrant materiality of the place. For instance, in the lamenting sound of the turbines, which "seemed to groan" (26) or, again, in the keening sounds around the farm, where "the wind would suddenly bawl, the air con would creak and whirr, the transformer would thrum from the floor below, and, deeper still, the waves would thud against the walls of the dock" (40). In a similar way, plastic bags and other types of junk are endowed with human qualities, rising from the depths of the North

102 *Angelo Monaco*

Sea "like bulbous light-seeking creatures" (5). While sailing across the turbines, Jem's attention is caught by their foundation jackets that congregate densely underwater, resembling a plethora of coloured plastic bags, "huge, silent creatures" that "swelled and pulsed like heart-beats" (178). The elegiac quality of these objects that resemble sentient beings resonates with Nayar's formulation of the "sublimity of waste" (73). As he observes, debris and objects have no boundaries "of either space or time" (73). Therefore, they can imbue the present with their own form of life. In this sense, waste can be read as "the uncanny replication of nature's elaborate and sublime landscapes" (67). Bearing in mind Jean-François Lyotard's understanding of the sublime as a failure of the imagination to provide an appropriate representation of the "incommensurability" (Lyotard 79) of nature,[5] the sublimity of waste can be read as a signifier of human uncertainty in "a landscape inhabited by broken or strange bodies" (Nayar 70). The narrative thus produces an enmeshment between the human and non-human that attests to the necessity of an equal distribution of grievability (Butler 2009, 22).

In *Doggerland*, both the boy and the old man seem to be aware of the uncanny sublimity of the landscape: the waste heap symbolically replicates the stratified sediments of Doggerland. Owing to its ubiquitous presence, waste outstands humankind, being implicitly a sign of the precarious nature of humanity itself. By rendering waste into something resembling a life form, *Doggerland* relocates the human in a wider web of connections and interactions. What is more, by attributing human qualities to inanimate objects, Smith gives voice to the non-human without enframing it as a thing. Smith's poetical strategy echoes Kate Rigby's words on the self-reflexive nature of ecopoiesis, understood as "a discourse on that which lies outside all enframings, all social systems, including that of language" (Rigby 437). By recognising the limits of all sorts of enframing, we are invited to participate in a polyphony that "contains more than human voices, for which we ourselves cannot stand in" (439). This emphasis on the common fragility of the human and non-human brings to mind Butler's contention that grief can "challenge the very notion of ourselves as autonomous and in control" (2004, 19).

Understood as an expression of grief, this form of polyphony can be observed in the similarly precarious configuration of the landscape as it is constantly shaped and reshaped by sweeping sea currents. This instability and fragility of Doggerland, that can be seen to invert the linear chronology of geological evolution, underscores the qualities of an "ecological uncanny" (Nayar). Drawing on Sigmund Freud's concept of the *Unheimlich* (1919), which captures the fear of the "primitive," Nayar defines the "ecological uncanny" as the lack of frames of knowledge and understanding of environmental changes, where familiar landscapes "are rendered unfamiliar because they *become* unhomely, inhospitable" (Nayar 49; original emphasis). In *Doggerland*, this sense of unfamiliarity

Ecological Grief and Human Grievability   103

is conveyed through the disruption of temporal linearity as Smith manipulates the alternation of various geological phases at discourse level, thus disregarding the chronological timeline of geological history. The fact that the seven chapters on the geological transformations of Doggerland follow a circular structure, rather than a chronological one, performs the overriding condition of environmental precariousness through the chaotic alternation of ice melt, coastline emersion and huge flooding. Moreover, the fragility of the place is built on an elegiac language that seems to ventriloquise human precariousness, thus making grievability audible. In the chapter entitled "c. 14,000 Before Present," for instance, the narrator indulges in the description of trees striking their roots in the woodlands, with "water turning to solid mass, taking its liquid forms [...] and translating them to tendril, flower, leaf" (Smith 2019, 134). Water repeats itself, "creasing into peaks and troughs [...] striving for circularity" (135). Smith's alternation of the past and present tense in the chapters devoted to the transformation of the landscape is indicative of a suspended temporality like that of limbo. These poetic vignettes abound in *Doggerland*, shedding light on the slow, transformative power of time and suggesting the idea of nature as being continuously disturbed, while residual forms of the past survive into the present.

Temporality, a salient feature of the vulnerable form of *Doggerland*, is hence handled with a troubled organisation that refracts the emotional wounds of the protagonists, linking the historical mutations of the landscape to the sense of temporal disorientation experienced by the boy and the old man. Significantly, the narrator evokes the protagonists' past by providing glimpses of their earlier life before moving to the wind farm. Also, the narration, particularly from Jem's perspective, is devoted to the recollection of his father's death, thus adding a further layer of temporal turbulence to the narrative. From the very first pages, the reader is introduced to a disturbing situation where human memories are as "hazy and indistinct" as "the turbines, in squally weather, [when they] would churn up so much spray that all edges and outlines disappeared" (16). Furthermore, repetitions and amnesia tend to affect people and landscape alike, disclosing a certain saturation with the past that is capable of dissipating clear-cut recollections. Ice caps break during the Würm glaciation (20,000 BCE), turning water into a frozen ground where lichens gradually grow (102), thus leading to the emergence of woods and, then, to the appearance of mammals. And yet, water eventually returns, flooding the area again around 8,000 BCE and thus completing its work (53).

Through the image of the alternation between water and earth, wetland and woods, the novel conjures up a temporal situation connoted by a cyclic flow, where the possibility of remembering and fixing things in mind is almost impossible. In many lyrical descriptions, *Doggerland* unveils this dialogic interplay between opposites that recalls the

104   *Angelo Monaco*

structure of the palimpsest in that it brings together different spaces and times into a composite communicative memory "so that one layer of traces can be seen through, and is transformed, by another" (Silverman 3). This figurative assemblage of different layers is conveyed, for instance, in the maps that the boy finds in the wind farm. The maps, where the oscillating configuration of the place is registered through notes and annotations, show the seabed as if it were land, and the lines describing valley and hills, with tracks of different rocks and minerals (Smith 2019, 49). Maps, as Rebecca Mills observes, are an instance of elegiac writing in that they act as "both a navigating device to orient themselves within the world of grief, and as an artifact to trigger memories associated with a certain place linked to the dead person" (497–98). This practice of interfacing with ancient times signals the persistence of not only the past but also its oblivion, because the landscape has eventually changed, while the map, in its cartographic attempt at archiving a specific moment, works as a palimpsestic assemblage of traces dating back to distant temporal layers, thereby recalling Max Silverman's model of palimpsestic memory.

This palimpsestic organisation is made clear in the various descriptive passages that enhance the relevance of the maritime trope as a symbol of an irruptive, ungovernable force. This is how the narrator invokes the mutability of water that challenges the linear flow of time:

> For a hundred thousand years the water waited, locked up as crystal, sheet and shelf. All was immobile, but for the slow formation of arc and icicle, which was water remembering the way it used to be and the waves it would become again. [...] solidity is nothing but an interruption to a continuous flow, an obstacle to be overcome, an imbalance to be rectified.
>
> (Smith 2019, 54)

Arguably, this vignette leaves no doubt that water can control time, anticipating its ability to change the place, turning the landscape into a vulnerable entity. Whereas ice pulls back, making space for rocks, lichens and the first reindeers (102–103), the sea levels continue to rise turning the earth into unstable ground (155).

Crucially, this more-than-human "polyphonic song" (Rigby 434) of Doggerland amplifies the condition of grievability epitomised by the protagonists' shattered and dislocated existences, thus making an ethical opening to a more-than-human confrontation with the fragility of life. Environmental precarity can be said to materialise a non-human form of bare life or, borrowing Rob Shields's words, to represent an instance of a "bare nature" that takes the form of "absence, gap, or ellipsis in discourse" (Shields 8). As Shields argues, when nature is seen as a "form without implication" (13), it can be sacrificed to be exploited and it is "reduced to its energy capacity" (8). Such a reduction similarly informs the depiction of Doggerland, where nature is viewed as a resource deprived of recognition and exploited for the production of hydroelectricity. Shields claims that bare nature is at the service of global capitalism and that it frames social relations as it "reifies the relationship between humans and their world by freezing it" (12). The elliptical conformation of Doggerland is distinctively perceivable in the spectral atmosphere of the environment, where drifting sand "reveals a trace of something" (Smith 2019, 214). The traces buried underwater constantly resurface, turning the present-day marine area into a ghost-like landscape with signs dating back to a deep geological past. As in the palimpsestic model, characterised by "different voices, sites and times" (Silverman 8), the scenery of Doggerland, with its changeable features, is like a "remnant" (Shields 13) of the natural world. Along a coastline that used to be a forest, ghosts appear, telling stories of a place that was once covered over with ice (Smith 2019, 215). Bare nature is hence a haunting manifestation, the paradoxical "presence of an absence" (Shields 14), unveiling, through fragmented, palimpsestic traces, residual features like blackened roots, clods of peat and petrified stumps (Smith 2019, 215). The ghost, a central trope of the elegy, is not only a symbol of dispossession and bare life; rather, it entails, as Judith Butler and Athena Athanasiou contend, an "unarchivable spectrality" (19) that, while turning nature into absence, transforms humans into forlorn figures. In many ways, the repeated exposure to vulnerability dramatises a permanent state of precariousness that, quoting Nayar, juxtaposes ecological fragility to human grievability by disclosing "the dependence of our lives upon precarious environments, people and processes" (Nayar 7).

The desolate landscape of Doggerland, with its vast emptiness, involves a sense of the uncanny with its weird sounds and spectral apparitions. Smith employs the stratification of Doggerland as an archiving palimpsestic structure where ancient settlements are buried and memories can change, transform and illuminate the past. Repetitions evoke a strangeness that also affects Jem and Greil as they follow strict routines and live in utter isolation. The prevalence of the modal "would" to describe regular habits, in an automatic and mechanical manner, is illustrative of this uncanny effect as the following quote demonstrates: "He *would* take his watch out of his pocket and count the numbers. [...] He *would* wait a minute. Then two" (Smith 2019, 41; emphasis added). This gesture, that entails an experience of alienation and dispossession, is how Smith depicts Jem's daily life in the wind farm. Incensed by loss and melancholia, the boy and the old man emerge as vulnerable and precarious subjects, totally immersed in an environment deprived of any form of comfort. This condition of ungrievability implies the central question of how we define what is grievable and what is not, alerting the reader to the risks of an unequal distribution of grievability. Grievability,

106   *Angelo Monaco*

Butler claims, is "a presupposition for the life that matters" (2009, 14), thus representing a necessary condition through which we can illustrate the relevance of human and non-human forms of life.

The Paradoxical Ethics of Bare Life and Dispossession

So far, I have highlighted the environmental over the human dimension and have discussed the disjointed temporal structure of the novel. Nevertheless, *Doggerland* is also a story about the bare existence of humanity under conditions of loss and alienation. The projection into the future and the allusions to a situation of totalitarian surveillance make the narrative edge towards the genre of dystopia. As already mentioned, the human condition that emerges in Smith's novel connotes wounds and grief, thus recalling the condition of *homo sacer* in Agamben's acceptation of the term. *Homo sacer* is a victim of the violence of law and, as Walter Benjamin famously remarked in his "Critique of Violence" (1921), this condition is "not the exception but the rule" (248).

What Agamben calls "bare life" converges with the precariousness and marginalisation of the human beings that populate *Doggerland*. In the initial pages, the reader realises that a sense of monotonous existence marks human life in the wind farm, where days, months and seasons "passed through untethered and indistinct among the flotsam" (Smith 2019, 5). The wind farm can be seen as a space of biopolitical control where Jem and Greil are placed under surveillance, isolated from the rest of society with a limited freedom of movement. This condition recalls Agamben's "zone of indifference, where inside and outside do not exclude each other but rather blur with each other" (Agamben 2005, 23). Linguistic evidence about this enigmatic corporation is so scanty that what the reader learns solely derives from the short conversations between Jem and Greil. Both men wear clothes and accessories displaying the logo of the Company. In such an anonymous setting, where one cannot understand what has happened to Britain and to the world, humans resemble passive spirits with "no way out" (34). Moreover, harsh weather conditions regulate the movements of the boy and the old man: immense waves breaking against the turbines and spraying water mixed with rain allow neither Jem nor Greil to go anywhere (119). As the narrator notes, this passive acceptance robs the subjects of agency, "as if they were being acted upon some enormous, sweeping magnet" (118). This suspension of life recalls Butler's contention that dispossession reduces humanity to bare life, a form of imposition that rules "the maintenance and control of bodies and persons" (2004, 56) insofar as they live in a state of total passivity and abjection. Agamben's *homo sacer* inhabits a legal state of exclusion "by virtue of *having entered* into an intimate symbiosis with death without, nevertheless, belonging to the world of the deceased" (1998, 99–100; original emphasis). Similarly, Butler and Athanasiou's

Ecological Grief and Human Grievability 107

dispossessed subject is bereft of the ability to act, living in a "condition painfully imposed by the normative and normalizing violence that determines the terms of subjectivity, survival, and livability" (2).

Instances of dispossession haunt *Doggerland*, giving prominence to the elegiac quality of the story. The old man, for instance, is featured as silent and suffering, unable to oppose the strict rules of the Company. His health is precarious and unstable and his stature so small that his physical aspect almost looked frail (Smith 2019, 8), like the geological conformation of the place. As the narrative progresses, Greil can be seen to suffer from chronic ailments such as coughing and spasming, manifestations of vulnerability that onomatopoeically find an echo in the deafening noise of the turbines. Thus, *Doggerland* makes the main tenets of grievability visible and even audible, particularly in the form of what Butler and Athanasiou define as "new idioms of 'saying,' 'hearing'" (132) that emerge when language fails to express oppressions and atrocities. Despite the fragmented and brief conversations, made of muttered, half sentences, a distinctive auditive feature that the novel materialises, beyond the hissing sound of the wind, is the old man's "rattling breath" (Smith 2019, 203) that metonymically reproduces the metallic noise of the turbines shaken by cold currents. This eerie sound blends human and non-human forms of grievability, eroding not only the metallic surface of the turbines but also human psychology. Greil is almost dispossessed of his voice: owing to his precarious health, the old man embodies a linguistic form of dispossession that enhances the precarity of his isolated life, without any affective ties in the external world. In the second chapter, entitled "Cracks," the narrative zooms in on the old man's state of bare life, establishing onomatopoeic connections between the cracks of the turbines and the physical and emotional wounds of the man, whose skin is as cold as the metal doorways (209). Among the various wounds that deprive him of voice and agency, Greil has a burn on his forearm, a non-healing bruise on the neck and a split thumbnail (209). These scars are all signs of his exhausting activity in the farm, displaying, like the maps of the coastline, the erosional changes of Greil's body.

Likewise, mechanisms of dispossession govern the life of Jem, who lost his father in the aftermath of a mysterious accident. The boy's existence seems suspended: he is forced to replace his father in the farm since the "terms of service had to be fulfilled" (34). There are only a few hints regarding his disappearance. What Jem and the reader can gather derives from the words of the quarterly supply boat pilot who brings the tinned food Jem and Greil live on. When Jem learns that a second maintenance boat exists and that his father had drowned after using it, he assumes that his father was trying to escape and return to the mainland to join him, thus feeling responsible for his death. A sense of grief also percolates through the boy's storyline, which is made visible and audible through the image of his aching stomach and ringing ears (71).

108 *Angelo Monaco*

Though displaced and deprived of their freedom, Jem and Greil become gradually sensitive to the vulnerability of the other. In its negative force, the subject, Butler and Athanasiou claim, "is moved to the other and by the other—exposed to and affected by the other's vulnerability" (1). Strikingly, then, dispossession is not only understood as a negative and disabling concept by Butler and Athanasiou. On the contrary, it can have positive and enabling effects in that it reminds the subject of its dependency on the other, thus opening up the possibility of relationality as "a necessary condition of the subject's survival" (2). *Homo sacer*, whose life seems ungrievable for the socio-political order, can therefore elicit some form of relationality, a concern that Smith's novel ultimately enhances. Despite their short and fragmented conversations, made of sighs and intermittent stutters, and notwithstanding the silence about Jem's father's death, a form of frail solidarity eventually emerges between the boy and the old man. The cracks in Greil's body tie in with "the fissuring of the subject" (Butler and Athanasiou ix), a space of psychic and ethical aperture that can enable relationality. This reminds us that livability depends on the care we receive from other people, a reliance that promotes "the formation of primary passion in dependency" (Butler 1997, 9). In this light, *Doggerland*, one could argue, unveils its powerful message of solidarity. In other words, Smith's novel can be read as a narrative that favours connectivity against a background of bare life and dispossession. The attachment between dispossessed subjects, hence, produces a paradoxical point of connection despite the portrayal of a persisting sense of human isolation and the impossibility to connect.

Apocalypse and/or Dystopia

In the afore-mentioned review, Warner argues that *Doggerland* can be defined as a dystopian fiction. However, the novel evinces a clear generic instability as the dual perspective on the grievability of both the human and the non-human reverberates with the conventions of apocalyptic fiction. Although absent at the level of discourse, the apocalypse is indirectly evoked through fragmented sounds and memories, its elliptical form recalling the absence/presence of bare nature. As Andrew Tate explains, if in dystopian worlds we find tension and friction between "a decadent ruling elite and [...] a vast, starving underclass," in apocalyptic tales there is "a brutal struggle eked out by the survivors" (3). Following Tate's argumentation, I would argue that *Doggerland* is a post-apocalyptic narrative with some dystopian elements, much like Margaret Atwood's *The Year of the Flood* (2009), Cormac McCarthy's *The Road* (2006) and Emily St. John Mandel's *Station Eleven* (2014), among others. In the aftermath of a catastrophe, humans are confronted with the remnants of a world where environmental devastation and a certain degree of hope are combined to reveal—in line with the etymological meaning of the

Ecological Grief and Human Grievability   109

term "apocalypse" from the Greek Ἀποκάλυψη—a "frequently foretold 'ruined future,' a future that counterintuitively often resembles our deep past" (Tate 13).

In the attempt to capture "the elements of loss and transformation" (Hicks 8) that inform contemporary post-apocalyptic novels, *Doggerland* shares, for instance, the same interest in exploring human survival in a post-apocalyptic world as in McCarthy's novel. Strikingly, the reader may note a certain parallelism between Smith's novel and *The Road* since both works are mainly centred on the feelings of grievability of two people living in a decayed world on the brink of destruction. McCarthy's influence on Smith's novel is evident at a number of levels. *Doggerland* presents a boy and an old man, while in *The Road* we find a father and his son struggling to survive against a backdrop of violence and destruction. In ways that echo McCarthy's characters, Jem and Greil repair equipment and scavenge to survive. This emphasis on the theme of salvage is, as Heather J. Hicks argues, a distinctive feature of contemporary post-apocalyptic novels in that "the characters are confronted with the remnants of the modern world—from the immaterial domain of words and ideas to the physical detritus of objects and machines" (3). This central preoccupation with survival is reflected in the collapse of global modernity, thus producing a condition of wreckage that leads characters to rely on their own resources and preserve the remnants of civilisation. As in McCarthy's novel, the protagonists of *Doggerland* endure hunger, ailments, isolation, storms and bad dreams. In addition, as in *The Road*, in Smith's narrative readers are not aware of why and how this post-apocalyptic world came to be, a point that intensifies the sense of disorientation. Unlike classical dystopias that are "historically aware" (Stock 2),[6] Smith's narrative lacks an in-depth knowledge of the historical events that inform the dystopian imaginary: many questions are left unanswered, while the reader does not know who is in control of the situation or what the turbines are powering.

What the reader clearly knows, however, is that the Company controls Jem and Greil's lives. Not only do they have to spend their days in the isolated farm in the North Sea, wearing clothes with the logo of the Company, their daily routine is ruled by the Company's norms as well. Eating habits, for instance, are rationed, and food is bland and unappetising: proteins and reconstituted vegetables are only available in tins delivered by the pilot. As the narrator observes, the boy seems to be accustomed to cooking food with a patina of congealed fat on vegetables— orange discs, bulbous white and green florets (Smith 2019, 31)—or to eating what tastes like fruit with "the bitter tang of melted plastic" (159). However, the old man reminisces about the food once farmed and grown in the soil. As these examples show, the dystopian imagination that permeates Smith's novel is infused with a sense of duality, where past and future are juxtaposed. If amnesia contaminates the future, with

110   *Angelo Monaco*

the boy and the man losing memories about how life used to be before the Company, the past returns through hazy recollections. Like trauma narratives, apocalyptic stories, John Berger argues, "must be reconstructed by means of their traces" (19), helping readers remember that "[t]here is always some remainder, some post-apocalyptic debris" (34) that can redirect the destructive force of the story.

Doggerland presents only a few allusions to the past of the country before the Company came into existence. These scattered images of the past occasionally resurface, just as the strong tidal currents carry rubbish and plastic bags to the surface of the North Sea. As Jem observes, while picking up plastic bags with the Company's logo, it "was easy to forget things that existed before the Company took over" (Smith 2019, 47). This comment reasserts the irregular temporal frame that governs Smith's novel, moving between the pre- and the post-apocalyptic moment, regardless of time linearity and proceeding by means of fragmentary and disconnected memories. The lack of historical depth reveals an apocalyptic mode that disrupts the traditional unitary conception of the apocalypse, thus calling into question what Frank Kermode terms the "sense of an ending" that allows readers "to see the structure whole" (8). Drawing a parallel between life and fiction, Kermode sees the apocalypse as a way to make sense of our lives as we live in the midst of time (3). By means of such formal solutions that give order and shape, Kermode adds, narratives attempt to create "an organization that humanizes time" (45) providing readers with the sense of an ending. The apocalyptic temporality of *Doggerland*, instead, seems more concerned with creating a temporal turbulence "to make space for unwritten futures which are key to agency" (De Cristofaro 2018, n.p.). As Diletta De Cristofaro argues, post-apocalyptic novels, like *Station Eleven*, do not rely on a "sense of an ending" in that they question "the passivity fostered by apocalyptic determinism" (119). Similarly, *Doggerland* articulates a critical temporality that complicates the sense of an ending. This is suggested firstly by the fragmentation of the chronological order; secondly, by the vignettes on the transformation of the place; and, finally, by the narrative sequences that disrupt the tedious routines in the wind farm that form the bulk of the plot. The search for the second boat (77–79), drinking homebrew and cooking tinned food (21–31), fishing for artefacts of a lost civilisation, and finding plastic and other objects from the seabed (1, 14) create gaps in the plot that undermine "the sense-making function of the apocalyptic paradigm" (De Cristofaro 2020, 75). In this respect, Smith's novel does not leave readers without possible hints of alternative options to the monotonous existence that the narrative charts from the initial pages, providing spaces for agency and scenarios for an unwritten future.

Notably, the maps that Jem finds in the farm keep spaces of possibility open, thus resisting closure and a deterministic ending. Though the

Ecological Grief and Human Grievability 111

maps are signifiers of a disconnected past, they also illuminate possible forms of survival. In the effort to unveil the truth about his father's death, the boy discovers a map showing a second maintenance boat. He finds out where this second boat is located and tries to reach it and leave the farm. While the insistence on past memories, emerging confusedly and without chronological linearity, recalls the elegiac form, Jem's investigation, instead, moves the temporal orientation of the novel towards the present and the future, thus veering towards the format of "critical" dystopias. By blurring genres, critical dystopias "allow both readers and protagonists to hope by resisting closure: the ambiguous, open endings of these novels maintain the utopian impulse within the work" (Baccolini and Moylan 7). These alternative possibilities emphasise the importance of shelter and salvage in conditions of precariousness, complicating the deterministic logic of dystopian fiction. Moreover, the maps portray a submerged world, making Jem aware of its precariousness, of "the feeling of crumbling earth" (Smith 2019, 68). The mapping process reconnects various temporal layers, contributing to thematise the various manifestations of grievability and making the feeling of the apocalypse uncannily present as an "absent referent" (Berger 108). In other words, Smith's novel engages with (un)grievability as a general condition that affects both the human and non-human in the age of the Anthropocene. This inter-human symmetry reconfigures Butler's concern with ethical relations, also from the perspective of the environment. This symbiotic relation finds a common ground in those practices that favour what Vikki Bell, in "From Performativity to Ecology" (2008), calls "cultural survival." In an interview with Bell, Butler claims that surviving depends on the boundary with the other, thus representing "a function of interdependency" (Bell 2010, 148). Survival implies contact, and this contact can be extended to the natural world. Survivability, therefore, arouses from a feeling of solidarity that unites various manifestations of vulnerability. As Bell observes, taking a cue from Isabelle Stengers's idea of an "ecology of practices" (2005),[7] survivability arises in everyday practices of caring for others beyond the human scale. In my view, the search for survival in *Doggerland* can be read in accordance with this theoretical combination as an ethical act of relationality with a world in its turn exposed to wounds, as the catastrophes that have changed Doggerland demonstrate. While readers can neither understand the nature of the environmental catastrophe that has altered the place, nor measure the human impact on such climatic changes, they can clearly perceive the sense of solidarity the novel hints at by its very conclusion.

Conclusion

There is in *Doggerland* a double valence in its representation of precariousness, due to the fact that forms of relationality can emerge from the

112 *Angelo Monaco*

exposure to grievability. This affective attachment, which interweaves human grievability with ecological grief, occurs in a moment of interdependence, not only between individuals but also in relation to the place. The final pages of *Doggerland* depict a landscape that has been turned red because of a dust storm from distant deserts. Symbolically, this new configuration seems to solidify the liquid landscape, bringing it back to its original continental nature. Through the image of the storm—which stands for a random pattern of chaos and complexity, made of the same molecules of water and air but always different in its proportions (132)—*Doggerland* reveals the circularity of time, thus representing both routine and change. Such an orientation breaks up the elegiac tone of the narrative, multiplying its contradictions and opening up the possibility of hope. The novel ends with Jem's meditating on what he still might find out, feeling that "he could see some way" (Smith 2019, 243) and that they still have a lot of time in their hands. This conclusion foreshadows possible unwritten scenarios, providing the sense that livability and survival prevail over the ungrievability of Jem and Greil's bare lives by means of affective ties of mutual care.

In summary, *Doggerland* emphasises in various ways the vision of human life and of the environment as sites of precariousness and critical survival. As my reading of Smith's novel has tried to demonstrate, the narrative revolves around some issues that find significant echoes in Butler's philosophy by enhancing the sense of grievability, precariousness and dispossession that affect humans and non-humans alike. As the analysis has shown, the novel thematises Smith's preoccupation with these issues both at the level of form and content. The disarrayed temporality of the novel and its generic hybridity, oscillating between elegy and apocalypse, constitute central elements of a fragmented form that highlights an overriding sense of grievability. Moreover, *Doggerland* enhances the concern with precariousness by addressing it with a sense of totalitarian control. For all this, however, what the reader is reminded of by the end of the novel is that, even in extremely aching conditions of grievability, precariousness and dispossession, it is still possible to find potential ways of arousing interconnections and strive for survival. When wounded humans are confronted with other forms of grievability, boundaries become the lines along which a new configuration of self and world can be constructed. In a place where everything shows a tendency to mutability and erosion, this ethical embrace provides the basis for livability and survival.

Notes

1 In the "Acknowledgments" (248), Smith makes a list of the bibliographical references employed to reconstruct the history of Doggerland, among them Crane's *The Making of the British Landscape.* The first archaeological

Ecological Grief and Human Grievability   113

traces of Doggerland were discovered in the early twentieth century when animal remains, dating back to the Neolithic period, were found. The toponym Doggerland, instead, refers to "doggers," Dutch fishing boats that used to traffic along the south-east coast of England for fishing cods during the Middle Ages.

2 According to Karen Barad (2003), Jane Bennett (2010) and Rosi Braidotti (2013), among others, humans are entangled with non-human actors and these tentacular associations can provide new insights into the ways in which we see human agency, its implications, limitations and boundaries.

3 According to the Italian philosopher, the formula *homo sacer* was employed in Roman law to describe "an obscure figure" (Agamben 1998, 8) dwelling in a marginal position between culture and nature that represents a form of exclusion from the law "stripped of every right by virtue of the fact that anyone can kill him without committing homicide" (183).

4 I am using here Kate Rigby's idea of "framing" through which she highlights the formal tension between human and non-human, "which lets things be in their obscure otherness in the very process of revealing them within the work of art" (Rigby 430).

5 As is well known, Lyotard revisits the Kantian aesthetics of the sublime, reading it as a concept "outside the horizons of presentation" (Lyotard 79).

6 In his *Modern Dystopian Fiction and Political Thought* (2018), Adam Stock investigates how modern dystopian fiction interacts with a wide range of political aspects, from environmental disasters to security. In his view, modern dystopias are not simply embedded into a specific historical background; rather, they tend to blend past, present and future.

7 Using the concept of the rhizome as theorised by Gilles Deleuze and Félix Guattari, Stengers advocates an "ecology of practices," understood as a complex interaction of knowledges and practices to better shape the future. Such an ecology of practices represent a "tool for thinking" (Stengers 185), concerned with both the human and the non-human.

Works Cited

Agamben, Giorgio. *Homo Sacer: Sovereign Power and Bare Life.* 1995. Trans. Daniel Heller-Roazen. Stanford, CA: Stanford UP, 1998.

———. *State of Exception.* 2003. Trans. Kevin Attell. Chicago, IL: The U of Chicago P, 2005.

Atwood, Margaret. *The Year of the Flood.* London: Bloomsbury, 2009.

Baccolini, Raffaella, and Tom Moylan. "Introduction. Dystopia and History." *Dark Horizons: Science Fiction and the Dystopian Imagination.* Eds Raffaella Baccolini and Tom Moylan. London and New York: Routledge, 2003. 1–12.

Ballard, James Graham. *The Drowned World.* 1962. London: Harper Perennial, 2010.

Barad, Karen. "Posthumanist Performativity: How Matter Comes to Matter." *Signs: Journal of Women in Culture and Society* 28.3 (2003): 801–31.

Bell, Vikki. "From Performativity to Ecology: On Judith Butler and Matters of Survival." *Subjectivity* 25 (2008): 395–412.

———. "New Scenes of Vulnerability, Agency and Plurality: An Interview with Judith Butler." *Theory, Culture & Society* 27.1 (2010): 130–52.

Benjamin, Walter. "Critique of Violence." 1921. *Selected Writings.* Vol. 1. Eds Marcus Bullock and Michael W. Jennings. Cambridge, MA: Harvard UP, 1996. 236–52.

114   *Angelo Monaco*

Bennett, Jane. *Vibrant Matter: A Political Ecology of Things*. Durham and London: Duke UP, 2010.

Berger, James. *After the End: Representations of Post-Apocalypse*. London and Minneapolis: The U of Minnesota P, 1999.

Braidotti, Rosi. *The Posthuman*. Hoboken, NJ: Wiley and Sons, 2013.

Butler, Judith. *The Psychic Life of Power: Theories in Subjection*. Stanford, CA: Stanford UP, 1997.

———. *Precarious Life: The Powers of Mourning and Violence*. London and New York: Verso, 2004.

———. *Frames of War*. London and New York: Verso, 2009.

Butler, Judith, and Athena Athanasiou. *Dispossession: The Performative in the Political*. Cambridge, MA: Polity, 2013.

Crane, Nicholas. *The Making of the British Landscape: From the Ice Age to the Present*. London: Weidenfeld & Nicolson, 2016.

Cunsolo, Ashlee, and Karen Landman. "Introduction: To Mourn beyond the Human." *Mourning Nature: Hope at the Heart of Ecological Loss and Grief*. Eds Ashlee Cunsolo and Karen Landman. Montreal: McGill-Queen's UP, 2017. 3–26.

De Cristofaro, Diletta. "Critical Temporalities: *Station Eleven* and the Contemporary Post-Apocalyptic Novel." *Open Library of Humanities* 4.2 (2018): 37, 1–26. DOI: 10.16995/olh.206. Accessed on 03/01/2020 at: olh.openlibhums. org/articles/10.16995/olh.206/.

———. *The Contemporary Post-Apocalyptic Novel: Critical Temporalities and the End Times*. London: Bloomsbury, 2020.

Freud, Sigmund. *The Uncanny*. 1919. Trans. David McLintock. London: Penguin, 2003.

Ganteau, Jean-Michel. *The Ethics and Aesthetics of Vulnerability in Contemporary British Fiction*. London: Routledge, 2015.

Gilmartin, Sarah. "The Old Man and the Sea and the Boy." *The Irish Times*. 20 April 2019. Accessed on 09/09/2021 at: www.irishtimes.com/culture/books/the-old-man-and-the-sea-and-the-boy-1.3853394/.

Hicks, Heather J. *The Post-Apocalyptic Novel in the Twenty-First Century: Modernity beyond Salvage*. New York: Palgrave Macmillan, 2016.

Hughes, Rowland, and Pat Wheeler. "Introduction. Eco-dystopias: Nature and the Dystopian Imagination." *Critical Survey* 25.2 (2013): 1–6.

Kennedy, David. *Elegy*. London and New York: Routledge, 2007.

Kermode, Frank. *The Sense of an Ending: Studies in the Theory of Fiction*. 1966. Oxford: Oxford UP, 2000.

Klein, Eileen. "*Sky Burials*: Review." *Dundee University Review of the Arts*. Accessed on 13/09/2021 at: https://dura-dundee.org.uk/2016/11/07/sky-burials/.

Lyotard, Jean-François. *The Postmodern Condition: A Report on Knowledge*. Trans. Geoff Bennington and Brian Massumi. Minneapolis: U of Minnesota P, 1984.

Mandel, Emily St. John. *Station Eleven*. London: Picador, 2014.

McCarthy, Cormac. *The Road*. London: Picador, 2006.

Mills, Rebecca. "The Elegiac Tradition and the Imagined Geography of the Sea and the Shore." *Interdisciplinary Literary Studies* 17.4 (2015): 493–516.

Nayar, Pramod K. *Ecoprecarity: Vulnerable Lives in Literature and Culture*. London and New York: Routledge, 2019.

Rigby, Kate. "Earth, World, Text: On the (Im)possibility of Ecopoiesis." *New Literary History* 35.3 (2004): 427–42.

Shields, Rob. "Bare Nature." *Space and Culture* 21.1 (2018): 4–17.

Silverman, Max. *Palimpsestic Memory: The Holocaust and Colonialism in French and Francophone Fiction and Film*. New York and Oxford: Berghahn Books, 2013.

Smith, Ben. *Sky Burials*. Tonbridge: Worple P, 2014.

———. *Doggerland*. London: Fourth Estate, 2019.

Stengers, Isabelle. "Introductory Notes on an Ecology of Practices." *Cultural Studies Review* 11.1 (2005): 183–96.

Stock, Adam. *Modern Dystopian Fiction and Political Thought: Narratives of World Politics*. London and New York: Routledge, 2018.

Tate, Andrew. *Apocalyptic Fiction*. London: Bloomsbury, 2017.

Walker, Drew. "Two Regimes of the Human: Butler and the Politics of Mattering." *Butler and Ethics*. Ed. Moya Lloyd. Edinburgh: Edinburgh UP, 2015. 141–66.

Warner, Alan. "*Doggerland* by Ben Smith. Review: A Watery Dystopia." *The Guardian*. 11 April 2019. Accessed on 09/09/2021 at: www.theguardian.com/books/2019/apr/11/doggerland-ben-smith-review/.

Part III
Outcasts

6 Ungrievable Incest

Ecology and Kinship in Michael Stewart's *Ill Will*

Maite Escudero-Alías

Introduction

The publication of *Ill Will. The Untold Story of Heathcliff*, by British novelist Michael Stewart in 2018, celebrating the bicentenary of Emily Brontë's birth, brings to the fore poignant questions on nature, vulnerability and kinship that have permeated our culture for centuries. In this midquel told by an autodiegetic narrator, we witness the story of Heathcliff after his hasty departure from the Heights. Under the name of William Lee, Heathcliff embarks on a journey through the English moors towards Liverpool in search of his mother, surrounded by the wild and arid landscapes of the region while witnessing the destruction of the environment for the sake of imminent progress. The novel, thus, posits concerns about the moors as the most forbidden and mysterious terrain, from South to North, linking past, present and future. According to historian William Atkins, the moors were first "described in the seventeenth and eighteenth centuries not by novelists but by horseback topographers and agricultural 'improvers' […]. The moors of England were apt for improvement" (xviii). Farming could indeed benefit from the meadows, pastures, cattle and sheep dispersed throughout the moors. In literature, the moors appear as places of extreme loneliness, as "ill-omened, sombrous, dreary, desolate and sinister" (xvii). In Emily Brontë's *Wuthering Heights* (1847), the presence of the moors works as an insubordinate space of individual struggle, where the categories of gender, race and social class are imbricated in modes of disavowal and erasure from the geographical and moral space of civilisation and order. More specifically, the moors preserve all that is backward and uncivilised, sustaining lifeblood, indispensable for the eternal love bond between Catherine and Heathcliff. For Brontë, the moors were "[e]ternity, where life is boundless in its duration, and love in its sympathy, and joy in its fullness. It was a sea stretching into infinity" (quoted in Atkins 186).

This timeless quality of the moors also endows it with a wilfulness of its own, highlighting a stone and tectonic time that best defines Heathcliff and Catherine's eternal love. By transforming the space of the moors, Brontë's novel underlined a new sense of ecological futurity that

DOI: 10.4324/9781003347811-10

120 Maite Escudero-Alías

foresaw the principles of interrelationality and interdependence among all types of entities, be they organic or inorganic. Such openness is evident throughout the protagonists' symbiotic relationship with the moors. In contemporary biology, symbiosis consists of "replacing an essentialist conception of individuality [...] leading us into directions that transcend the self/nonself, subject/object dichotomies that have characterized Western thought" (Gilbert, Sapp and Tauber 326). Interestingly, the concept of symbiosis originated in the nineteenth century as a way of understanding the complex assemblages among different entities. Heathcliff and Catherine's transcendental love, I argue, is forged in a very specific geographical site—the moors—that not only expands and deviates from chrononormativity, as understood in traditional realist Victorian novels, but also transforms the space of human and non-human boundaries. Inevitably, fused as the couple is with a landscape that evokes freedom, openness and eternity, symbiosis also encompasses "a range of more or less asymmetrical relations as notable for their complexity and interdependence as for their draining and destruction" (Samyn 244). From the outset, their sublime love entails both interdependence and self-destruction, emphasising an intrinsic and intricate relationship among nature, society and economics. The novel, thus, spins around a double paradox: while it forecasts Heathcliff and Catherine's eternal love in relation to its surroundings, it foreshortens the contingency of such possibility, for the boundaries of Heathcliff's race and social class intervene in and interrupt such a natural scenario, if only to erase his insubordinate space and assert, instead, the totalising principle of social stability over the spatial and temporal openness of the moors, existing in a permeable relation to uncontrolled hybridisation and species crossing. In a similar vein, Heathcliff transgresses the boundaries of sexual and ethnic normalcy, being singled out for his otherness as a heightened vulnerable body. In *Precarious Life. The Powers of Mourning and Violence* (2004), Judith Butler thoroughly examined the social and political exclusion of vulnerable subjects and the conceptions of who is normatively human. The question that preoccupies her is "Who counts as human? Whose lives count as lives? And, finally, what makes for a grievable life?" (2004, 20). For Butler, we are all done and undone by each other; there is always a relational vulnerability that constitutes us socially. Yet, specific political conditions exacerbate such vulnerability, triggering violence, grief, loss and other models of dispossession. Although Heathcliff's experience of otherness merges into an encounter with alterity that is mainly attached to grief and revenge, his vulnerable condition also opens up the possibility of action and transformation, thus emphasising his sheer vitality and hopefulness.

Drawing on an interdisciplinary theoretical framework of queer ecologies, animacies and other articulations of non-normative embodiments of humanness and kinship, the present chapter offers a reading of *Ill Will* that carries a textual and ideological fixation with *Wuthering Heights* in the representation of both ecology and kinship, an interpretation that accentuates those contested and violent histories through which natural and cultural systems continue to produce each other. As Butler points out,

> some lives are grievable, and others are not; the differential allocation of grievability that decides what kind of subject is and must be grieved, and which kind of subject must not, operates to produce and maintain certain exclusionary conceptions of who is normatively human: what counts as a livable life and a grievable death?
>
> (2004, xiv–xv)

What is at stake here is whether these novels articulate and engender an ethics of life that can transgress and challenge kinship norms. As will be argued, while *Wuthering Heights* understandably reinforces a normative patriarchal kinship that celebrates human law and order and annihilates otherness and excess—be it physical, moral or sexual—, it strikes a chord that *Ill Will* continues re-establishing the very boundaries that the former attempted to transgress by means of the incestuous relationship between Heathcliff and Catherine. The implications of such moral and natural disruption are their own expulsion from the boundaries that regulate normal citizenship and sovereignty, accentuating their status as ungrievable lives. In contrast to the Romantic celebration of nature and culture as a non-conflictual and concordant community marked by beauty, both novels align themselves with a merely utilitarian ethics that excludes such a harmonious and beautiful ideal, both ontologically and ethically. This place is mostly marked not only by the otherness of Heathcliff but also of the moors. According to LeiLani Nishime and Kim D. Hester Williams (2018), the term "ecology" might be opened up to "include urban environments and agricultural systems, which in turn can help us recognize the historical traffic between racial identities and ecological space and place" (4). My concern for ecology, then, stems from the mutual implication of human society and natural systems, from the messy entanglements that physicist Karen Barad coined as "intra-action." The notion of intra-action

> recognizes that distinct agencies do not precede, but rather emerge through, their intra-action. It is important to note that the 'distinct' agencies are only distinct in a relational, not an absolute sense, that is, agencies are only distinct in relation to their mutual entanglement; they don't exist as individual elements.
>
> (Barad 33)

Crucially, we can establish the mutual entanglement of Heathcliff and Catherine's romance within the spatial openness of the moors, an idea

122   *Maite Escudero-Alías*

that underlines vitality and mutability. However, they end up struggling against the wider entanglements of human action and law. Entwined in this messy web of life that in nature has no limits, they find themselves foreclosed by a mesh of cultural and social ties that congeal their natural vitality and desire. It is my contention that due to Heathcliff's racial and social otherness, the novels cannot seem to disentangle modes of ontological and physical violence that permeate and penetrate the very heart of nature. An open ecology, to use Deving Griffiths and Deanna K. Kreisel's words, demands that we "reconceptualize modes of violence, from the environmentalism of the poor and the ecologies of race to the reframing of toxicity, threat, and predation" (15). In arguing that Heathcliff is depicted as a non-human figure, one can also build up upon conversations with the writings of Giorgio Agamben (1998), Judith Butler (2000), Mel Chen (2012) and Achille Mbembe (2013), to name but a few. At the core of both novels rests Heathcliff's "bare life," the othered dark "gypsy brat" (Brontë 35) who was considered in the Earnshaw family as a thing—"they entirely refused to have *it* in bed with them" (35; emphasis added). This vision of Heathcliff as an enigmatic portrayal of a dark race has allowed critics to put forth a myriad of interpretations, ranging from Marxist approaches envisaging him as an enslaved Irish immigrant into 1840s England (Eagleton 1995), up to postcolonial studies that consider him as "the energy of rebellion" (Meyer 20) against the oppressive power of the imperial gaze.

More recently, however, there are other studies that focus on the importance of the corporeal in Heathcliff, thus pointing to the enforced state "of animal life, of *zoe*, in the colonized subject" (Delacy 144). What interests me here is the connection between Heathcliff's allegedly animal life and his dislodging from citizenship and society, since his condition as an outsider propels his exclusion from the legal system of inheritance and forces him to run away from the Heights. More fiercely, Heathcliff's untamed spirit and torment can be interpreted as the result of a foreclosed and ungrievable status that is granted by the prohibition of his desire towards Catherine and by his sheer reluctance to follow the moral order of cultural and social norms. In other words, my argument is that Heathcliff's status as an animal-being or *zoē* agrees well with the foreclosure of his incestuous desire towards Catherine, thus removing him from the realm of normative kinship and citizenship. Based on the Aristotelian distinction between *zoē* or *bare life* and *bíos*, or *qualified life* of the citizen, Agamben elaborates on the concept of *homo sacer* as "a zone of indistinction between the human and the animal, a werewolf, a man who is transformed into a wolf and a wolf who is transformed into a man—in other words, a bandit, a *homo sacer*" (105). Unlike the sovereign, who has the right of a qualified life, the *homo sacer* inhabits a zone of human exclusion and, more often than not, such exclusion is grounded on the individual's biopolitical position. There are numerous

Ungrievable Incest 123

examples of bare lives, such as those of the poor, the migrants, the refugees, the sick and the disabled, the non-human animals, plants and other organic creatures. In the case of Heathcliff, he is presented as animalistic and demonic, "a lying fiend, a monster, and not a human being" (Brontë 136). Even Catherine recognises his animal nature, calling him "a fierce, pitiless, wolfish man" (102), thus rendering his dark body and unknown origins as the basis for his discrimination and exposing him to a permanent death-in-life.

Interestingly, Heathcliff's objectification and further dehumanisation as an "unreclaimed creature, without refinement—without cultivation; an arid wilderness of furze and whinstone" (102) positions him within the realm of "animacy," a specific affective and material construct that "is not only nonneutral in relation to animals, humans, and dead things, but is shaped by race and sexuality" (Chen 5). Building upon queer theory's turn to new materialism, I locate Heathcliff's animacy not only in his evident animalisation but, more discerningly, in both his inseparable intimacy with natural elements and his impossible marriage with Catherine, making him an extremely vulnerable subject. In all their facets, these accounts refer to a painful and violent process of living-in-death, rejected and ungrieved by the normative society, from which he will not be able to escape. Ultimately, it is his sacred love towards Catherine that situates him apart from social conventions, prolonging the intensity of their love even beyond their own bodies, and resulting in a violent affirmation of life within death. In what follows, I will articulate these premises in three separate sections so as to forge a renewed thread of interpretation that relates both Heathcliff's aberrant position as a non-human person and his expulsion from the realm of the normative sexual laws that regulate desire and love.

"An arid wilderness of furze and whinstone"

Heathcliff's Romantic spirit endorses a steady care for nature and an attachment to the English moors. Blended with the landscape of the Heights, he is often associated with natural elements that spur vitality, strength, wilderness and roughness to the same extent. Such a duality echoes a dialectical movement between freedom and vulnerability, thus ranking him as sympathetically identifying with the landscape, despite his hardness and predatory overtones. Not coincidentally, Nelly describes Heathcliff as "a bleak, hilly, coal country" (Brontë 69), in comparison to Edgar's "beautiful fertile valley" (69). This metaphor allows for a queer materialist reading of Heathcliff through the lenses of Aristotle's *De Anima* (*On the Soul*) in which he discussed the notion of "the soul" (from the Latin *animus*) as the animating principle for humans, animals and vegetables. For Aristotle, the soul is related to the *form* or *essence* of any living things, unlike the *attributes*, which are not considered as

124 *Maite Escudero-Alías*

partaking of this character. In his treaty, Aristotle describes the soul as the main principle of animal life, and yet, "there seems to be no case in which the soul can act or be acted upon without involving the body; e.g. anger, courage, appetite, and sensation generally" (Book I, Part I). The existence of the soul is not possible without the body, even in the case of thinking: "but if this too proves to be a form of imagination or to be impossible without imagination, it too requires a body as a condition of its existence" (Book I, Part I). Quite revealingly for my analysis, Aristotle did not include as an animating principle "dead" matter such as "stones, bricks, and timbers" (Book I, Part I), as he considered them passive materials, attributes not considered essential. The main criterion for his classification is that the soul is to be identified with what is eminently productive of movement. Accordingly, the soul moves and is susceptible of being moved: "if the soul is moved, the most probable view is that what moves it is sensible things" (Book I, Part I). In this hierarchy of sensible things, what is compelling for me is that rocks, metals and stones are excluded altogether, as they are not endowed with a soul and thus are not conceived of as vulnerable entities.

New materialism pays attention to inanimate things and looks back on Aristotle's animating principle, the soul as the spark of life, insisting that things can generate a multiplicity of meanings. From the humanities and social sciences to physics, scholars are drawing on posthumanist conceptions of animate and inanimate things, advocating the vitality of inert matter. Jane Bennett's *Vibrant Matter: A Political Ecology of Things* (2010) stands out at the forefront of this field, opening up new venues of research in which the vitality of non-human bodies, "the capacity of things—edibles, commodities, storms, metals—not only impede or block the will and designs of humans but also act as quasi agents or forces with trajectories, propensities, or tendencies of their own" (viii). Bennett's political project aims at building on a new ecological sensibility in which all bodies form alliances with other bodies, sharing Spinoza's faith that "everything is made of the same substance" (Bennett x). Likewise, Rosi Braidotti's position accounts for practices that define the mattering of the world; that is, she envisages a radical continuum between nature and culture, a "nature-cultural and humanimal transversal bonding" (1), which stems from Spinoza's monistic ontology. Although the ethical significance of human affect is relevant in these studies, Bennett focuses on the agency of the things that "produce (helpful, harmful) effects in human and other bodies. Organic and inorganic bodies, natural and cultural objects *all* are affective" (xii; original emphasis). Thus, she theorises a vitality intrinsic to materiality as such, arguing that this vibrant matter is not exclusively the raw material employed by humans or God in the creation of things, but rather is a variety of bodies such as stem cells, electricity, food, trash, worms, chains, etc. I would like to extend this argumentation a bit further and claim that rocks and stones have

Ungrievable Incest 125

a capacity to act and be acted upon. Stones are not considered part of the hierarchy of animacies, and yet their constant changeability through time allows for debates about life and liveliness. This entails a willingness to theorise stones from a literary perspective, an idea that stems from my attentive readings of Romantic and Victorian poetry, as well as from my personal conviction about the force of nature to act and to be acted upon, thus becoming another vulnerable and grievable entity that we should all recognise as such.

Suggestively, the name "Heathcliff" is always already invested with natural elements, screening him within the vitality and roughness of the Yorkshire moors. Among the diverse references to nature, his description as "an unreclaimed creature, without refinement—cultivation; an arid wilderness of furze and whinstone" (Brontë 102) becomes the foundation of his subsequent mistreatment and exclusion from legitimate citizenship. And yet, the fact that Heathcliff is not compared to any type of rock, but to whinstone or basalt, positions him in the realm of agency and will. Firstly, and unlike Aristotle's claim, there is geological evidence that allows us to state that rocks and stones are moved by compression and distension, resulting in tectonic movements that modify and transform the Earth. As geologist Marcia Bjornerud points out:

> unfortunately, stone has an underserved reputation for being uncommunicative. The expressions *stone deaf*, *stone cold*, *stony silence*, and, simply, *stoned* reveal much about the relationship people have to the rocks beneath their feet. But to a geologist, stones are richly illustrated texts, telling gothic tales of scorching heat, violent tempests, endurance, cataclysm, and reincarnation.
>
> (4–5; original emphasis)

Secondly, whinstone is a type of volcanic and igneous rock capable of metamorphosis when it cools and contracts, forming sets of polygonal prisms or columns known in geology as columnar jointing, which displays astonishing interlocking shapes. When Catherine utters "he's [Heathcliff] more myself than I am. Whatever our souls are made of, his and mine are the same, and Linton's is as different as a moonbeam from lightning, or frost from fire" (Brontë 80), she is obviously rendering Heathcliff's soul as fire, full of passion and vitality. Very much like the volcanic rock, Heathcliff's natural attributes convey not only hardness and wilderness but also passion and beauty— the furze may also evoke these qualities as it is an arid bush but beautiful when in bloom. By extension, the love between Catherine and Heathcliff conjures up an interconnectedness or assemblage that transgresses the cultural limits of personhood: "My love for Linton is like the foliage in the woods. Time will change it. I'm well aware, as winter changes the trees—My love for Heathcliff resembles the eternal rock beneath—source of little visible

126 *Maite Escudero-Alías*

delight, but necessary" (82). Remarkably enough, such rock beneath is the bedrock that sustains the ground, the whinstone, the furze. As if it were an intact and unaltered rock, their love remains the essence of their vitality, a whole world of resemblances and resonances of nature.

In *Ill Will*, the allusions to the natural environment and stonewalls are highly revealing too: Heathcliff's journey through the moors is guided by "the buzzing of the flies for company," the grass and moss next to a rowan tree he rests by, the dandelions leaves that were "a bit bitter for breakfast" (Stewart 9) or some plants that nourished him.

Moreover, he comes across all types of animals, such as rabbits, sparrows, butterflies, frogs and even "lays down on the straw with the swine" (24), while he recalls Catherine teaching him the names of all the plants at the moors: "dog rose, gout weed, earth nut, fool's parsley, goat's beard, ox-tongue, snake weed" (25). Concomitantly, the autodiegetic narrator tells us about the harsh working conditions of farm labourers and pitmen who spend day and night doing mill work, building canals or setting fire to coal: "It's not natural to never see the sun. A pit is hell on earth. A mill is not much better. Folks call it progress" (30). According to William-Heathcliff, there exists a sharp contrast between his and Catherine's moors as a place of solace and wonder, and the presence of enclosures as a man-made intrusion disturbing the freedom of nature:

> I [William] looked around at the landscape around me. Meadow, pasture and field enclosed by stone walls and beyond the moorland. Walls that reached up steep cloughs and marked who owned what and marred the land they squatted upon.
>
> (41)

Fences and stone walls are a sign of progress and stand in opposition to uncountable types of birds, flowers and natural beauty he encounters during his journey to Liverpool. As these descriptions suggest, stones are associated here with artificiality, confinement, somehow spurring the limits between nature and culture, stealing the freedom of nature in favour of social and economic interests and accentuating environmental degradation.

Through posthuman understandings of non-human bodies, both organic and inorganic, we can resort to questions of animacy as a site of connectivity and relationality. In this case, William's position as *zoē* uncovers the link between human normalcy and conventional reproductive accounts of sex and intimacy. That is, while he is relegated to the realm of an inanimate life, imbued with raced and class toxicity, the sense of vitality that emanates from his will is immanent to transgressions, "violating proper intimacies, including between humans and nonhuman things" (Chen 11). In *Wuthering Heights*, Heathcliff's violation also affects the normative boundaries of kinship and desire towards Catherine, as he defies both the *oikía* (the private household) and the *polis* (the public realm). Being ruler and ruled, Heathcliff paradoxically exerts his power and strength if only to be deprived of them. In *The Human Condition*, Hannah Arendt turns to such a distinction in order to reveal the conditions for political action. Action is transgressive in nature, as it "always establishes relationships and therefore has an inherent tendency to force open all limitations and cut across all boundaries" (190). Accordingly, action entails a creative act of springing up a new beginning. While Heathcliff-as-ruled fits such a definition, he is disavowed and erased from the public realm because of his violent behaviour as a ruler: "to be political, to live in a polis, meant that everything was decided through words and persuasion and not through force and violence" (Arendt 26). Heathcliff's position allows him to play the tyrannical ruler and to simultaneously enact an ethics of full responsibility for his actions, even as he knows that his erasure as an ungrievable subject will lead him to death.

Kalos Thanatos: A Beautiful and Noble Death

In her work *Antigone's Claim* (2000), Butler explores the various ways in which kinship, social order and the state are constituted by foreclosing the power of the feminine. Her approach to Sophocles' myth appears as a necessary claim for a progressive queer feminism and sexual politics. The main interpretations on this mythic figure have been carried out by Hegel, Lacan and Lévi-Strauss, who represent Antigone as the embodiment of a destructive and unethical impulse against the social and political order that also denies the possibility of an incestuous relationship. In their readings, the heroine finds no place as a citizen because she is positioned outside the terms of the state. As Hegel puts it, "she is not capable of offering or receiving recognition within the ethical order" (quoted in Butler 2000, 13), simply because she has transgressed the natural roles of her feminine gender and, therefore, she is accused by the chorus of adopting "manly" manners. Steeped in incestuous legacies—she is the daughter of her brother-father Oedipus—, Antigone defies Creon's orders and disobeys the law when she buries her brother Polyneices after Creon, her uncle and king, prohibited such a burial, on grounds of betrayal and infidelity. Antigone buries her brother and commits the subversive act of refusing to deny that she performed the deed, thus appropriating "the rhetoric of agency of Creon and assimilating the very terms of sovereignty that she refuses" (Butler 2000, 11). Antigone's confession both defies and inhabits the language of sovereignty, speaking in and against it. And yet, because of her defiance, Antigone, a woman who is not married and has no sons, finds no place within citizenship as she has transgressed the biological and cultural limits of intelligible kinship.

128   *Maite Escudero-Alías*

In his work *The Elementary Structures of Kinship*, Claude Lévi-Strauss contends that the incest taboo is the mechanism by which "biology is transformed into culture, and so is neither biological nor cultural, although culture itself cannot do without it" (quoted in Butler 2000, 19). Culture, here, is understood as a set of universal rules that are not alterable or subject to change. The domain of this universal role of culture is what Jacques Lacan defined as symbolic or linguistic rules, and these rules reinforce normative kinship relations. Furthermore, Lacan "establishes Antigone at the threshold of the symbolic, understood as the linguistic register in which kinship relations are instated and maintained; he understands her death as precipitated precisely by the symbolic insupportability of her desire" (Butler 2000, 29). Thus, Antigone does occupy a position within the symbolic-kinship, but only to be expelled from it. Her self-conscious act challenges the limits of the symbolic order and banishes her to a living death: by pronouncing the words "I say that I did it and I do not deny it" she expresses a daring desire that will sententiously declare her guilt. In stating these words, Antigone both acknowledges her act and pronounces it, thus posing an overt hostility against universal law and the symbolic norms of culture. In this way, her words accuse her of being guilty, depicting her kinship position as the reiterative and performative process of a set of linguistic practices *that do what they say.*

For Butler, such a structuralist account of language is designed to establish the ontological origin of the cultural and legal state apparatus, inasmuch as this paradigm imposes and defines *a priori* which forms of existence and kinship are legitimate and which ones are not. Remarkably, Butler attempts to reconceptualise both the incest taboo and the forms of kinship that are legitimised within culture. More specifically, she is interested in defending the performative possibilities of subversive agency and change: is it not the case, she wonders, that this norm may be "temporarily opened to subversion from within and to a future than cannot be fully anticipated?" (2000, 21). If Antigone were not her words, if her words were not her deeds, if her deeds were not a frozen performative act, would it not be possible to legitimise other different forms of contingent relationships which may entail their own iterability and resignification within the regulatory terms of a less restrictive culture and sexuality? In Butler's words: "if kinship is the precondition of the human, then Antigone is the occasion for a new field of the human" (2000, 82). Certainly, while we cannot say that Antigone is not heterosexual, she refuses to become a mother and a wife, "by scandalizing the public with her wavering gender, by embracing death as the bridal chamber and identifying her tomb as a 'deep dug home'" (76). Her move towards death may also be read as her love for her brother, a love that cannot be consummated and that presupposes a domain of the ungrievable. In this sense, Antigone is an anomaly and, as such, she is not a human. As Fanny Söderbäck points out, "as a woman, she simply cannot be equal [...]. Woman is this outside. The polis would not exist without her. Yet the polis can only exist without her [...]. She inaugurates the very order that will exclude and destroy her" (74).

At a time in which the notion of the human requires participation in a normative sense of the family, Antigone represents a deformation and a displacement of kinship: "her fate is not to have a life to live, but to be condemned to death prior to any possibility of life" (Söderbäck 23). She is guilty of a crime against the state and is further relegated by the chorus to an inhuman status, or, in Agamben's terms, to the status of *homo sacer* (sacred man), that "obscure figure of archaic Roman law, in which human life is included in the juridical order [...] solely in the form of its exclusion (that is, of its capacity to be killed)" (8). Since the publication of this work on Antigone's myth, Butler has recurrently delved into questions about whose lives count as lives worth defending and grieving for, that is, whose lives are eligible, intelligible and worth sustaining, and whose are disposable and ungrievable, "already lost and, hence, easy to destroy or to expose to forces of destruction" (2020, 17). This raises the question of how a normative kinship condemns and forecloses unliveable and aberrant desires, such as Antigone's, incest itself, "making of her life a living death, that has no place within the terms that confer intelligibility on life" (2020, 23). Butler's reading of Antigone attempts to rethink the Lacanian notion of the symbolic order and to productively acknowledge its contingency to go beyond self-destruction and death in the case of individuals who do not conform to such norms. For Butler, Antigone's subversive claim takes place within the very terms of the symbolic that anticipate its own perversion, laying out the possibility of new forms of kinship arising from the incest taboo. In the play, the prohibition of incest becomes the basis for the configuration of exclusionary patterns of kinship that deny "a thoroughly *egalitarian approach to the preservation of life*" (2020, 56; original emphasis), and impose a monolithic account of grievability, exercising an adamant form of political agency.

Indeed, as argued in the previous section, Agamben talks about a set of lives whose ontological status as legal subjects is suspended and whose humanness is not fully recognised. Arendt also refers to the "shadowy realm" that haunts the public sphere of the political and exercises a violent process of subjection, "where the human is constituted through words and deeds and most forcefully constituted when its word becomes its deed" (81). The issue of violence, then, is intrinsically related to grievability, and when we ask whose lives count as selves worth living, we should account for nonviolent practices of social equality and interdependency that highlight openness to alterity and the dispossessed. In her latest work, *The Force of Non-Violence* (2020), Butler foregrounds the importance of social bonds and interdependency to "accept the notion

130   *Maite Escudero-Alías*

that all lives are equally grievable" (2020, 56), encouraging us to consider an ethics of non-violence that "proves to be an integral dimension of biopolitics and of ways of thinking about equality among the living" (2020, 56). This means that we must embrace a convincing position of relationality that respects not only persons but also animals and all living processes and forms of life. The presumption of equal grievability should be an ethical principle sustaining and organising all spheres of our lives, be them private or public.

Heathcliff's Claim: A Transgression of Kinship Norms

Interestingly for Butler, of the three Theban plays by Sophocles, *Antigone* (c. 442 BC), *Oedipus the King* (c. 449 BC) and *Oedipus at Colonus* (405 BC), *Antigone* precedes its prehistory, as the former was written before the two plays on Oedipus. The prohibition against incest is more strikingly accentuated by the force of reading it retroactively, contextualised with the historical effectiveness of Oedipus. Concomitantly, the novel *Ill Will* belatedly affirms the spectre of incest that haunts Heathcliff and Catherine's Romantic relationship in *Wuthering Heights*. Both original texts posit a dialectical sense of textual interdependence in order to fully convey the perversion of desire, thus entailing a form of uncertain temporality whose force precedes the utterance of the events. While some critics have discussed the relationship between Heathcliff and Catherine as incestuous (Goetz 1982; Perry 2004; Kuper 2009), I argue that *Ill Will* presupposes the same ideological premises of kinship as *Wuthering Heights* inasmuch as the protagonists' familial bonds confirm Heathcliff and Catherine's incestuous blood link, thus foreclosing the possibility of imagining other structures of kinship and grievability. Their blood relation makes marriage impossible between sister and brother, despite their desire for one another.

In his quest for his origins, William Lee, Heathcliff's avatar, discovers that Mr Earnshaw used to invest money in a business proposition related to the transportation of "gin and cotton, as well as a variety of worsted goods" (Stewart 226), that is, slaves from the West coast of Africa to the West Indies. Like many other men, Mr Earnshaw carefully selected the most pleasant black women who were sold into prostitution and, as Hardwar tells him, "he made a special attachment to one of the negresses. Your mother" (227). To which William replies, "are you saying that Mr Earnshaw is my father by blood?" (227). After this revelation, William is informed that his mother, named Lilly, died "a few years after he was born, as she took her own life. As many do" (228). Born a slave, Lilly was called "Negro Number Twenty-nine" (229), "Twenty-nine times a night" (310) and was devoid of human traits: "Niggers are natural thieves. And cannibals. Slavery stops thievery, slavery stops cannibalism [...]. Niggers are an inferior race, incapable of living as free men, or free women" (229). William pictures his mother's condition as a prostitute "being passed from one man to the next" (236) in a state of confusion and bewilderment. The truth can indeed be a terrible thing, as it unveils aberrant practices of abuse and violence at the hands of his surrogate father. His position as the son of a female slave carries a sense of ungrievability that is exacerbated when his relationship with Cathy cannot be consummated. Doubly relegated to the margins of legibility and normative kinship, he undergoes a process of transformation that implies showing sympathy and generosity towards Emily, a girl he saves from death while she is being whipped by two men in a barn. His connection with Emily is brought about by the memories of Hindley beating him, as he "felt the girl's pain as if it were my [his] own" (59). From this moment on, Emily becomes his best companion, allowing them to make money and survive because "Emily was blessed with the power of talking to dead people" (72). Together with Emily's friendship, William clings to the moors and the forest, the rooks, crows, rabbits and hares, flowers and berries, as a way of grieving over the loss of Catherine. The brutal nature attributed to him in *Wuthering Heights* is transformed here into affective bonds with nature and with his friend Emily.

Dorothy J. Hale develops the Levinasian phrase "ethics of alterity" to describe a wide variety of understandings of otherness: "this can include otherness within [...] the human encounter with nonhuman states of being, the lives of animals, states of divinity, or even the nature of fiction" (6). The value of inhabiting otherness is that "it brings into visibility the socially disenfranchised, the ignored, the abject" (7), thus revealing emotional responses that may disrupt one's ideological and ethical positionings. Although Emily Brontë's representation of Heathcliff as a social and racial other succeeded in offering an encounter with otherness, *Ill Will* gives voice to William Lee and favourably appraises his internal focalisation and use of free direct style in order to set emphatically the attachment of otherness: "seeing the interest of everything is all that it is his vision, his conception, his interpretation" (Hale 29). Stewart credits his main character with an empathetic understanding of Emily's condition and emotions and a fondness of animals and nature, all of which foregrounds an ethical position of respect and sympathy about the other in Hale's wider acceptation of the term. Such characterisation of otherness challenges traditional representations of characters who are not simply strangers but "unconventional, odd, aberrant —even violent, criminals" (Hale 49). Yet, when the reader is compelled to intimacy and awe towards such characters, as is the case with Heathcliff/William, we must value the role of fiction as the main agent of profound self-transformation. As Toni Morrison reminds us, "imagining is not merely looking or looking at; nor is it taking oneself intact into the other. It is, for the purposes of the work, *becoming*" (4; original emphasis).

132 *Maite Escudero-Alías*

The experience of otherness, then, demands a move towards openness, expanding the limits of intelligibility and vulnerability.

Conclusion

Whereas in *Wuthering Heights* Heathcliff's ethical transgressions, even to the point of sadism and violence, qualify him as a moral stranger and challenge the limits of humanness, the autodiegetic narrator in *Ill Will* performs his own capacity for otherness as a self-conscious act of empathy and care, thus enacting an aesthetics of alterity that also opens the possibility of seeing through oneself to understand the other, albeit temporarily. As William explains to Cathy, during his trip to Liverpool with Emily, they encountered children on street corners and poor women selling goods. What moved them to such pity was a "poor freak," a chimney sweeper, whose pain and misery is ignored by the opulent and privileged gentlemen and ladies passing by, as no one "even seem to notice this miserable wretch" (Stewart 109). Yet, William's imagined transformation also entails acquiring education and wealth and using it for the unethical aim of taking revenge against all inhabitants at the Heights, including Cathy. He would use his wealth to witness the destruction of Hindley and the Heights, coming between Edgar and Cathy so that he "would make sure that you [Cathy] never be happy. Just as you had ensured that I would never be other than cast out and alone" (315). This desire for revenge may be interpreted as evidence that William is as fiendish as Heathcliff, since this accomplishment takes place through the recollection of memories, without which remembrance as action would be impossible. Yet, through the reification of vengeance, William/Heathcliff inaugurates the very order that will destroy them, as both are intertwined in the tragedy of an impossible love, thus incarnating a transgression that is fatally linked to a death-drive and incest. The impossible reconciliation between both characters is further emphasised at the very ending of the novel by the use of italics and an explicit "you" addressed to Catherine as the sole recipient of their own tormented acts and deeds: "*everything runs in a circle, the river and the rain, the moon around the earth, the earth around the sun, even revenge*" (321; original emphasis). William/Heathcliff's attachments to nature and unrequited love are but a trace of their constant mourning for the grievable life they are denied to live, a life in which Heathcliff/William is no longer the "half-man, half-monster," the devil that Hindley named him. Like Antigone, they act benevolently but without full citizenship; theirs are the lives that haunt the normative constitution of the human and surely die from a lack of recognition. While Antigone is not allowed into the public sphere, where the human is constituted through its linguistic acts, because she is a woman, Heathcliff/William also remains outside its terms because of their lack of entitlement to intelligibility and sovereignty. As indomitable and ungrievable subjects, is their transgression part of their deathly desire that originally constitutes them as such? Or rather, do their solitude, freedom and persistence in their actions serve to sustain the spectre of incest as the prohibition without which social norms could not possibly emerge?

By posing a threat to normative kinship, Heathcliff/William's transgression exposes the vulnerability of kinship's norms, thus opening up the possibility of recognition under a different symbolic order. If the rule of prohibiting incest is universal and produces unintelligible subjects, both Heathcliff and Cathy are condemned to lead a living death in a society that refuses the public recognition of their loss, thereby triggering feelings of violence, masochism and sadism and, in the case of William's narration, relegating him to an aberrant violation of the norm, and making impossible his status as a human and grievable body. When the incest taboo forecloses a love that persists in spite of its textual exclusion, what emerges is the occasion for its literalisation and reconfiguration. Yet, *Ill Will* replicates Heathcliff/William's banishment from the ontological certainty of kinship, depriving them of legitimation and figuring the non-human at the border of the human.

Acknowledgements

Research for this chapter was funded by the Spanish Ministry of Science and Innovation (MICINN) (code PID2021-124841NB-I00) and by the Government of Aragón and the European Social Fund (ESF) (code H03_20R).

Works Cited

Agamben, Giorgio. *Homo Sacer: Sovereign Power and Bare Life.* Trans. Daniel Heller-Roazen. Eds Werner Hamacher and David E. Wellbery. Stanford, CA: Stanford UP, 1998.

Arendt, Hannah. *The Human Condition.* Chicago, IL: U of Chicago P, 1998.

Aristotle. *On the Soul.* (c. 350 BC) 1931. Trans. J. A. Smith. Accessed on 11/02/2022 at: http://classics.mit.edu/Aristotle/soul.1.i.html/.

Atkins, William. *The Moor. Lives, Landscape, Literature.* London: Faber and Faber, 2014.

Barad, Karen. *Meeting the Universe Halfway. Quantum Physics and the Entanglement of Matter and Meaning.* Durham and London: Duke UP, 2007.

Braidotti, Rosi. "A Theoretical Framework for the Critical Posthumanities." *Theory, Culture, Society* 36.6 (2018): 1–31.

Bennett, Jane. *Vibrant Matter: A Political Ecology of Things.* Durham: Duke UP, 2010.

Bjornerud, Marcia. *Reading the Rocks. The Autobiography of the Earth.* New York: Westview P, 2005.

Brontë, Emily. *Wuthering Heights.* 1847. Oxford, New York: Oxford UP, 1995.

134   *Maite Escudero-Alías*

Butler, Judith. *Antigone's Claim. Kinship between Life and Death.* New York: Columbia UP, 2000.

———. *Precarious Life. The Powers of Mourning and Violence.* London and New York: Verso, 2006.

———. *The Force of Non-Violence.* London and New York: Verso, 2020.

Chen, Mel. *Animacies. Biopolitics, Racial Mattering and Queer Affect.* Durham: Duke UP, 2012.

Delacy, Eamonn. "*Wuthering Heights* Must Be Defended!: Heathcliff and Necropolitics in the Yorkshire Moors." *Victorians: A Journal of Culture and Literature* 134 (2018), 139–50.

Eagleton, Terry. *Heathcliff and the Great Hunger.* London and New York: Verso, 1995.

Gilbert, Scott F., Jan Sapp, and Alfred I. Tauber. "A Symbiotic Way of Life: We Have Never Been Individuals." *Quarterly Review of Biology* 87.4 (2012): 325–41.

Goetz, William. "Genealogy and Incest in 'Wuthering Heights'." *Studies in the Novel* 14.4 (Winter 1982): 359–76.

Griffiths, Deving, and Deanna K. Kreisel. "Introduction: Open Ecologies." *Victorian Literature and Culture* 48.1 (2020): 1–28.

Hale, Dorothy J. *The Novel and the New Ethics.* Stanford, CA: Stanford UP, 2020.

Kuper, Adam. *Incest and Influence.* Cambridge, MA: Harvard UP, 2009. Lévi-Strauss, Claude. *The Elementary Structures of Kinship.* 1949. Revised ed. Trans. James Harley Bell and John Richard von Sturmer. Ed. Rodney Needham. Boston, MA: Beacon P, 1971.

Mbembe, Achille. "Necropolitics." *Biopolitics: A Reader.* Eds Timothy Campbell and Adam Size. Durham: Duke UP, 2013. 161–92.

Meyer, Susan. *Imperialism at Home: Race and Victorian Women's Fiction.* Ithaca, NY: Cornell UP, 1996.

Morrison, Toni. *Playing in the Dark. Whiteness and the Literary Imagination.* New York: Random House, 1992.

Nishime, LeiLani, and Kim D. Hester Williams. "Introduction: Why Racial Ecologies?" *Racial Ecologies.* Eds LeiLani Nishime and Kim D. Hester Williams. Seattle: U of Washington P, 2018. 3–15.

Perry, Ruth. *Novel Relations: The Transformation of Kinship in English Literature and Culture 1748–1818.* Cambridge: Cambridge UP, 2004.

Samyn, Jeanette. "Intimate Ecologies: Symbioses in the Nineteenth Century." *Victorian Literature and Culture* 48.1 (2020): 243–65.

Söderbäck, Fanny. *Feminist Readings of Antigone.* Albany: SUNY P, 2010.

Sophocles. *The Three Theban Plays: Antigone, Oedipus the King and Oedipus at Colonus. c. 442 BC, c. 449 BC, c. 405 BC. Introduction and Notes Bernard Knox.* Trans. Robert Fagles. Penguin Classics. Harmondsworth: Penguin, 1984.

Stewart, Michael. *Ill Will. The Untold Story of Heathcliff.* London: Harper Collins, 2018.

7 (Un-)Grieving Celestial in Toni Morrison's *Love*

Paula Martín-Salván

Introduction

Toni Morrison's *Love* (2003) is structured as a collection of juxtaposed female perspectives on a central but absent male character. The late Bill Cosey is husband, lover, friend … to a long list of mostly female characters, including his daughter-in-law May, his granddaughter Christine, two of his employees (L and Vida Gibbons) and his wife, Heed. The titles of the chapters emphasise precisely the relational nature of Bill Cosey's identity: Portrait, Friend, Stranger, Benefactor, Lover, Husband, Guardian, Father and Phantom.[1] Through these relational categories, his story is woven into a dense textual network. One female character, however, is markedly absent from the main textual nodes and emerges only marginally as a ghostly presence, vague but recurrent. This is Celestial, a scarred-face prostitute who is said to have been Cosey's lifelong true love. As noted by Cynthia Wallace, the narrative is "notably reticent" about Celestial (382).

Most criticism of the novel hardly mentions Celestial at all (Humann, Mellard, Roynon), and those who do write about her focus on the ways in which she appears to be a mediating figure, compared to Heed (Palladino 350), actualised in the younger figure of Junior (Bouson, Harack, Vega-González) or evoked as mediator between Heed and Christine, a symbol of their bond in childhood (Carden and, again, Harack). In a sense, this emphasises her subsidiary position within the novel. But while she is clearly what we may call a secondary character,[2] most readings tend to obviate her central position in the plot dynamics. She may indeed be identified as a disruptive or oppositional kind of secondary character (Woloch 25), expelled from the narrative both within the discourse and the story (25).

Critics like Wallace (384) or Megan Sweeney (446) have identified the novel's plot with the "murder mystery" genre. In so doing, they emphasise the organisation of the narrative as a retrospective unveiling of the cause and circumstances of Bill Cosey's death and its consequences for his potential heirs, Christine and Heed. The conflict between them over Cosey's will, ambiguously leaving everything he owned to "[his] sweet

DOI: 10.4324/9781003347811-11

136 *Paula Martín-Salván*

Cosey child" (Morrison 2003, 88), constitutes the plot's motor force. Yet, as L eventually confesses her intervention in the Cosey affairs, that version of the will is revealed to be a forgery to replace Cosey's earlier, authentic will, in which Celestial was to be his heiress (200). The forged will, then, may be perceived as an attempt to erase Celestial not only from Cosey's inheritance but also from the narrative focusing on the characters' lives after his death.

Like Cosey himself, Celestial is also dead in the diegetic present, only remembered and evoked feebly by the rest of the characters. Unlike Cosey's, her death is not mourned explicitly by any character. While Cosey's very public funeral constitutes a central scene in the novel—a pivotal point joining the remembered past and the diegetic present—, the reader is offered no glimpse of Celestial's ageing and death. The fact that she seems to disappear from the narrative without a trace, that her death is not registered, points to the way in which their lives are marked by inequality, echoing the concept of "grievability" theorised by Judith Butler: "those who are grievable would be mourned if their lives were lost; the ungrievable are those whose loss would leave no trace, or per-haps barely a trace" (Butler 2020, 74–75).[3]

Taking cue from the observation that her death is "unnarrated," explic-itly failing to "tell what is supposed to have happened, foregrounding the narrator's refusal to narrate" (Warhol 220), I would like to propose the hypothesis that, since her loss is not registered as such in the novel, not marked and definitely not mourned (Butler 2020, 75), Celestial is an ungrievable character. As Judith Butler has claimed, "[w]ithout griev-ability, there is no life, or, rather, there is something living that is other than life" (2009, 15). Presented as "the other woman" in Cosey's domes-tic life, Celestial, the lover, has no place in his public, visible existence. Even if everyone around Bill Cosey knows about her, she belongs to the subterranean, secret life that takes place underneath the surface of the shiny family portrait. Quoting Jeanette Winterson's narrator in *Written on the Body*, one may observe how "[o]dd that marriage, a public dis-play and free to all, gives way to that most secret of liaisons, an adul-terous affair" (Winterson 16). Celestial's status regarding the Coseys, and by extension the entire community of Silk, is further complicated by the fact that she is a prostitute. An additional level of social exclusion and secrecy is thus associated to her, for, as Julia O'Connell Davidson claims, the prostitute is the community's "constitutive outside" (1997, 181). Haunting the community, talked about but never part of it, pushed to precarity (Butler 2009, 25), Celestial's ghostly presence in the novel is both enduring and elusive.

In this chapter, I would like to explore how Celestial is constructed as an ungrievable subject through structural and social mechanisms that bring about her exclusion. My reading of the novel, and specifi-cally of this character, tries to establish a correlation between the social dynamics of gender and class prejudice that the story dramatises (most visibly through the relationship between Heed and Christine) and the narrative structure of the text, in its treatment of Celestial as a paradoxically central but ungrievable character. Regarding the first aspect, it seems quite evident that Morrison seeks to establish Celestial as a figure of marginality and otherness, whose relationship with Cosey can never be legitimated and, hence, socially visible. Her structural position may be explained by reference to Morrison's own words on the figure of the "outlaw woman" that features recurrently in her fiction: "The women who step outside the borders, or who think other thoughts, define the limits of civilization, but also challenge it" (O'Connor 2003).

Celestial's social status is paralleled, as I will argue, by the position she holds within the narrative stance of the novel. The text is narrated in the third person through variable focalisation combined with an enigmatic first-person narrator, L. Through this complex technique, which in fact is part of Morrison's characteristic style, the text reconstructs the story of the Cosey household over a period of several decades, from his raising as model citizen to his death and its aftermath. It is quite noticeable that Celestial is the only female character whose perspective is never offered through focalisation. She is only present in the text to the extent that she is seen or remembered by others, like Heed and Christine, or L. However, the very fact that she is mentioned in the text at all, I would claim, points to the failure in obliterating her from collective memory. I will argue, therefore, that Celestial joins the cohort of Morrison's ungrieved ghosts. My analysis of the character focuses, firstly, on the sociological implications of her condition as a prostitute, and the way in which she is constructed as socially dead, and hence, as potentially ungrievable. After reviewing the specific moments in the novel when Celestial features explicitly, I set out to consider her marginalisation from the core of the text in terms of narrative structure. A relevant aspect of how she is presented as a character that I set out to explore is the way in which the narrative replicates in its construction the social mechanisms that bring about Celestial's exclusion. Simultaneously, the novel dramatises the impossibility of erasing her completely and shows her as a persistent but ghostly presence. As argued in the concluding section of this chapter, however, the novel offers a final twist to the notion of grievability in connection to Celestial, as it focuses on her claim to grieve her lover rather than to be grieved herself. The image of Celestial grieving Cosey's death at the very end of the novel invites further reflection on Butler's conceptual framework.

The Prostitute and Social Death

In *Love*, Celestial is presented in terms that may be familiar to Morrison's regular readers. An obvious precedent for this character and its textual

138 *Paula Martín-Salván*

function regarding the protagonists is to be found in the three prostitutes from *The Bluest Eye*, China, Poland and Miss Marie (Morrison 1970, 50), with whom Pecola Breedlove spends her time. Like them, Celestial is an enigmatic prostitute who fascinates the two main characters, Heed and Christine, during their childhood. Their first meeting features prominently in the text, as the then little girls observe this woman in a red dress walking along the beach with her head held high (Morrison 2003, 188). The moment is significant because it exceptionally reverses the scopophilic regime established in the text by focusing on Celestial's gaze rather than on how she is observed by others.[4] Here, it is Celestial who looks at the girls: "Her eyes locking theirs were cold and scary, until she winked at them, making their toes clench and curl with happiness" (188). From here on, Heed and Christine identify Celestial with everything that is forbidden and daring. In Carden's view, "she represents female fearlessness, independence and possibility" (138). She is a dangerously attractive model of womanhood that stands at the margins of the socially acceptable. While most adult characters pretend that she is not even there, the girls' fascination rescues her from utter social death.

In sociological terms, Celestial falls into the realm of the unthinkable, except for those who have not fully assimilated the exclusionary conception of the normatively human (Butler 2004, xiv–xv). Following Davidson, we may analyse the social dynamics established in the novel regarding Celestial's status as a prostitute. In a model of community that upholds a partial recognition of women as citizens entitled to sovereignty over their own bodies, the prostitute is the extant figure that guarantees the satisfaction of men's sexual urges regardless of such sovereignty (Davidson 2016, 179). Therefore, Davidson claims,

> prostitute women thus have to be imagined as outside the community. Because they 'agree' to sell their sexuality as a commodity, prostitutes are held to have placed themselves outside the remit of the socially agreed rules which govern sexual life. They are expelled and excluded from the community.
>
> (2016, 179)

Both Butler and Davidson refer to the construction of the prostitute as "socially dead" (Butler 1997, 27; Davidson 2013, 134). Guillaume Le Blanc, in turn, identifies the prostitute as socially invisible (146). Orlando Patterson's concept of "social death," coined in his seminal study *Slavery and Social Death* (1982), describes the invisibility of individuals whose existence is not acknowledged by a community with which they nevertheless interact, as a process that "involves the paradox of introducing him as a nonbeing" (38).[5]

Writing about *The Bluest Eye*, Jennifer Gillan states: "When the abstract, disembodied citizen is figured as white and male, all others

(Un-)Grieving Celestial 139

cannot embody such citizenship because they are hyperembodied by the racial and/or gendered markings visible on their bodies" (Gillan 283). In *Love*, Morrison places all her characters on the same side of the racial divide, but the limits of citizenship are still marked on the characters' bodies. Celestial is marked both by the red dress that L identifies with her wild nature, and by the scar on her face; but these markers paradoxically turn her into a socially dead entity, a non-being in the Silk community. L refers to her as "a local woman I know" (Morrison 2003, 67), and May, when asked by Christine about her, tells the girls to stay away from her (188). May's words point towards the mechanisms of social exclusion that try to erase Celestial from view, despite her persistent physicality in the novel. Thus, she illustrates Butler's point that grievability is "already operative in life," to the extent that "to be grievable is to be interpellated in such a way that you know your life matters" (2020, 59).

Cosey, on the other hand, may be the figure of abstract citizenship, but he is hypervisible in the text, constantly looked up to by his neighbours and employees and raised to the status of role model by the community. This is evinced in that he is depicted in the "benefactor" mode, paying for other neighbours' funerals, doctor bills, college fees (103), etc. In Tessa Roynon's terms, "Cosey is an obvious embodiment of the American dream" (33). Morrison is intent on showing through the opposition between the socially invisible Celestial and the hypervisible Bill Cosey that class and gender intersect to establish the borders of citizenship in this fictional universe. Cosey himself, male and wealthy, occupies the central position in such a universe, while all the other characters are marked as peripheral. Celestial is simultaneously closest to Cosey—through her lifelong relationship with him—and displaced to the farthest margins precisely because of the unacceptability of the transgression represented by such a relationship. Sweeney emphasises this point when commenting on the words used to describe Bill Cosey upon his death as an "ideal husband" and "perfect father" (Morrison 2003, 201): "These hermetic legal categories pretend full adequation with Cosey's persona while writing Celestial out of the equation" (Sweeney 459).

A moment in the novel that perfectly illustrates such a contrast is the description of the portrait of Cosey that features prominently at several points in the story. Recalled by Sandler Gibbons through focalisation, the portrait is said to have used as model a photograph in which Cosey appears to be looking at her (Morrison 2003, 112). The portrait itself becomes a token of the position of authority held by Cosey both in business and at home, as it is said to have hung first at the back of Vida's desk, at the hotel's office and then above Heed Cosey's bed (112). In the painting, though, his gaze looks to someone who remains out of the frame, and thus cannot possibly have been captured by the camera. Once more, Celestial is the invisible but permanent companion of Bill Cosey's lifetime. Pushed out of the frame, she can be said to exist only to

140   *Paula Martín-Salván*

the extent that he looks at her, that he sees her. If the portrait symbolises the way Cosey is seen by the community, it also illustrates the way in which the community is willing to see him, but refuses to acknowledge Celestial within the same frame of existence.

J. Brooks Bouson describes Celestial in already ghostly terms: "for the true love of Cosey's life was the sporting woman, Celestial, a woman Heed never acknowledged knowing about even though she was aware that Celestial had the power to summon her husband at will" (366). Cosey's refusal to acknowledge Celestial as his mistress is noted in the novel by L, who claims that he would deny knowing her if asked (Morrison 2003, 67). Indirectly, when the issue of Cosey's will is mentioned by L, she refers to Celestial as the only woman around Cosey who would never be interested in his patrimony, as it reminded her of the fact that she was not allowed to enter the Cosey house or hotel (201). Critics tend to focus on Cosey's disavowal of Celestial as a symptom of his hypocritical nature or simply as a statement of "communal norms" (Sweeney 459). However, the novel actually underscores Cosey's attempts to bring her to visibility, and how these seem to be thwarted by the collective disapproval of the community and by L in particular. Mary Paniccia Carden observes, interestingly, the irony involved in the fact that Cosey is only willing to make public his feelings for Celestial in a posthumous way, in his will (141).

Celestial's banishment from Cosey's communal, public life is symbolised in the idea that their meetings normally take place on Cosey's boat, a fact mentioned by L at the end of the novel (Morrison 2003, 201), but anticipated as the narrative focalises Sandler Gibbon's memories about the carnivalesque boat parties hosted by Cosey for his white and wealthy friends (111). Sweeney points out that "Celestial counts only in the 'invented' and 'counterfeit world' of Cosey's infamous boat parties" (459). However, this critic also claims that Celestial is the only character that disrupts the norms of commodification and property in the novel by defying any attempt to reduce her to communal narratives (460).

Celestial in *Love*

My interest in the character, however, lies not only in the sociological depiction Morrison offers *per se* but on the textual strategies used to performatively enact Celestial's unthinkable, ungrievable nature. I would claim that Morrison's deft use of these strategies allows her to show simultaneously Celestial's invisibility and centrality to the novel. On the one hand, Morrison replicates what has traditionally been, as argued by Laura Hapke, the tendency in American fiction to "refuse to imagine the prostitute at all," or to have her "relegated to the status of a minor character" (1). On the other hand, she underscores Celestial's centrality to the text by making her the main subject of the novel's kernel event and by giving her a prominent position in the closing scene. A further piece of evidence on how Celestial haunts the narrative of *Love* was provided by Morrison herself, in an interview with Evan Solomon, where she recalls that the original title she had in mind for the novel was "The Sporting Woman" (Solomon n.p.). Given that she changed the title at her editor's suggestion, we may add the figure of the editor as an additional agent in bringing about the erasure of Celestial from the narrative.

It seems necessary, in order to assess Celestial's place within the narrative structure and plot dynamics, to identify the specific moments in which she appears explicitly in the novel. Celestial's name is mentioned for the first time on page 67, in one of the italicised sections narrated in the first person by L, a former employee at the Cosey household. The connection with Junior is made, as L claims that "something about her puts [her] in mind of a local woman [she] know[s]. Name of Celestial" (Morrison 2003, 67). Several aspects about this passage illustrate the way in which Celestial typically appears in the text: firstly, she is evoked indirectly in connection to another character, Junior.[6] The similarity between them is established and immediately denied, reinforcing L's tendency to contrast the past with the present (67). Secondly, she is referred to in the present tense. This may go unnoticed on a first reading, but turns out to be relevant as we find out later that both L and Celestial have been dead for quite some time in the diegetic present. Thirdly, the reference to Celestial is just a passing moment in L's rambling monologue as, soon after mentioning her, she turns her attention to Mr. Cosey, and then to his first wife, Julia.

Celestial is mentioned again on page 92 when Christine, Bill Cosey's granddaughter, arrives at a brothel called Manila House: "This is Celestial territory, she thought, remembering a scar-faced woman on the beach" (92). The reference to her is brief, but loaded with relevant information. It is at this point that we learn of Celestial's profession, and also of Christine's process of "social fall" after leaving the Cosey house. Additionally, the description of a "scar-faced woman" triggers a backward connection to something mentioned earlier in the text, as L, in the opening section of the novel, talked about "wild women [...] who wear scars like presidential medals" (4).

L's monologue in the chapter entitled "Benefactor" confirms that Celestial is the love of Cosey's life by pointing to how, even after marrying the 11-year-old Heed Johnson, he eventually goes back to Celestial (105). Also significant is that Celestial's clientele is said to be reduced to Cosey himself, which confirms in passing a shift in her status, from prostitute to Cosey's mistress (106). In the passage, L elaborates on Celestial's beauty, a recurrent thought whenever she is mentioned (106). Additionally, a sense of distinction is attributed to her, one which is similarly echoed in other moments of the novel (106, 111). Celestial's name is only mentioned again by old Christine and Heed in the diegetic present,

142   *Paula Martín-Salván*

as they remember hearing a man call "Hey, Celestial" to a woman in a red dress while playing on the beach as children (187–88). "Hey Celestial" becomes, we are told, their private code word (188):

> Fascinated, they tried to imagine the things she does not hesitate to do regardless of danger. They named their playhouse after her. Celestial Palace. And from then on, to say 'Amen', or to acknowledge a particularly bold, smart, risky thing, they mimicked the male voice crying 'Hey, Celestial.'
>
> (188)

The passage reinforces the constellation of textual references around Celestial, including her association to the ideas of danger and boldness, the seashore, the red colour and the scar on her face. It is through such associated lexical items that we are able to identify other moments in the text where she may be indirectly spotted, without her name ever being mentioned. Most salient in this regard is a passage, included in the narration of the relationship between Bill Cosey and his son Billy Boy, about how they helped to remove a hook from a girl's cheek, an anecdote that would explain the scar on Celestial's face (101). This is probably the time when Bill Cosey met her for the first time. L will evoke several times the image of Celestial boldly walking into the waves (106).[7] The reference to her age, moreover, resonates and retrospectively anticipates his marriage to 11-year-old Heed.

Cosey's Will as a Legal and Narrative Device

All in all, Celestial remains a fleeting, intermittent presence in the novel. Mentioned explicitly only four times, she occupies the very margin of the text and her interactions with other characters are nearly nil.[8] Her marginality may be read along sociological and narratological lines. In the socio-political canvas the novel portrays, Celestial is the subaltern. Like other "wild women" in Morrison's fiction, she is physically and symbolically displaced to the margins of social structures. As argued by Sweeney (2006) or Vega-González (283–84), Celestial corresponds, in this regard, to a "type" including Wild (*Jazz*), Pilate (*Song of Solomon*), the prostitutes from *The Bluest Eye* or even Beloved (*Beloved*) herself. From the point of view of narrative structure, the fact that she is the only character whose perspective is never offered in the text through internal focalisation makes her a most enigmatic, opaque character. It also dramatises her subaltern nature, as her story is never presented in her own terms, but always through the others' gaze on her. Read along the lines of Miranda Fricker's concept of testimonial injustice, Celestial may be said to be doubly wronged, not only intradiegetically, as her social marginalisation prevents her from participating in social and discursive practices involving Bill Cosey, but also at the discursive level, as the novel's narrative stance replicates what the story thematises: the rejection of Celestial's testimony as someone who knew Cosey intimately. Celestial is the victim of a clear "prejudicial credibility deficit" (Fricker 27) exercised both diegetically and discursively.

Harack points out, in connection to L's role as a narrator: "After all, she provides only one perspective, and when she observes Celestial's ghost sitting on Cosey's tombstone, the reader is prompted to consider what Celestial's story might have been *if she had told it herself*" (11; emphasis added). Even within the scope of L's version of the story, she is to be looked at, yet has no voice. Significantly, her narrative disenfranchisement is identified with the absence of vocality. The only time when her voice is actually mentioned in the novel calls the readers' attention to its divergence from human speech, by calling it "a sound," "a tune" and "a scream" (Morrison 2003, 106). This is symptomatic of Celestial's condition as a socially invisible subject, along the lines of Le Blanc's connection between the subject's voice and social invisibility: "the voice itself of the invisible woman or man is considered as a toneless voice" (Le Blanc 55; my translation).

Celestial would remain a marginal character (in textual and sociological terms) were it not from the way in which Cosey eventually brings her to the centre of his universe, and that of the story. This is recounted by L in a fragmentary way, scattered through her monologues. She alludes to this change in Cosey's attitude to her when, shortly after his son's death, she mentions that Bill Cosey had his silverware engraved with "hooked C's": "But if double C's were meant to mean Celestial Cosey, he was losing his mind" (Morrison 2003, 104). This already hints at Cosey's desire to make Celestial a visible presence in his life and household. It is only at the end of the novel that L confesses the contents of Cosey's 1964 testament: "They never saw the real thing—witnessed by me, notarized by Buddy Silk's wife—leaving everything to Celestial. Everything. Everything" (200). By making Celestial his legal heiress, she would have become the central figure whose visibility is constantly thwarted in the text. Cosey's intention, however, is never fulfilled, for L's confession goes further and includes her intervention in order to prevent this version of the will from leaving his other heirs, Heed and Christine, penniless (201).[9] Through L's act, Celestial is once more pushed into the margins of the story.

Sweeney, who discusses the legal conflicts featured in the novel, claims that L's intervention in forging Bill Cosey's will serves her notion of justice, placing her in the role of "rogue lawyer" (Sweeney 458). Yet, in her reading of this event, she claims that "L's interventions guarantee that May, Christine, and Heed will not be disenfranchised by virtue of their precarious status as women within patriarchal norms of property transmission" (459). Thus, Sweeney argues, "L's interventions seal Celestial's disenfranchisement" (461). The issue of how she may have

144   *Paula Martín-Salván*

been restored to the status of visible citizenship through the will and the subsequent property ownership is never considered explicitly in L's narrative, thus confirming what the text assumes as a "given": Celestial's disenfranchised, marginal and precarious status, which for the rest of the Cosey women would represent a "fall."[10] As Ho Wen-Ching observes, L's action has the effect of "underscoring the fault lines of class difference between Celestial and the Cosey women" (659). Although, as Sweeney notes, "L assumes that Celestial does not need Cosey's property and would not have respected it because she lives outside the patriarchal economy of domesticity and property transmission" (461), in fact, her actions confirm such a system by writing her out of the law and locking her out of the house (462). Bearing in mind Elisabeth Bronfen and Sarah Goodwin's question on the notion of the testament—"What kind of voice does the body have in the text, the linguistic traces, it leaves behind?" (6)—we may go back to the idea that the document establishes a prolongation of Bill Cosey's identity as the "Big Man" who had no one to stop him and could get away with anything he wanted (Morrison 2003, 133). As Elizabeth Hallam, Jenny Hockney and Glennys Howarth argue, the will as a plot device points to "the social agency of the dead as mediated through writing practices" (88). It should be mentioned, in this regard, that as the plot revolves around the issue of Bill Cosey's will, his death may be connected to the testamentary text as a mechanism through which he exerts his agency even after death. It should also be noted that L's intervention is, from this perspective, an act of usurpation of the patriarch's agency, a defiance of his authority and, perhaps, the only time he would not have his whim satisfied.

Conclusion: Celestial's Claim

In *Frames of War*, Butler introduces the idea of a "differential distribution of public grieving" (2009, 38) in order to sustain her argument that "grievability" may be perceived as an index of how societies build conceptions of citizenship based on the possibility to claim a life as a potential loss. It is from the consideration that "some lives are grievable, and others are not" (Butler 2004, xiv), that a dialectical opposition may be established between the representation of the deaths of Bill Cosey and Celestial in *Love*. While Cosey's death is publicly recognised and amplified through the funeral ritual attended by the Silk community and their later continuous grieving of him, Celestial's own death is unthinkable (because unrepresented) and, hence, ungrievable. Because she has never been acknowledged as a member of the community, we may argue, her life is not perceived as lost (Butler 2009, 15) in the novel. While Cosey's and Celestial's grievability may be said to be already operative in life, the novel underscores such differential grievability at the moment of the characters' death.

(Un-)Grieving Celestial   145

Bill Cosey's funeral features prominently in the novel. It is an event recurrently returned to in the narration, in an example of Morrison's typical spiralling "technique of suspension" (Page 33). In the different fragments narrating this event, the focus is on the fight between Heed and Christine after a twenty-four year-long separation. It is first mentioned in a passage focalising Vida Gibbons' memories of the Cosey household, on page 34 of Morrison's novel, and again on page 37, as "the dignified funeral he deserved." When it is mentioned for the second time the focus is on May's mental deterioration, and on how L tried to persuade her not to wear a military helmet to the funeral. Pages 98–99 feature a longer, detailed version of the fight over Cosey's coffin, including L's two-word intervention—"I'll tell"—which enigmatically puts a stop to the quarrel. In this passage, the idea that Cosey's funeral is a social event meant to grieve a notable member of the community is underscored by contrast: "The tacky display, the selfish disregard for rites due the deceased whom each claimed to honor, angered people" (99). The funeral becomes an occasion for the community to come together, so that Cosey's death becomes a mechanism for the reinforcement of social cohesion, threatened by Heed and Christine's confrontation. "Death," Jean-Luc Nancy claims in *The Inoperative Community*, "is indissociable from community, for it is through death that the community reveals itself—and reciprocally" (14). From this perspective, Cosey's death epitomises the idea of a community reabsorbing or sublating death itself and, by so doing, revealing itself as a community (Nancy 13–14).

All the "Cosey women" are said to have attended the funeral and are mentioned in at least one of the fragments narrating the event. All of them, except Celestial. She is never mentioned, and we do not even know whether she is alive in 1971, when Cosey is said to die. In fact, to the extent that she is only mentioned as part of other characters' memories, her status in the text is already ghostly, her emplacement indeterminate (we cannot know when and where she is). It does not really matter, we could argue, because she was never perceived as a person, citizen or member of the Silk community. Excluded from society, she remains a disavowed, inaccessible subject. Yet, her irreducible materiality (her scar, her red dress, her good looks, …) haunts the rest of characters.

As already mentioned, Celestial remains ungrieved in the novel to such a point that, even when she reappears in the very last paragraph, L (who acts as narrator in this section) does not even mention whether she is dead or alive.[11] Critics, however, tend to assume that she is dead (Bouson 372; Palladino 350; Harack 11).[12] This is the passage:

> *Her scar has disappeared. I sit near her once in a while out at the cemetery. We are the only two who visit him. She is offended by the words on the tombstone and, legs crossed, sits perched on its top so*

146   *Paula Martín-Salván*

> *the folds of her red dress hide the insult: "Ideal Husband. Perfect Father". Other than that, she seems content.*
>
> (201; original emphasis)

How do we know, then, that she is dead, and therefore ungrieved? I would claim that the recurrent textual signs evince her status: first, the fact that her scar has disappeared, suggesting an afterlife, without traces of bodily wounds. Then, the fact that she is still wearing the (already iconic) red dress she was mentioned to wear on the beach the day Heed and Christine first saw her.

A further note may be added on the differential distribution of grieving in the novel, as there seems to be a clear asymmetry in the deceased characters' afterlife existence. While Cosey remains voiceless, disembodied, brought back to life through a sort of prosopopoeia, and in the ghostly haunting on the living from his (Dorian Gray-like) portrait, Celestial seems to be an embodied ghost, one who is able to perch on Cosey's tomb, to cover the stone's words with her dress and to sing. Celestial's ghostly reappearance at the end of the novel, of course, features as a motif that fits into Morrison's *oeuvre*. The host of (mostly female) ghosts, led by Beloved, would easily accommodate her. As Brian Norman argues, "[i]n the American literary tradition of dead women talking, such women demand much more than commemoration on the part of the living. The intervention they demand is what they were denied in life: social justice" (3). This is indeed the case of Celestial, I would claim, as she may be identified as a victim of testimonial injustice (Fricker 7), to the extent that she has been consistently barred from the social rituals around Cosey's death. Hence, her presence in the last pages of the novel does not seem to respond to a need to be grieved, remembered or commemorated by the community that ignored her in life. Celestial does not haunt the community in search of recognition, in an attempt to be grieved and, thus, apprehended as someone who lived. Rather, the passage suggests a vindication to partake in the mourning and grieving of others.

In the final paragraph of the novel, both Celestial and L are said to acquire a degree of "vocality."[13] Celestial "sings to him. One of those down-home, raunchy songs that used to corrupt everybody on the dance floor" (Morrison 2003, 201–202). The song sung by Celestial, which L joins by humming, may represent a last act of claiming for herself what the Silk community refused her in life: the right to mourn her lifelong companion as her own. This act of appropriation is further confirmed by the physical act of sitting on his tombstone mentioned above, as the lyrics of the song are a call to return to her: "Come on back, baby. Take me by the hand" (202). Cosey has been sublated, absorbed by the communal tissue of Silk through the stories about him. Therefore, Celestial's "appeal for a posthumous form of citizenship" (Norman 1) does not involve a claim to be grieved by the community, but the claim to grieve

(Un-)Grieving Celestial   147

her beloved, to claim him as her own.[14] It is the reparation of the testimonial injustice she has suffered that may be said to be at stake here. L's identification of her song, and the fact she joins her, may be regarded as an act of recognition of Celestial's claim, a reparation for the way in which her voice, her story, had been previously silenced.

Through her, Morrison comes to question the social dynamics established around the grieving of Cosey's death, in terms close to those expressed by Judith Butler: "which social arrangements can be recognized as legitimate love, and which human losses can be explicitly grieved as real and consequential loss?" (2000, 24). Celestial thus emerges at the end of the novel as an Antigone-like figure. Like Antigone in Hegel's reading, as recalled by Butler, she is "an outside without which the polis could not be" (2000, 4). She remains outside the social body constituted by the community of Silk, and her grieving does not partake of customary rituals. Yet, her greatest act of defiance and vindication is her claim to grieve her lover.

Notes

1 The novel's structure works as a critical reflection on the idea of Bill Cosey as "referential core" of the novel, the "protagonist, who stands at the center of the text's symbolic structure" (Woloch 18). This in turn formally articulates the interrogation of Cosey's centrality in the female characters' lives at the thematic level. The novel's conclusion points to the missed opportunity in Heed and Christine's lives, in terms that seem to address both the formal and the thematic structure of the text (Morrison 2003, 189).

2 On the notion of secondary or minor characters and the distribution of character-space in fiction, see Woloch.

3 Christina Sharpe's *In the Wake* (2016) and Achille Mbembe's *Necropolitics* (2019) may be mentioned as relevant theoretical takes on the issue of grievability and race. Work that specifically addresses issues of grievability and mourning in a contemporary African American context includes Henry A. Giroux (2006) and Lisa M. Perhamus and Clarence W. Joldersma (2016). As Perhamus and Joldersma argue, discussion of African American public mourning as protest goes as far back as W.E.B. Du Bois' references to "sorrow songs" in *The Souls of Black Folks* (1903).

4 On the use of the term "scopophilia," see Mulvey.

5 The figure of the prostitute may be regarded as illustrative of the two mechanisms for the representation of social death established by Patterson: the "intrusive" one, whereby the individual is identified as the "enemy within" (39), which corresponds to the figure of the captured slave-prisoner of war; and the "extrusive" mechanism that categorises the individual as "one who ceased to belong and had been expelled from normal participation in the community because of a failure to meet certain minimal legal or socioeconomic norms of behavior" (41). Morrison does not specify the process whereby Celestial's social death has come to be represented, but she has L describe how she conducts her business "in such a quiet, reserved way you would have thought she was a Red Cross nurse" (Morrison 2003, 106). Such a view of Celestial as a social outcast turned into a figure of mercy and assistance to the community may connect her to one of the most celebrated "socially dead"

148 *Paula Martín-Salván*

characters in US literature, Hester Prynne, and the way she is depicted in *The Scarlet Letter*: "Her breast, with its badge of shame, was but the softer pillow for the head that needed one. She was a self-ordained Sister of Mercy" (Hawthorne 152). Both characters are presented as carrying themselves with a greater dignity and attitude of service to the community, while paradoxically being identified by such community as morally deficient.

6 The connection between Junior and Celestial is also noticed by Heed herself when Junior winks at her on one occasion and this triggers the memory of the time when she and Christine first saw her on the beach, and Celestial winked at them (this moment is recalled on page 188): "She winked, startling Heed into a momentary recall of something just out of reach, like a shell snatched away by a wave" (Morrison 2003, 27).

7 L mentions later how their encounters would normally take place on a boat owned by Cosey (Morrison 2003, 201), thus emphasising the idea of Celestial's removal from his landed property.

8 Were we to apply Franco Moretti's character network theory to Morrison's *Love*, Celestial would emerge as a relatively peripheral dot in an otherwise densely interwoven network of characters' interactions. Her only connecting lines would indeed be to Bill Cosey, L, Heed and Christine. Yet, without her, much of the plot would be lost, thus bringing to our attention the relevance of the distinction between a character's centrality in a character network and the stability it may provide to the network (Moretti 222).

9 It is most significant, I would claim, that L's understanding of the testament is not the result of an act of love towards Celestial but rather of revenge against his relatives: "his hatred of the women in his house had no level" (Morrison 2003, 201).

10 L's intervention therefore thwarts the possibility for Celestial to "fall up," a term used by Nina Auerbach to describe the kind of plot in which prostitution works as a step in social climbing, towards respectable marriage and social position (Auerbach 158).

11 Palladino (2012, 350) claims that the passage is ambiguous and may actually refer either to Celestial or to Heed. She argues, in fact, that it is such ambiguity which confirms the perceived identification between both characters: "In the final italicised section, narrated by L, Heed and Celestial almost conflate into one ghost [...]. Unquestionably mirroring each other, at this stage they are indistinguishable" (350–51).

12 In Bouson's reading of the character, Celestial comes to life through Junior, as she arrives into the Coseys' Monarch Street house to work as Heed's secretary. Bouson points to how Junior becomes an embodied mediator for the ghostly relationship between Cosey and Celestial—along the lines of the character dynamics of Henry James' *A Turn of the Screw*—and refers to her as Junior-Celestial. Cosey seems to look at her and talk to her from his portrait, which Junior becomes enthralled about (Bouson 2008, 369) as she feels that the portrait is summoning her to his presence (156).

13 See Wallace (382), on the musical character of Celestial's voice and the call-and-response structure of her enunciation, to which L is drawn.

14 In other words, it is a claim to occupy the position of bride that she has been denied in life. On the bride-death connection, see Bronfen.

Works Cited

Auerbach, Nina. *Woman and the Demon. The Life of a Victorian Myth*. Cambridge, MA: Harvard UP, 1982.

Bouson, J. Brooks. "Uncovering 'the Beloved' in the Warring and Lawless Women in Toni Morrison's *Love*." *The Midwest Quarterly* 49.4 (2008): 358–73.

Bronfen, Elisabeth. *Over her Dead Body. Death, Femininity and the Aesthetic*. Manchester: Manchester UP, 1992.

Bronfen, Elisabeth, and Sarah Goodwin. *Death and Representation*. Durham: Duke UP, 1993.

Butler, Judith. *The Psychic Life of Power. Theories in Subjection*. Stanford, CA: Stanford UP, 1997.

———. *Antigone's Claim. Kinship between Life and Death*. New York: Columbia UP, 2000.

———. *Precarious Life. The Powers of Mourning and Violence*. New York: Verso, 2004.

———. *Frames of War. When Is Life Grievable?* New York: Verso, 2009.

———. *The Force of Non-Violence*. New York: Verso, 2020.

Carden, Mary Paniccia. "'Trying to Find a Place When the Streets Don't Go There': Fatherhood, Family, and American Racial Politics in Toni Morrison's *Love*." *African American Review* 44.1/2 (2011): 131–47.

Davidson, Julia O'Connell. *Prostitution, Power and Freedom*. 1998. London: Wiley, 2013.

———. "'Does She Do Queening?' Prostitution, Sovereignty and Community." 1997. *Reclaiming Sovereignty*. Eds Laura Brace and John Hoffman. London: Bloomsbury, 2016. 171–87.

Du Bois, W.E.B. *The Souls of Black Folks*. 1903. Harmondsworth: Penguin Classics, 1996.

Fricker, Miranda. *Epistemic Injustice. Power and the Ethics of Knowing*. Oxford: Oxford UP, 2007.

Gillan, Jennifer. "Focusing on the Wrong Front: Historical Displacement, the Maginot Line, and *The Bluest Eye*." *African American Review* 36.2 (2002): 283–98.

Giroux, Henry A. *Stormy Weather: Katrina and the Politics of Disposability*. New York: Routledge, 2007.

Hallam Elizabeth, Jenny Hockney, and Glennys Howarth. *Beyond the Body: Death and Social Identity*. London and New York: Routledge, 1999.

Hapke, Laura. *Girls Who Went Wrong: Prostitutes in American Fiction, 1885–1917*. Madison: Popular P, 1989.

Harack, Katrina. "'Not Even in the Language They Had Invented for Secrets': Trauma, Memory, and Re-Witnessing in Toni Morrison's *Love*." *The Mississippi Quarterly* 66.2 (2013): 255–78.

Hawthorne, Nathaniel. *The Scarlet Letter*. 1850. London: Penguin, 2012.

Humann, Heather Duerre. "Family and Violence in *Love*." *Women's Studies* 43 (2014): 246–62.

Le Blanc, Guillaume. *L'invisibilité sociale*. Paris: Presses Universitaires de France, 2009.

Mbembe, Achille. *Necropolitics*. 2016. Durham, NC: Duke UP, 2019.

Mellard, James M. "'Families Make the Best Enemies': Paradoxes of Narcissistic Identification in Toni Morrison's *Love*." *African American Review* 43.4 (2009): 699–712.

Moretti, Franco. *Distant Reading*. London and New York: Verso, 2013.

Morrison, Toni. *The Bluest Eye*. New York: Holt, 1970.

———. *Song of Solomon*. New York: Alfred A. Knopf, 1977.

———. *Jazz*. New York: Alfred A. Knopf, 1992.

———. *Beloved*. New York: Alfred A. Knopf, 1997.

———. *Love*. New York: Vintage, 2003.

Mulvey, Laura. "Visual Pleasure and Narrative Cinema." 1975. *Film Theory and Criticism: Introductory Readings*. Eds Leo Braudy and Marshall Cohen. New York: Oxford UP, 1999. 833–44.

Nancy, Jean-Luc. *The Inoperative Community*. Ed. Peter Connor. Minneapolis: U of Minnesota P, 1991.

Norman, Brian. *Dead Women Talking. Figures of Injustice in American Literature*. Baltimore, MD: Johns Hopkins UP, 2013.

O'Connor, Anne-Marie. "*Love* and the Outlaw Women." *Los Angeles Times*, 15 October 2003. Accessed on 9 December 2021 at: https://www.latimes.com/archives/la-xpm-2003-oct-15-et-oconnor15-story.html/.

Page, Philip. *Dangerous Freedom: Fusion and Fragmentation in Toni Morrison's Novels*. Jackson: UP of Mississippi, 1995.

Palladino, Mariangela. "Aphrodite's Faces: Toni Morrison's *Love* and Ethics." *Modern Fiction Studies* 58.2 (2012): 334–52.

Patterson, Orlando. *Slavery and Social Death. A Comparative Study*. 1982. Cambridge, MA: Harvard UP, 2018.

Perhamus, Lisa, and Clarence W. Joldersma. "Interpellating Dispossession: Distributions of Vulnerability and the Politics of Grieving in the Precarious Mattering of Lives." *Philosophical Studies in Education* 47 (2016): 56–67.

Roynon, Tessa. "A New 'Romen' Empire: Toni Morrison's *Love* and the Classics." *Journal of American Studies* 41.1 (2007): 31–47.

Sharpe, Christina. *In the Wake. On Blackness and Being*. Durham, NC: Duke UP, 2016.

Solomon, Evan. "The Toni Morrison Interview." *Word. The Soul of Urban Culture*, 27 March 2016. Reprinted from CBC News World on 18 November 2003. Accessed on 9 December 2021 at: http://wordmag.com/the-toni-morrison-interview/.

Sweeney, Megan. "Commensurability, Commodification, Crime, and Justice in Toni Morrison's Later Fiction." *Modern Fiction Studies* 52.2 (2006): 440–69.

Vega-González, Susana. "Toni Morrison's *Love* and the Trickster Paradigm." *Revista Alicantina de Estudios Ingleses* 18 (2005): 275–89.

Wallace, Cynthia R. "L as Language: *Love* and Ethics." *African American Review* 47.2/3 (2014): 375–90.

Warhol, Robyn R. "Neonarrative; or, How to Render the Unnarratable in Realist Fiction and Contemporary Film." *A Companion to Narrative Theory*. Eds James Phelan and Peter J. Rabinowitz. Malden, MA: Blackwell, 2005. 220–31.

Wen-Ching, Ho. "'I'll Tell'—The Function and Meaning of L in Toni Morrison's *Love*." *EurAmerica* 36.4 (2006): 651–75.

Winterson, Jeanette. *Written on the Body*. London: Jonathan Cape, 1992.

Woloch, Alex. *The One vs. the Many: Minor Characters and the Space of the Protagonist in the Novel*. Princeton, NJ: Princeton UP, 2009.

Part IV

Contamination

8 What Remains of (Un-)Grievability in Hollinghurst's and Tóibín's AIDS Fiction

José M. Yebra

Introduction

The outburst of AIDS in the 1980s constituted a mass traumatic event, especially for gay men and other disenfranchised groups. Indeed, for Susan Sontag, the disease was grander than a metaphor, "an invader" (106) and "a construction" (109), becoming a sort of homophobic dystopian fantasy. In *The Burning Library: Writings on Art, Literature and Sexuality 1969–1993*, Edmund White addressed it as a climactic narrative closing in an anti-climactic aftermath: "To have been oppressed in the fifties, freed in the sixties, exalted in the seventies, and wiped out in the eighties is a quick itinerary for a whole culture to follow. For we are witnessing not just the death of individuals but a menace to an entire culture" (151). Simon Watney, in *Practices of Freedom: Selected Writings on HIV/AIDS* (1994), also recalled the spectacularisation of this collective trauma, though adding ethical undertones: "The spectacle of AIDS calmly and constantly entertains the possible prospect of death of all Western European and American gay men from AIDS […] without the slightest flicker of concern, regret, or grief" (58). In other words, it is not only that, using Butler's terminology, the lives of these diseased men do not "qualify as a life and [are] not worth a note" (2004, 34) but also that the spectacle of their prospective departure resides in its "purifying" ungrievability.

AIDS was the symptom of an undercurrent violence that sexual dissidents have systematically suffered. They were blamed for being actively responsible for their own fate: "The press divided people living with HIV into the 'guilty'—those thought to have brought HIV infection upon themselves, like gay men—and 'innocent victims' like those with haemophilia who were infected with HIV from donated blood" (Catalan n.p.; original emphasis). As perpetrators of (self)infection and death, gays were rendered ungrievable. Hence, their scars did not turn them into vulnerable victims but marked them as disenfranchised. The infected challenged biopolitics because their bodies could not be disciplined and controlled to meet socio-political regulation of life. They often became living dead, rejected not only in biopolitical terms but, in many cases, by

DOI: 10.4324/9781003347811-13

154   *José M. Yebra*

their own families. This only accelerated the process of marginalisation of sexual dissidents and drug-injecting users. Threatened by AIDS, they were literally ungrievable for normative institutions such as the family and the state and more dependent than ever on alternative families and subsidiary networks (D'Emilio). In this sense, Butler's words on those whose life is not worth living are very relevant: "They cannot be mourned because they are always already lost or, rather, never 'were,' and they must be killed, since they seem to live on, stubbornly, in this state of deadness. Violence renews itself in the face of the apparent inexhaustibility of its object" (2004, 33–34). It is for these reasons that some media, politicians and religious leaders spectacularised the AIDS crisis as unthinkable and ungrievable. Gay annihilation was allegedly a "purifying" event, one that eliminated dissidence, difference and death from a pretended normalcy.

All the above leads to the main contention of this chapter, namely, that gay fiction has diversely reacted to this homophobic fantasy of ungrievability. It is not my purpose to systematise the multiple reactions to this mass trauma especially when, as White points out, "gay literature [wa]s healthy and flourishing as never before" (1991, 35) during the 1980s. This chapter will focus instead on what remains in the texts after loss, especially when the actual impact of AIDS recedes and yet the dystopian effects and discourse are still evident. To illustrate my point, I will make reference to two novels that respond in quite different terms to the homophobic fantasies of the 1980s: Alan Hollinghurst's *The Line of Beauty* (2004) and Colm Tóibín's *The Blackwater Lightship* (1999). In Hollinghurst's novel, what remains is the elegiac testimony of the narrator recalling oversexualised bodies and lifestyles before the AIDS outburst. There is thus a melancholic identification with (and attachment to) the departed, which problematises actual grievability. By contrast, in *The Blackwater Lightship*, the protagonist's diseased body is de-sexualised and overtly mourned in Catholic Ireland. By de-spectacularising AIDS, the novel recasts Catholic redemption, sanctions grievability and paves the way for a socio-cultural change on sexual dissidence. Gust A. Yep's analysis of loss and its remains in the context of AIDS (2007) is quite revealing to understand the complex elegiac discourse of both novels. Quoting the words of David L. Eng and David Kazanjian, Yep explores the inextricable connection between loss and what remains: "We might say that as soon as the question 'What is lost?' is posed, it invariably slips into the question 'What remains?' That is, loss is inseparable from what remains, for what is lost is known only by what remains of it, by how these remains are produced, read, and sustained" (quoted in Yep, 683). To answer these questions, Yep explores how viewers of the docufilm *Common Threads* (on the Quilt of Names of AIDS victims displayed in Washington) are confronted with different types of remains: "the AIDS body and the sexuality of such bodies" (686); "spatial remains," especially "large gay meccas" (689) and "the uniqueness of the individual and the ideal of justice, activism, and affective life" (691). This chapter explores which of these types of remains are addressed in Hollinghurst's and Tóibín's novels.

The Line of Beauty as Melancholic Elegy

Hollinghurst's Booker Prize winner *The Line of Beauty* revisits the AIDS London of the 1980s that his first novel, *The Swimming-pool Library* (1988), portrayed in real time. *The Line of Beauty* is not simply a return, though, because it continues where *The Swimming-pool Library* ended and works through previously unresolved traumata. Will Beckwith, the protagonist of *The Swimming-pool Library*, was originally to die of the disease and write his story while very ill, as Hollinghurst has confessed in an interview (Canning 337). However, the novel recalls his promiscuous lifestyle (Hollinghurst 1998, 3), before allegedly getting ill. Beckwith's first-person narration renders an oversexualised approach of the gay community, one of mechanical sex and anonymous sexual encounters in saunas, discos and clubs. In this sense, *The Swimming-pool Library* addresses gay bodies in the early-AIDS years as full of life, enjoying— in Yep's terms (688)—the possibilities of gay meccas and challenging the classic images of ravaged bodies waiting for death in the popular imagination. In any case, AIDS works as a turning point that splits the novel in specular terms whereby this oversexualised gay underworld is about to be lost and doubly replaced. At first, the novel announces a prospective world where diseased bodies and corpses are ungrieved because they are ungrievable. When Will enters a gay porn cinema he cannot recognise the prognostic scene (before the porn film itself) in which an ant-eater's "freakishly extensile tongue come[s] flicking towards us, cleaning the fleeing termites off the wall" (Hollinghurst 1998, 48). The protagonist can only feel threatened and thrilled by the metaphor of dying gays/termites. Gays are animalised and rendered disposable and therefore deserving no human value. Likewise, in terms possibly evocative of Holocaust victims in gas chambers, Will witnesses how gay men at the gym "queu[e] for the hair dryer and cloud the air with Trouble for Men, with a kind of foreboding, as an exotic species menaced by brutal predators" (223). The fact that these men willingly enter their death scenarios perversely suggests what homophobic fantasies do, namely, gays giving in to their ungrievable deaths. Despite Will's overt sexuality and privileged status, his narration is what actually remains, as a testimony of a bygone period. In other words, *The Swimming-pool Library* renders some elegiac omens valid as long as Will's oversexualised scenario is operative in "the last summer of its kind there was ever to be" (3). Eventually, however, this gay underworld is replaced and sublimated by Charles Nantwich's pre-gay world and testimony. Will's *alter ego*,

156   *José M. Yebra*

Charles, is an old aristocrat who, after their accidental encounter, asks the youth to write his biography. In reading Nantwich's nostalgic diaries, Beckwith recalls same-sex desire in colonial Sudan and post-WWI London through the old man's several lives (129). Charles's testimony is an extended elegy where he mourns idealised homoerotic friendships, especially with non-whites and marginal men. Taha, his Sudanese servant, is delicate and elegant (206), and of Webster, his first black lover, he recalls "his colour, among the trees, the green water & the faded grass [which] struck me [Charles] like a Gauguin" (113). He even idealises and finds redemption in his Wildean downfall when he is imprisoned for gross indecency in the 1950s, paradoxically by Will's grandfather. The scene in which Lord Beckwith proudly witnesses Charles going down (260) is the prelude to the latter's embracing of gay liberation in prison. Henceforth, Charles attempts to recall an ideal homoerotic scenario getting acquainted and allegedly favouring marginal men from Africa or jail. His pre-gay underworld is thus a melancholic sign of its own absence because his elegiac discourse reveals his idea of a same-sex idyll that never existed and thus cannot be grieved.

The elegiac is a continuum in homoerotic and homosexual literature (Guy-Bray 205–207) and in Hollinghurst's in particular. In Guy-Bray's words, an elegy is

> a poetic response to the death of a greatly loved person. The typical elegy contains a lament and a celebration of the dead person and ends with the poet finding consolation in the contemplation of something that is considered to be more important than the life or death of any one person
>
> (205)

The genre, which was commonplace in homoerotic and homosexual writing until the late nineteenth century, was revalued as a consequence of the AIDS pandemic (207). In being seriously threatened with extinction, gay and queer literatures have updated elegy to conjure up grievability and neutralise mainstream homophobic fantasies. As long as the elegiac voice addresses those to whom, as Butler argues, governments and *de facto* power deny grievability (2009, 39), elegy constitutes a counter-narrative, especially when it comes to sexual dissidence. The Quilt of Names of AIDS victims, which Yep refers to, is a case in point. As a reaction to mass death,

> in the initial years of the AIDS crisis in the US, the public vigils, and the Names Project broke through the public shame associated with dying from AIDS, a shame associated sometimes with homosexuality, and especially anal sex, and sometimes with drugs and promiscuity. It meant something to state and show the name, to

put together some remnants of a life, to publicly display and avow the loss.

(Butler 2009, 39)

The Names Project and public vigils constitute mass-scale elegiac events. If the classic elegiac poet finds personal consolation in something that transcends his beloved and the liminal space between life and death he inhabits, elegy is especially complex when a whole culture is under threat and loss seems to overcome any remnants.

The Line of Beauty is what remains after (a melancholic aftermath to) the prospective departure of Will Beckwith and his peers as part of a homophobic agenda of ungrievability. Indeed, *The Line of Beauty* establishes a complex relationship with *The Swimming-pool Library*, one which recalls the duality grief-grievability in Butler's *The Force of Non Violence* (2020). In Butler's view, "there is a difference between someone being grieved and that same person's bearing, in their living being, a characteristic of grievability. The second involves the conditional tense: those who are grievable *would* be mourned if their lives *were* lost; the ungrievable are those whose loss would leave no trace, or perhaps barely a trace" (Butler 2020, 74–75). It is a question of perspective between factuality and potentiality; *The Line of Beauty* grieves *The Swimming-pool Library* in recalling the same decade, the 1980s, and the same traumata, namely AIDS mass extinction. When so many gays die, the most privileged, such as Will and Charles, are given a voice because they are grievable for the sake of their peers. In any case, they eventually come to understand their vulnerability and grievability as personal and generational, something that the protagonist of *The Line of Beauty* only does far too late.

Nick Guest, a naïve guy down from Oxford, lives at his upper-class friend Toby Fedden's house for unknown reasons while he writes his PhD on Henry James. Ashamed of his middle-class family, Nick falls in love with the Feddens, for whom he plays the role of aesthete and "perfect courtier" (Hollinghurst 2004, 121). The fact that *The Line of Beauty* was published in 2004, but is set in the 1980s, allows Hollinghurst to explore the AIDS trauma more overtly than *The Swimming-pool Library*. Like Will Beckwith, Nick still focuses on an oversexualised gay London and its abrupt end. In coming back to the 1980s, *The Line of Beauty* revisits Thatcher's neoliberal and homophobic politics and hence grieves those whom *The Swimming-pool Library* could not. Hollinghurst's debut novel is about memory, Will coming to terms not only with the end of his generation but with the stories that came before and that made "the tragic queer" (Woods 229–38) recurrent along the twentieth century. When *The Line of Beauty* returns to the 1980s, the tone is elegiac yet again: Nick mourns his two lovers, who die of AIDS, although he fails to see his tragic error or *hamartia* (Yebra 2011). He

158   *José M. Yebra*

thinks that beauty is grievable and can conceal the ultraconservative ideology of Thatcher and the Feddens. As the family aesthete, Nick feels so protected that he cannot recognise his otherness and foresee his eventual ungrievability. His first encounter with his lodgers' house is very revealing:

> He loved letting himself in at the three-locked green front door, and locking it again behind him, and feeling the still security of the house as he looked into the red-walled dining room. [... He admired] the pictures, the porcelain, the curvy French furniture so different from what he'd been brought up with. [...] Like his hero Henry James, Nick felt that he could stand a great deal of gilt.
> (Hollinghurst 2004, 6)

Nick's surname reveals he does not belong: he can only be a guest, a sycophant begging for attention from those he admires and envies. For the Feddens, he is an outsider, unworthy of real attention, evolving in response to their needs: "a friend, pet, factotum, errand boy, and finally scapegoat" (Marcus 182). In other words, he is misrecognised and deprived of true attention: his insignificance explains his confinement in "the children's zone" (Hollinghurst 2004, 4) at the Feddens'; as for his gayness, it is ignored and/or sublimated in and through art. When Nick chooses the Feddens and Thatcherism, he essentially misrecognises himself as who he "really" is, a middle-class gay youth in the era of AIDS. His life, contrary to what he believes, is "not conceivable as [a life] within certain epistemological frames" (Butler 2009, 1) such as neoliberal conservatism. In this sense, his life is "never lived nor lost in the full sense" (1) as long as he cannot discern it from aesthetics. His misrecognition of himself as other and his imperfect consideration of the other turn out to be fatal as his aesthetic fantasy is replaced by a homophobic dystopia, the fantasy of ungrievability mentioned in the introduction. That is, concerning the bodily, sexual and geographical remains after loss addressed by Yep, Hollinghurst's novels recall the ambivalence between sexuality and the memory of liberation and the actual effects of the disease; in other words, the ambivalence between loss and its remains that elegies have always represented. Oversexualisation, gay meccas and bodies in large cities are enjoyed and lost by Will and Nantwich and newly again by Nick.

The Swimming-pool Library grieves the end of an idealised world, which announces a prospective dystopia in retrospect. The elegiac in *The Line of Beauty* is more disturbing, "perhaps [because] it is less about attempts to heal and salve, and more about rupture" (Perry and Iggulden n.p.). In other words, Nick does not invest so much in overcoming the death of the beloved other(s)—as is the case of classic elegies—as he does in grieving his delusive representation of himself. This is patent in

What Remains of (Un-)Grievability   159

the way he refers to his lovers' deaths as a consequence of AIDS and his own downfall. Leo just disappears and Nick can only regret his demise through an intertextual reference to Henry James's words on Poe's death *"The extremity of personal absence had just overtaken him"* (Hollinghurst 2004, 411; emphasis added), which Leo's mother cannot understand. However, the sentence gains meaning when Nick thinks of his own loss and what will remain of him: "The words, which once sounded arch and even facetious, were suddenly terrible to him, capacious, wise, and hard. [... T]hen he saw himself in six months' time perhaps, sitting down to write a similar letter to the denizens of Lowndes Square" (411). Like Leo's, Wani's beauty also fades. He is initially modelled after Hogarth's Line of Beauty (hence the title): "He [Nick] didn't think that Hogarth had illustrated this best example of it, the dip and swell [of Wani]" (200). Likewise, Catherine Fedden reduces Wani's body, following Hogarth, to "a few curves, cheekbones, lips, lashes, heavily inked squiggles of hair" (348). Thus, the transformation of Wani when he gets ill is paradigmatic of what remains after the loss caused by AIDS: "He commanded attention now by pity and respect as he had once had by beauty and charm" (431). Although Leo is dead and Wani only provokes "a cringing smile of condolence" (431) in those he previously thrilled, Nick breaks away from their loss and clings to the remains of beauty, especially his memories and the aesthetic projects he developed with them. However, it is especially in his beauty fantasy with the Feddens that Nick relies for post-AIDS survival. Art, the line of male beauty and gay meccas do not last long, though. James Wood insightfully refers to the collapse of Nick's delusive world:

> Everything unravels, as we knew it would. Leo dies of AIDS, and Wani is now deadly ill; his parents continue to maintain that he caught it from a lavatory seat. Gerald Fedden narrowly retains his parliamentary position in the general election of 1987. But he is soon investigated for financial irregularities. The baying press, now camped outside his Notting Hill mansion, discovers that his lodger, one Nick Guest, is the lover of Wani Ouradi, the son of the supermarket millionaire and Tory Party donor. Gerald is finished as soon as this story is revealed, and the Feddens turn on Nick, who has kept, it seems, so much from them.
>
> (2004, 49)

Nick eventually fails to protect himself as well. He qualifies as a life worth living and grieving, or so he thinks, until what has remained hidden—his homosexuality, Fedden's business and AIDS—unravels, as Wood points out (49). When tabloids recall the scandal at the Feddens', "Gay Sex Link to Minister's House" (Hollinghurst 2004, 469) being one of the headlines, the protagonist's delusive fantasy comes to an end.

160   *José M. Yebra*

As soon as the scandal comes out, the protagonist is not only expelled but misrecognised by those he considered his loyal friends. Gerald Fedden makes it particularly clear in their last encounter. His so-far covert homophobia erupts, denying Nick his elegiac wish-fulfilment fantasy: "It is an old homo trick. You can't have a family, so you attach yourself to someone else's. [...] Who are you? What the fucking are you doing here?" (482). Nick cannot still understand the rules of the game and cannot come to terms with his withdrawal. Likewise, it is only too late that he recognises that (Henry James's) aestheticism is not enough to grieve his multiple losses (from his lovers, to his family and the Feddens), which derives in melancholia.

Unlike classic elegies, which mourn the dead lover, Nick ultimately grieves himself in narcissistic terms. In this sense, *The Line of Beauty* plays with the stereotype of gayness as an excess of sameness, a desire for the same instead of the other. The protagonist is unable to grieve actual death because he can only grieve his own conception of beauty (Yebra 2011). In other words, his narcissism is extreme because he paradoxically does not pity himself as much as he pities his delusive conception of himself. Almost at the end of the novel, he looks back on the past in terms of loss: "It was a sort of terror, made up of emotions from *every stage of his short life, weaning, homesickness, envy and self-pity*, but he felt that the self-pity belonged to a larger pity" (Hollinghurst 2004, 501; emphasis added). In the first three stages Nick still addresses his complex cathexes with his mother (weaning), his background (homesickness) and the Feddens (envy). All of them imply a process of disassociation from the other. However, it is in his last narcissistic stage, which overcomes the previous ones, that the protagonist fully disassociates from himself, for he witnesses his own disgrace and prospective death. When he is traumatically expelled by the Feddens, accused of envy and revenge as a "gay parasite" (481), his beauty fantasy comes to an end and Nick falls into a larger pity or melancholia because, as mentioned above, he is unable to cope with loss. Using Freud's words, it can be argued that Nick "knows whom he has lost but not what he has lost in him" (245). In other words, the protagonist cannot come to terms with himself if it is not through the other.

Nick's hamartia cannot be addressed from normal mourning, as happens in elegy. In it, the ego mourns the lost object in order to overcome the loss itself. However, in cases of melancholia, there is "an extraordinary diminution in [one's] self-regard, an impoverishment of his ego on a grand scale" (Freud 244). That is why, Freud argues, melancholic egos rely on self-punishment rather than on assuming the loss of the other. However, this self-hatred derived from the loss of the object-choice conceals a much more complex process. The melancholic overidentifies with his object-choice, which would imply an object cathexis and self-sadism that would conceal an extreme narcissism, "an immense ego self-love"

(Freud 252). Unlike the straightforward pain for the lost beloved one experienced in mourning and expressed in manifestations of it such as elegy, in melancholia there is an ambivalent "struggle over the object" which is intimately and traumatically linked with the ego and unconsciously comes back. Nick Guest's object-choice is an idealisation of beauty that he systematises in Hogarth's Line of Beauty, Henry James's convoluted discourse and the opulence and manners of the Feddens (Yebra 2011). In repressing his original libidinal sources, coinciding with the first two stages of his life, he starts a melancholic process, feeling envy for those he admires (especially the Feddens) and self-pitying or tormenting himself even before the apparent loss takes place. In other words, his being expelled from the Feddens' and everything they represent is a mere performance of the actual loss, which takes place as soon as he enters their house and narcissistically rejects his former self.

What remains after Nick's downfall and the novel's return to the 1980s, gay oversexualisation and the homophobia resulting from AIDS, is a "fake" elegy. He does not mourn those who died and suffered the ungrievability of a perverse regime. Instead, *The Line of Beauty* (or rather, the lie of beauty) reveals the perils of accepting a wish-fulfilment fantasy of make-believe and eventual extinction. When Nick assumes a sentimental discourse whereby his narcissistic self-pity belongs to a larger pity, he implicitly acknowledges the ambivalence of melancholia: in being disempowered, his "'self is exuberantly discarded' and there occurs 'the terrifying appeal of a loss of the ego, of a self-abasement'" (Dollimore 303). However, (Nick's) fantasy of dissolution resulting from loss is no longer a "struggle to redeem or transcend it" (Dollimore 305). The novel addresses and warns against this ambivalence, the twofold fantasy between self-abasement and transcendence, which recalls and rebuffs Yep's "uniqueness of the individual." Indeed, the hero's self-indulgence develops into acquiescence with sentimentalism and power, which only justifies the act of "purifying" ungrievability of sexual dissidents like himself.

The Blackwater Lightship as Redemptive Elegy

The excess and spectacularisation of gay sexuality, corporeality, death and ungrievability in Hollinghurst's *The Line of Beauty* (and *The Swimming-pool Library*) contrast with the de-sexualised/spectacularised account of gayness and death in *The Blackwater Lightship*. Thus, Tóibín's novel is *a priori* in line with the classic iconography of the AIDS-infected body as "desexualized" (Yep 694), "ravaged, disfigured and debilitated by the syndrome" (686). Declan Devereux, the protagonist, is a gay man who returns home very ill with AIDS. Once there, he confesses and recalls his coming to terms with his sexuality abroad: "we did things in France that we didn't do in Ireland" (Tóibín 1999,

162 *José M. Yebra*

167). Back in rural Ireland, he can only remember those times of "pure happiness" (167) now that he has become a living corpse. Sexuality (especially of the dissident type) is identified and placed elsewhere, not in Ireland, which apparently remains stuck in time along *The Blackwater Lightship*. Or so it seems at first sight because, for authors such as Eibhear Walshe, the country has been adjusting its traditions—its Catholic culture in particular—to accommodate new ideas and lifestyles. In Walshe's view, Tóibín's own process of coming-out mirrors the evolution of Ireland, more specifically the way in which same-sex desire has "made its way out" ("'This Particular Genie'" 116). Likewise, *The Blackwater Lightship*, especially Declan's deadly body, constitutes first an elegiac instrument and later a galvaniser of change and redemption.

Unlike classic elegies, *The Blackwater Lightship* mourns Declan while he is agonising. Moreover, instead of the lover who laments the beloved's death (or agony), Declan's prospective loss is grieved by his friends and family, namely, by his sister Helen, their mother Lily and their grandmother Dora. However, when they all meet around Declan at Dora's, the house, like his body, is unfathomable. In fact, Helen feels her grandmother's house "was gone. She pictured the house empty and ghostly" (Tóibín 1999, 118). Although Declan looks forward to a final reconciliation of the women in the family, scars are too deep to heal. In fact, Helen confirms those scars when, moving around the house, "[s]he felt she needed to revisit the rooms of the old house [...] knowing that something had ended. She needed [...] to let it end" (119). The house is the scenario where the three women evade each other and reluctantly meet Declan's gay friends from Europe and Dublin. Talking to Paul, a gay Dubliner, Helen confesses her feud with her mother and grandmother. When her father died, Helen recalls, her mother and grandmother did not comfort her and hence, she argues, "these two women are the parts of myself that I have buried" (187–88). Restraint and silence on their part prevented Helen from properly mourning her father. Both women apparently avoided expressing their feelings and welcoming the other as a protective shield, which Helen keeps wailing about: "My mother taught me never to trust anyone's love [...]. I associated love with loss" (188). Lily's teaching contradicts the logic of elegy because, for her, it is not the death of the beloved but his love that is grievable. In other words, love is disarming and, therefore, to be avoided as a way of pre-emptive self-protection. This philosophy of (un)grievability is put to the test when Helen breaks with her mother and grandmother to set up a new family with her husband and children (188) and also when Declan comes back home to spend his last days.

With the coming of gay liberation, elegy withdrew the classic "absence of consolation" and could focus on celebrating gay sexuality (Guy-Bray 207). As a matter of fact, as Guy-Bray argues, elegy was timely again when the AIDS pandemic erupted. However, the axis of AIDS elegies was "the fragility of human life" (207) rather than (or together with) homosexual celebration. The confluence of both, the embryonic gay liberation of the 1980s in Ireland and the impact of AIDS, characterises *The Blackwater Lightship*. In this Irish AIDS elegy, it is not Declan's lover who mourns his suffering and imminent death, but his friends and family. In the narrative, the physical symptoms of the disease—such as bruises, diarrhoea, pain in the stomach and a blind eye (Tóibín 1999, 204–205)—run parallel to the conflicts between his sister, mother and grandmother. In other words, Declan's body, like his father's before (214–15), lies at the core of these women's recriminations. Even in the Devereux matriarchy, the male corpse is a prerequisite for them to come to terms with their conflicts. Yet, Declan's corpse is more problematic than his father's, when Lily was, Helen recalls, "utterly placid" (215). His imminent death is special because he is a gay man dying of a shameful disease that must remain secret to the public eye; otherwise, the victim would be ungrievable as Declan's disease has been for his family for far too long. In this sense, Larry recriminates about his friend's family for ignoring Declan and his "gay" disease "during very difficult times" (223), when his alternative gay family was next to him. With all this in mind, one of the main issues the novel deals with, in my view, is whether vulnerable Declan is grievable and/as a redemptive force, which has obvious religious undertones.

Christ's grievability derived from his radical ungrievability. As a rebel and an outsider both for Roman and Jewish authorities, his death was officially ungrievable. However, the exceptionality of his message and the radical grievability his followers eventually granted him became valuable narratives for the Roman Empire. His message of extreme love for the other, even and especially the enemy, grants humans "in their living [...], a characteristic of grievability" (Butler 2020, 75). Christ's ultimate act, whereby he recognises universal grievability, is his own redemptive death. Declan is also an outsider and a redeemer begging for a revision of values. As a gay man, he problematises his family's conception of motherhood. He also questions masculinity, most men of the family being absent or dead. Thus, he challenges the women of his family and, indirectly, the country, to come to terms with less restrictive conceptions of gender roles, as the ones they endorse often make interpersonal, intergenerational and transgenerational understanding virtually unfeasible. When the effects of AIDS are almost unbearable for Declan, Lily overcomes her inarticulacy and kneels down "in front of him [holding] his hands" (Tóibín 1999, 253). Although she may recall the Virgin Mary mourning for her suffering son on the verge of death, her gesture may lack transcendence, but is still relevant. By holding hands with Declan, she mainly breaks with the emotional constraints she had imposed on herself in order to thrive as a strong woman in neoliberal Ireland. What is more, by attending a

164 *José M. Yebra*

very ill Declan when he wishes "it was over" (255), Lily situates her-self in a position next to that promoted by the ethics of care, caring for the vulnerable other. In this sense, the novel revises the poetics of ungrievability of AIDS victims claimed by religious bigots back in the 1980s and 1990s (Capehart n.p.). Instead, Lily relinquishes her moral and religious prejudices to accept her son without restrictions, welcom-ing his otherness. The scene is intimate, pre-verbal between a caring mother and her suffering son: "He was saying: 'Mammy, Mammy, help me, Mammy.' [...] Declan's tone when he spoke was abject, childlike [...]. Lily whispered to him words which Helen could not hear" (Tóibín 1999, 258). The communication between both is unfathomable to the outsider, even to Helen, who becomes a mere spectator. As he cries for help and Lily responds instinctually, she grants him a primordial sense of grievability.

The Blackwater Lightship responds to homophobic fantasies of extinction and ungrievability by revising family values and gender roles in Catholic Ireland. Declan's body stands as a symbol of redemption and prospective change, as Walshe suggests (2013, 91). In fact, as the dis-ease advances, Declan's imminent demise increasingly recalls an act of sacrifice, an updating of Christ's redemptive death in liminal terms: "In an advanced state of decomposition, his body is an interstitial territory between being and non-being, life and death, Irish tradition and foreign lifestyles" (Yebra 2014, 99). Although conservatism and the influence of Catholicism disappear from the country and the Devereux family, the novel shows how both are rearticulated to meet a changing reality. What may remain after Declan's sacrificial and redemptive death is, in any case, something new. His body is de-sexualised but heavily politicised as his (*a priori* ungrievable) life is rendered grievable. The main problem is, in my view, whether his life/death is worthwhile or not for its own sake but because it helps make a change.

At the beginning of the novel, Helen goes to appease her son Manus, who is having a nightmare and is "fending off some unknown terror" (Tóibín 1999, 1). The echoes of Manus's nightmare resonate later on, when Declan's spasms require Lily's attention. Towards the end of the novel, along a conversation with her mother, Helen hints at Manus's likely homosexuality: "'I was just thinking [...] that I have a son who reminds me of my father sometimes, just like you said about Declan'. [...] 'He's Cathal [...] he's quiet, like the men down here. [...] And then the other is the opposite'" (243). Thus, *The Blackwater Lightship* depicts and predicts a changing country where "once Declan is dead, a new gen-eration of gays will allegedly find their way into the future" (Yebra 2015, 133). The implications of this conclusion are rather problematic because the hope of a new generation depends on the redemptive demise of the previous one. The value of Manus's and his family's future is some-how related to a sacrificial death, not really to a homophobic fantasy of extinction of the other. That is why, although the novel assumes the need of an end to foresee a new beginning it cannot be concluded that the novel complies with homophobic politics at all.

Both in *New Ways to Kill Your Mother* (2012) and in his essay "New Ways of Killing Your Father" (1993), Tóibín explores the complexity of intergenerational and transgenerational relations. In the latter, he fantasises with the idea of re-imagining history as fiction so as to be free, to start "from scratch, creating a new self" (1993, 3). In similar terms, Paul Delaney points out how Tóibín's fiction focuses on issues like "loss, [...] melancholy, elegy and grief [...] and the changing shape of Irish society and law" (10). *The Blackwater Lightship* is all this because it explores what remains when Declan's dying body returns home to be grieved and thus end up the status quo. However, the novel goes beyond Declan's death to cope with "purifying" fantasies that are apparently transcendental instead of homophobic. In the moment of transition for the country that the novel represents, Declan's illness and the ups and downs of the Devereux family "were nothing [...] as she [Helen] stood at the edge of the cliff. [...] It might have been better [...] if there never had been people, if this turning of the world [...] happened without witnesses, without anyone feeling, or remembering" (Tóibín 1999, 260). Like Nick Guest, Helen fantasises with utter dissolution of consciousness. In Nick's case, it is the gay character about to die who turns sentimental. However, in *The Blackwater Lightship* there are significant differences. It is the survivor who fantasises with loss and dissolution, the gay body being elusive, "linked metaphorically with the eroding landscape of County Wexford" (Walshe 2013, 89); and besides Declan and Helen, the novel itself may be said (using Dollimore's words) to "struggle to redeem or transcend" loss (305). Yet, in both cases, "loss is embraced as dynamic and liberating, the condition of ecstatic renewal" (305). The overall melancholia of *The Swimming-pool Library* and *The Line of Beauty* contrasts with the redemptive hopefulness of *The Blackwater Lightship*.

Conclusion

Hollinghurst's and Tóibín's novels respond to crises and portray what remains after the AIDS dystopia in different, almost contradictory ways. Drawing on *The Swimming-pool Library*, *The Line of Beauty* oversexualises the gay body and recalls and fantasises pre-gay times in elegiac terms. Yet, oversexualisation is menaced, either by a homophobic status quo (the novel starts with Thatcher's landslide) or by the coming of AIDS, which was instrumentalised to justify homophobic campaigns, discourses and politics by those Nick calls friends. In the context of a dystopia in which, as Watney argues, gays are annihilated (Hollinghurst 2004, 58), elegy does not operate and so *The Line of Beauty* spells doom and melancholia

166 *José M. Yebra*

instead. It can be argued that Nick's (and somehow the novel's) self-indulgent fantasy of gay extinction is a form of embracing nothingness when, in the 1980s, AIDS was becoming a historical event. *The Blackwater Lightship*, by contrast, de-sexualises the gay body into a corpse to paradoxically overcome the constraining discourses (de-sexualisation being one) of a country in a process of change. The implications of Irishness and especially Irish Catholic undertones are essential to comprehend the sacrificial discourse and intergenerational conflicts around Declan's last days. Be it as it may, both novels grieve the prospective departure of the protagonists to denounce the dangers of homophobic discourses on "purifying" ungrievability, that is, gay mass eugenics. Both texts may feature oceanic dissolution as a metaphor of extinction and nothingness; yet, what remains after imagined or real dystopias is the complex transition between the generation ravished by AIDS and those that survived to give testimony.

Hollinghurst's and Tóibín's novels address the remains of (un)grievability in dissimilar terms, mostly derived from the traditions and contexts they belong to. *The Line of Beauty* (and *The Swimming-pool Library*) lament how gay lives and bodies were rendered ungrievable, especially when they were both assimilated and loathed by mainstream culture and politics. In other words, what remains is the posthumous grievability of oversexualised gay lives and bodies in melancholic terms. In *The Blackwater Lightship*, what remains of (un)grievability is ambivalent: the gay body (here represented by Declan) cannot be grieved in institutional terms, but is actually grieved by his family in sacrificial terms, thus re-adapting Catholic redemption to repair gays' ungrievability. Among the different losses left behind by AIDS, as mentioned above, Yep makes reference to the uniqueness of the individual and some ideals (691). It is quite an idealistic stand, even though movements and vindicatory voices have paved the way for memory, rehabilitation and the recognition of the rights of sexual dissidents. Hollinghurst's and Tóibín's novels address these issues. However, they do not do it self-indulgently because, together with the uniqueness of the individual and the ideal of justice, they recall the hardships of the process, which even sexual dissidents themselves assume: internal homophobia, self-sacrifice on behalf of something grander than oneself or extreme sentimentalism characterise their updating conception of elegy.

Acknowledgements

Research for this chapter was funded by the Spanish Ministry of Science and Innovation (MICINN) (code PID2021-124841NB-I00) and by the Government of Aragón and the European Social Fund (ESF) (code H03_20R).

Works Cited

Butler, Judith. *Precarious life. The Power of Mourning and Violence*. London: Verso Books, 2004.

———. *Frames of War. When Is Life Grievable?* London: Verso Books, 2009.

———. *The Force of Non Violence. An Ethico-Political Bind*. London: Verso Books, 2020.

Canning, Richard. *Conversations with Gay Novelists. Gay Fiction Speaks*. New York: Columbia UP, 2001.

Capehart, Jonathan. "Pat Robertson's 'Vicious Stuff' about Gays and AIDS." Last accessed on 07/01/2022 at: https://www.washingtonpost.com/blogs/post-partisan/wp/2013/08/29/pat-robertsons-vicious-stuff-about-gays-and-aids/.

Catalan, Jose. "It's a Sin: How the Media Fuelled the Homophobic Response to the HIV Crisis." Channel 4 Series: *The Conversation*. 8 March 2021. Last accessed on 07/01/2022 at: https://theconversation.com/its-a-sin-how-the-media-fuelled-the-homophobic-response-to-the-hiv-crisis-154504.

Delaney, Paul. "Introduction." *Reading Colm Tóibín*. Ed. Paul Delaney. Dublin: The Liffey P, 2008. 1–20.

D'Emilio, John. *Making Trouble*. New York: Routledge, 1992.

Dollimore, Jonathan. *Death, Desire and Loss in Western Culture*. New York and London: Routledge, 2001.

Freud, Sigmund. "Mourning and Melancholia." *The Standard Edition of the Complete Psychological Works of Sigmund Freud* Vol. XIV. Trans. James Strachey. London: Hogarth P, 1958. 239–58.

Guy-Bray, Stephen. "Elegy." *The Gay and Lesbian Literary Heritage*. Ed. Claude Summers. New York and London: Routledge, 2002. 205–207.

Hollinghurst, Alan. *The Swimming-pool Library*. London: Vintage, 1998.

———. *The Line of Beauty*. London: Picador, 2004.

Marcus, J. S. "Fiction in Review. Alan Hollinghurst." *Yale Review* 93.3 (2005): 180–85.

Perry, Gaylene and Annette Iggulden. "Breath & Elegy Moments of Grief and Art." *Anatomy and Poetics*. Last accessed on 27/12/2021 at: http://www.doubledialogues.com/article/breath-elegy-moments-of-grief-and-art/.

Sontag, Susan. *Illness and Metaphor and AIDS and Its Metaphors*. New York: Picador, 1989.

Tóibín, Colm. *The Blackwater Lightship*. London: Picador, 1999.

———. *New Ways to Kill Your Mother: Writers and Their Families*. New York: Scribner, 2012.

———. "New Ways of Killing Your Father." *The London Review of Books* 15.22 (November 18, 1993). Last accessed on 12/12/2021 at: https://www.lrb.co.uk/the-paper/v15/n22/colm-toibin/new-ways-of-killing-your-father/.

Walshe, Eibhear. "'This Particular Genie': The Elusive Gay Male Body in Tóibín's Novels." *Reading Colm Tóibín*. Ed. Paul Delaney. Dublin: The Liffey P, 2008. 115–30.

———. *A Different Story*. Dublin: Irish Academic P, 2013.

Watney, Simon. *Practices of Freedom: Selected Writings on HIV/AIDS*. Durham, NC: Duke UP, 1994.

White, Edmund, ed. *The Faber Book of Gay Short Fiction*. London: Faber, 1991.

White, Edmund. *The Burning Library: Writings on Art, Literature and Sexuality 1969–1993*. London: Picador, 1995.

Wood, James. "The Ogee Curve." *The New Republic* December 13, 2004: 47–49.

Woods, Gregory. *A History of Gay Literature. The Male Tradition*. New Haven, CT and London: Yale UP, 1998.

Yebra, José M. "A Terrible Beauty: Ethics, Aesthetics and the Trauma of Gayness in Alan Hollinghurst's *The Line of Beauty.*" *Ethics and Trauma in Contemporary British Fiction*. Eds Susana Onega and Jean-Michel Ganteau. Amsterdam and New York: Rodopi, 2011. 175–208.

———. "The Interstitial Status of Irish Gayness in Colm Tóibín's *The Blackwater Lightship* and *The Master.*" *Estudios Irlandeses* 9 (2014): 96–106.

———. "Transgenerational and Intergenerational Family Trauma in Colm Tóibín's *The Blackwater Lightship* and 'Three Friends'." *Moderna Språk* 2 (2015): 122–39.

Yep, Gust A. "The Politics of Loss and Its Remains in 'Common Threads: Stories from the Quilt'." *Rhetoric and Public Affairs* 10.4 (2007): 681–99.

9 Overcoming Grief and Salvaging Memory
Rebecca Makkai's *The Great Believers*

Giulio Milone

Introduction

Writing in response to the post-9/11 global conflict, philosopher Judith Butler ponders on what makes for a grievable life, given that "specific lives cannot be apprehended as injured or lost if they are not first apprehended as living" (2009, 1). Her concerned outrage, best argued in the essays *Precarious Life: The Powers of Mourning and Violence* (2004) and *Frames of War: When Is Life Grievable* (2009), is rooted in how media were reporting on the so-called "War on Terror" launched by the Bush administration. Throughout, Butler exposes how the dynamics of the US war against terrorism was marred by a complex cultural Western frame which dictated "who [would] be human, and who [would] not" (Butler 2004, XVI). Practical examples of this attitude can be found in the biased news coverage, which only focused on US losses, "consecrated in public obituaries that constitute so many acts of nation-building" (XIV). At the same time, the act of erasing any public representation of the names, images and narratives of those killed by the US is suggestive of the coercive process of de-humanisation of Arab people and practitioners of Islam, which ultimately resulted in their essential ungrievability, on account of their not having ever been considered "human" at all (32).

In this respect, Butler observes that "[t]he derealization of the Other means that it is neither alive nor dead, but interminably spectral" (2004, 33–34), as she notes that similar ontological limitations to human intelligibility were already made at the peak of the AIDS epidemic, where few to no deaths from AIDS were publicly grievable losses. As she forcefully argued: "If a life is not grievable, it is not quite a life; it does not qualify as a life and is not worth a note. It is already the unburied, if not the unburiable" (34). This is but a passing remark in Butler's broader argument, though one which resonates with other accounts of the "plague" that ravaged the US from 1981 to 1996, until the introduction of the first antiretroviral therapies.

In *Illness as Metaphor & AIDS and Its Metaphors* (1989), Susan Sontag expands on the theoretical observations she had begun in *Illness as Metaphor* (1978), and muses on the vocabulary used to describe the

DOI: 10.4324/9781003347811-14

170 *Giulio Milone*

rapidly escalating AIDS epidemic. She is particularly puzzled by the use of the term "plague" as it harkens back to a premodern era in which illnesses were understood as collective calamities that were "inflicted, not just endured" (Sontag 2002, 131). Framed in this light, AIDS emerges as "a disease incurred by people both as individuals and as members of a 'risk group'—that neutral-sounding, bureaucratic category which also revives the archaic idea of a tainted community that illness has judged" (132). Sontag is equally bewildered by the sectarian distinction made by society between the disease's putative carriers and those defined as "the general population," a rather vague category employed to describe, in this case, "white heterosexuals who do not inject themselves with drugs or have sexual relations with those who do" (113).

Leo Bersani also picks up on the same dichotomy while reflecting on the biased media coverage of the AIDS epidemic, highlighting that any potential course of action was suggested and discussed only as preventative for the general population, rather than for those at risk or already infected. Bersani mentions playwright Larry Kramer's provocative claim that, in order to stop the ever-growing hostility towards homosexuality, AIDS should spread out widely into the white nondrug-using heterosexual population: "What a morbid, even horrendous, yet perhaps sensible suggestion," Bersani smirks, "[that] only when the 'general public' is threatened can whatever the opposite of a general public is hope to get adequate attention and treatment" (8).

In her memoir *The Gentrification of the Mind: Witness to a Lost Imagination* (2012), activist and historian Sarah Schulman meditates on the historicisation of AIDS, which has been filtered through a "mellow tone" and "slightly banalized, homogenized" (2). In her felt recollection, Schulman highlights the spectral quality of the lives of all the friends she lost to AIDS along the years. Their deaths went unnoticed, barely cracking the surface of public discourse:

> Every gay person walking around who lived in New York or San Francisco in the 1980s and early 1990s is a survivor of devastation and carries with them the faces, fading names, and corpses of the otherwise forgotten dead. [...] Our friends died and our world was destroyed because of the neglect of real people who also have names and faces. Whether they were politicians or parents, as people with AIDS literally fought in the streets or hid in corners until they too died or survived, others—their relatives, neighbors, "friends," coworkers, presidents, landlords, and bosses—stood by and did nothing.
>
> (45–46)

What these disparate but first-hand accounts of the AIDS epidemic share is the bitter acknowledgement of a punitive and discriminatory hierarchy that progressively stigmatised and excluded members of a vast and decimated community at risk, detached from the general population purported to constitute the sole group worthy of treatment and protection. Sontag investigates this line of demarcation by probing into its linguistic and metaphoric undertones, ultimately uncovering the very same moral agenda that enrages Bersani and fuels his provoking arguments. By the same token, Schulman stresses how this outright discrimination resulted in complicated, delegitimised and socio-politically muted grief for all survivors, as she notes that the progressive gentrification of major city areas contributed to the definitive erasure of all traces of the people who died of AIDS.

In this context, a recent US novel, Rebecca Makkai's *The Great Believers: A Novel* (2018), is worthy of critical discussion as it seems to exemplify and fictionalise these theoretical observations, while simultaneously showing the protracted and evolving nature of traumatic grief over the years, and the multifarious ways in which the AIDS epidemic has been experienced, witnessed, remembered and written about in the US.

Writing and Telling

First published in 2018, Rebecca Makkai's *The Great Believers* belongs in the trend of recent and ambitious LGBTQ+ fiction that has quickly gained academic interest (Parson 2019). Like Alan Hollinghurst's novels and Hanya Yanagihara's *A Little Life* (2015), it charts the lives of a close-knit group of friends through the decades. Like the novels of Garth Greenwell and Adam Mars-Jones, it relies heavily on character introspection and frank depictions of sexuality. However, in terms of the location of AIDS stories—including not only novels but also seminal plays like Larry Kramer's *The Normal Heart* (1985) and Tony Kushner's *Angels in America* (1991)—Makkai's is unusually set in Chicago, the author's hometown, a metropolitan area that has often been overlooked in official audio-visual accounts of the epidemic. As one character observes early in the novel, Chicago was neither San Francisco nor New York, and things moved more slowly there—even the spreading of a new infection.

The novel employs two timelines, structured in alternating chapters: the first is set in Chicago in the mid-1980s, the second in Paris in 2015. In the first timeline, we follow young art curator Yale Tishman as he is about to bring in, for free, a valuable collection of paintings dating back to the Paris School of the 1920s. This is a remarkable career achievement that is offset by the fact that all his friends, gay men like him, are rapidly dying from a yet unknown and lethal virus. This section of the novel juggles between the dynamics in Yale's circle and his own work for the acquisition of the paintings. Thirty years later, Fiona Marcus is

172   *Giulio Milone*

in Europe tracking down her estranged daughter Claire, who somehow was enmeshed in a cult called Hosanna Collective, its leader being one Kurt Pearce, former lover of Claire and son of Cecily Pearce, a woman who helped Yale with the paintings. The book opens in 1985 with a wake for Nico, one of Yale's best friends and Fiona's older brother. At this stage, the collection of paintings is owned by Nora Marcus, Nico and Fiona's grandmother, who relates to Yale memories of her years in Paris as a young woman.

The handling of such a delicate subject matter, in which suppressed voices and marginalised identities occupy centre-stage, requires a brief consideration of who narrates such stories. In the Acknowledgements, Makkai elaborates on how she attempted to recreate the atmosphere of Chicago in the 1980s: she explicitly mentions her sources, which include oral testimonies, graphic novels, newspaper libraries, multifarious cultural artefacts and documentaries. Furthermore, in an ancillary piece published online, Makkai explains in detail how she, a straight white woman who did not experience the epidemic first hand, managed to build a convincing and respectful AIDS narrative centred on a fictional gay man without oversimplifying or exploiting the accounts of those men who actually lived through the events. She follows an ethical imperative that is as simple as it is disarming. In Makkai's own words:

> Representation of the other, when done poorly, upsets many people. Other people see that upset as censorship. [...] I don't need to apologize for writing across difference; I need to apologize if I get it wrong. [...] In order to write this, I had to satisfactorily answer two questions: Was I reinforcing stereotypes, or combatting them? And was I stealing attention from first-hand narratives, or shedding light on them? The first question was a matter of good writing—something I had control over. The second was stickier.
>
> (2018, n.p.)

Through her writing, Makkai attempts to honour what she learned via her research and oral testimonies, hoping that the final result could "guide readers to direct accounts of that time, or art by those who lived through it" (n.p.).

From a narratological standpoint, the novel is told by an external narrator that alternates between Yale's and Fiona's perspectives in their respective chapters. In its early drafts, the plot revolved only around Yale in the 1980s and the AIDS epidemic, but Makkai felt that focusing exclusively on Yale's perspective was "an attempt at ventriloquism" (n.p.), an appropriation of a story that was not hers to tell. Therefore, when she decided to expand the timelines and insert a second narrative centred on Fiona—a fictional character closer to her own identity—she found "the whole thing click[ing] into place. Suddenly [she] had a

Overcoming Grief and Salvaging Memory 173

populated universe, the depth and echoes of history, resonance between generations and across continents" (n.p.).

Devastating events such as the AIDS crisis have been rightfully framed and discussed as traumatic, as the final chapter of Cathy Caruth's *Trauma: Explorations in Memory* (1995) demonstrates. In one of the foundational texts of trauma studies, Caruth is in conversation with activists, historians and psychotherapists who all dealt with and lived through the epidemic. From their exchanges, the AIDS crisis emerges as an undoubtedly traumatic event, though one experienced and perceived only by certain people, "while the society as a whole [didn't] appear to be experiencing it at all" (Caruth 255). Taken together, Caruth's, Butler's and Bersani's similar observations may be said to point clearly towards the slow construction of the ungrievability of men dying from AIDS.

However, the most recent advancements in trauma studies share a certain preoccupation with the overabundance of trauma narratives in contemporary fiction and with their potential, mostly ethical, risks. For example, in a critical overview at the end of *Trauma and Literature* (2018), Roger Kurtz expressed his perplexity on the limits of the field, arguing that one criticism concerns

> its all-embracing nature, the fact that it is a large and baggy concept that soaks up other approaches (in the manner of a category like cultural studies), and that, as a result, it loses its analytical purchase. If trauma becomes synonymous with any kind of oppression or injustice,

the scholar warns, "it loses effectiveness as a discrete category" (335). In a recent op-ed for "Harper's Magazine," British author Will Self voiced the same concerns, bitterly suggesting that, in the end, the proliferation of such narratives in fiction benefits only literary critics and their agendas (n.p.). In *The New Yorker*, critic Parul Sehgal extends the issue to other fictional forms of storytelling such as films and TV shows, noting that trauma has become "synonymous with backstory" (n.p.) as the present must now give way to the past, where all mysteries can be solved. After arguing that the trauma plot often "flattens, distorts, reduces character to symptom, and, in turn, instructs and insists upon its moral authority" (n.p.), Sehgal illustrates what she considers to be the most reasonable antidote by stating that the most successful (and honest) stories about trauma do not resolve themselves in the past, but rather point towards the future. In Sehgal's own words:

> In deft hands the trauma plot is taken only as a beginning—with a middle and an end to be sought elsewhere. With a wider aperture, we move out of the therapeutic register and into a generational,

174 *Giulio Milone*

social, and political one. It becomes a portal into history and into a common language.

(n.p.)

Makkai seems to follow the route recommended by Sehgal, because in *The Great Believers* she does not handle the trauma of AIDS as a mere backstory to the present-day storyline. On the contrary, through a careful tuning and weaving of its interlocking stories, the novel provides a multigenerational backdrop against which several issues are investigated in their evolution across the decades, such as bearing witness to unspeakable events, mourning losses deemed ungrievable by the rest of society, exploring alternative notions of communities and families and how art can play a crucial role in all of these endeavours.

Living and Experiencing

Yale Tishman is one of the main characters in *The Great Believers*, and his perspective dominates the Chicago sections. At the beginning of the novel, he is having a long-term relationship with Charlie Keene, a journalist. The two live together and are thinking about buying a house of their own. They have also agreed to be monogamous, though Charlie often dwells on the possible unravelling of their coupledom, as he projects feelings of insecurity towards Yale, who, by contrast, seems unconcerned. Charlie is particularly jealous of two of their friends, Julian Ames and Teddy Naples, and he is convinced that sooner or later Yale will yield to their advances.

The issue of monogamy becomes crucial because it is opposed to sexual promiscuity, a potentially dangerous practice that increases the chances of exposition to HIV. Like Yale, Charlie and their friends try to protect themselves from an infection of which they still know little. Therefore, non-monogamous lifestyles such as Teddy's are frowned upon, and discussions of illness rapidly assume moral and condemning undertones, in terms that are strongly reminiscent of those highlighted by Sontag and Bersani. For example, when Yale tells Teddy: "I feel like we're all caught up in some huge cycle of judgment. We spent our whole lives unlearning it, and here we are" (Makkai 2019, 326), his words echo Sontag's idea that AIDS was received and discussed as an inflicted punishment, where their lives are at risk but, in the end, undeserving of being grieved in the public sphere.

Yale's world breaks into pieces when he finds out that Charlie has cheated on him and that he is now seropositive, while he was sanctimoniously lecturing Yale about the risks of having sex with other persons. As Yale's story takes a tragic turn, Makkai uses her character to show how gay men handled and endured the necessary precautions, from the blood tests (which many avoided due to shame) to the excruciating work of contact tracing, "the world's worst logic puzzle" (Makkai 2019, 180).

Overcoming Grief and Salvaging Memory   175

As a paratextual token of the traumatic blow, the moment in which Yale finally receives his diagnosis of seropositivity is relayed in the only chapter of the whole book that has a full date (15 July 1986), instead of just the mention of the year.

Yale tries to find a balance between the personal turmoil of having caught HIV and the professional task of protecting Nora's paintings from her money-hungry relatives. The novel also shows the young man's complex feelings for Charlie, whom he holds in contempt for his lies but cannot help but feel affection for. Through his chapters, firmly grounded in the reality of the 1980s, Makkai captures the anger and the progressive grief of that period, as Yale and his friends try to come to terms with the substantial indifference with which their friends' deaths were generally met. In Yale's own words: "A handful of dead astronauts and Reagan weeps with the nation. Thirteen thousand dead gay men and Reagan's too busy" (Makkai 2019, 246). This remark is strongly reminiscent of Butler's broader observations on the hierarchies of grief:

> Lives are supported and maintained differently, and there are radically different ways in which human physical vulnerability is distributed across the globe. Certain lives will be highly protected, and the abrogation of their claims to sanctity will be sufficient to mobilize the forces of war. Other lives will not find such fast and furious support and will not even qualify as "grievable."
>
> (Butler 2004, 32)

Yale's health gradually worsens, so that he is eventually taken to hospital. At this stage, Fiona cannot take care of him because she is in another ward of the same building, in the final stage of pregnancy. Yale dies alone in 1992, after dreaming of Fiona. When she gives birth to her daughter Claire, Fiona chooses "Yale" as her middle name, in what may be interpreted as the beginning of a complex and painful act of remembrance that will send ripples through the following decades.

The character of Yale Tishman occupies a curious position in the novel because his life story begins and ends in the Chicago sections. In terms of structure, Yale's life story can be said to provide a thematic bridge between Paris in the 1920s and later in the 2010s through his relationships with members of the Marcus family. However, Makkai develops Yale's personal story not exactly as a meditation on grief and ungrievability, but rather as a fictional rendering, drawn from her collected oral testimonies, of how gay men learned about AIDS and navigated society's judgement through the epidemic's first muddled and hysterical years.

Enduring and Remembering

In *The Great Believers*, the complications and hurdles of grief in relation to the AIDS epidemic are explored in the Paris chapters, set some thirty

176 *Giulio Milone*

years after the events narrated in the Yale-focused sections. In this novel, the traumatic burden of memory is carried out by at least three other characters on two planes, one more psychological and the other more material, though with varying degrees of involvement. These characters are Nora Marcus, her granddaughter Fiona and photographer Richard Campo, a secondary character in the 1980s section who becomes more prominent in the Paris chapters.

Nora Marcus's prized collection is comprised of sketches, drafts and finished items of several artists of the Paris School of the 1920s. Among well-known and real figures such as Amedeo Modigliani, Tsuguharu Foujita and Chaïm Soutine, Nora's collection includes works by Ranko Novak, an obscure fictitious artist with whom Nora had been romantically involved. Novak died in the war and Nora kept the sketches for which she posed as a model. Yale's bosses are more than ready to acquire the collection, but they could easily make do without Novak's work because of his anonymity, which also jeopardises the worth of the collection as a whole. Unsurprisingly, Nora does not agree with leaving Novak behind: after sixty years of silent grief, she is now trying to find a way of giving physical, exterior expression to it and to her traumatic memories as well. As she confesses to Yale, after his lover's death, Nora had spent most of her life wandering around galleries and thinking of the works that were not exhibited, such as Ranko's. She describes them as "shadow-paintings [...] that no one can see but you" (Makkai 2019, 252). This suggestive image is particularly apt in exemplifying what might happen when one is grieving loved objects whose lives and interpersonal relationships are unremarked and unrecognised by society.

The Great Believers takes its title from a short autobiographical piece by Francis Scott Fitzgerald, "My Generation." The conjuring of the Paris School through Nora's recollections makes this borrowing clearer. Fitzgerald writes:

> We were the great believers. [...] Well, many are dead, and some I have quarreled with and don't see anymore. I have never cared for any men as much as for these who felt the first springs when I did, and saw death ahead, and were reprieved—and who now walk the long stormy summer.
>
> (155, 161)

Here, Fitzgerald is referring to the Lost Generation, and Makkai's novel establishes a parallelism between the community of artists in Paris in the 1920s—frequented by Lost Generation writers like Fitzgerald himself, Ernest Hemingway, Gertrude Stein or T.S. Eliot—and Nico's second, chosen family. Nora observes that Paris welcomed boys landing from everywhere and she describes the city as a haven for all these misfit artists, in a way that strongly resembles large American cities like Chicago

Overcoming Grief and Salvaging Memory   177

that gave solace to LGBTQ+ youths coming from suburban areas. The arts scene in Paris was dislocated by World War I, and between the war and the influenza epidemic of 1918, a whole generation of artists was decimated. Nora gets acquainted with the survivors and later becomes their confidante, carer and even muse. Her attitude is mirrored by Fiona, who is immediately presented in the book as a sort of little sister to her "two hundred big brothers" (Makkai 2019, 8) and is later even labelled as "Saint Fiona of Boystown" (399). Before dying, Yale manages to display Novak's work alongside the other more famous artists, thus fulfilling Nora's life-long wish.

Providing an audio-visual testimony of this community of friends, who built themselves a family after their biological ones disowned them, is the artistic mission of photographer Richard Campo, whom we first meet taking pictures at Nico's wake. As the narrator points out in one of Yale's chapters, "[w]hat had started as a strange quirk had become [...] something essential. Whatever happens—in three years, in twenty—that moment will remain" (9). Richard's endeavour exemplifies the inherent complexities of memories about AIDS in which, as Christopher Castiglia and Christopher Reed observe, "the project of memory is frustrated by the sometimes startling divergence between our recollections of people or events and the way they are captured on film" (212). Home videos, candids and polaroids arranged in curated slideshows play a crucial role in reaffirming the actual liveliness of all the young men whose lives were deemed ungrievable and, as such, not properly mourned—as happens, for example, with Nico's family-arranged funeral, in which his lover and friends are prevented from participating, and where estranged relatives who did not accept his sexual orientation tell stories about him as a child, as if he had died in adolescence, thus invalidating his adult life as an out and proud man. Public eulogies serve the same goals as obituaries, in which "lives are quickly tidied up and summarized, humanized, usually married, or on the way to be, heterosexual, happy, monogamous" (Butler 2004, 32). The parallel unfolding of these two wildly different wakes for Nico reinforces Butler's suggestion that such forms of public grieving are often biased, almost parochial in a sense. Most importantly, they stress the gap between those parts of a certain life that are thought to be remembered, celebrated and grieved, and those others which, in contrast, are deemed unworthy of public interest, care and empathy.

Thirty years later, Fiona is a guest of Richard's in Paris, where he moved and furthered his career through a series of photographs described as "deathbed shots" (Makkai 2019, 24). He is about to launch a new exhibition at the Centre Pompidou, aptly named "Strata" (395), in which old photos and videos of the 1980s are revisited and updated. In the exhibition, the line between past and present is deliberately blurred, as the images both trigger and convey conflicting emotions of nostalgia, affection and rage. The images shown in "Strata" provide a continuation

178   *Giulio Milone*

or a conclusion to the stories begun thirty years earlier, as is the case of Julian Ames's portrait series. Julian was thought to have died of AIDS, and he unexpectedly reappears in Paris. Upon finding him again, Richard adds another portrait to his series, focusing on the changes in his physical appearance: the illness might have had an undeniable impact on him, but he is still there.

Fiona, finally, is the emotional centrepiece of the story. She spends the better part of her adult life feeling guilty for having failed in her motherly role of carer, of her brother and his friends, and her daughter Claire as well. She is perpetually haunted by the memories of her twenties, often daydreaming of Chicago in the 1980s, when Nico was still alive and well. The stark reality, however, is as hard as that described by Schulman, when the cities become actual graveyards made up of streets "where there had been a holocaust, a mass murder of neglect and antipathy" (Makkai 2019, 184). Indeed, Fiona's Chicago is strongly reminiscent of Schulman's apocalyptic description of New York, and comes to metaphorically embody the "lesions and echoing coughs and the ropy fossils of limbs" (Makkai 2019, 185) of the real victims of AIDS, unmourned by the normative society in cities where the political hierarchies of grief dictate who, how and when to grieve someone's death.

Fiona's character is given further psychological complexity when the narrative voice acknowledges the moral failings—or rather, complications—of her personal trauma, for example, when, years later, she is ashamed because she cannot bring herself to care about the ongoing AIDS crisis in the Third World. This moral conflict is even more evident in another episode. By setting a part of the Paris section in the autumn of 2015, the narrative includes in it the Bataclan theatre massacre, thus shocking Fiona into awareness of her numbness and lack of empathy:

> Was it because it wasn't her city, or because the rituals of outrage and grief and fear felt so familiar now, so practiced? [...] [She thought that] she'd been in the middle of a different story, one that had nothing to do with this. She was a person who was finding her daughter, making things right with her daughter, and there was no room in that story for the idiocy of extreme religion, the violence of men she'd never met.
>
> (Makkai 2019, 317)

The passage strikingly confirms and renders Butler's observation that our contemporary over-exposure to acts of senseless violence has made us progressively desensitised to them (2004, 149). Makkai's narrator probes into Fiona's reasonably distressed state, earnestly portraying the selfishness often felt by trauma survivors as they strive to reaffirm the legitimacy of their feelings. Confronted with public and broader issues, survivors like Fiona constantly ask themselves whether they are allowed to be grieving and in pain.

Thus, throughout the novel, Fiona, Richard and Nora are seen struggling with the burden of their memories, aware that what they remember is often the only trace left of someone whose death has not been properly recognised and grieved. In *The Great Believers*, Makkai makes a case for how the task of enduring and remembering traumatic past events is often as complicated and painful as it was experiencing them, as the act of witnessing translates into a complex act of survival in and out of itself. Indeed, the very notion of survival is imbued with ambivalent meanings, as Rudolf Freiburg and Gerd Bayer have aptly pointed out:

> On first glance, survival seems to be closely associated with 'happiness', 'luck', 'bliss' and 'felicity': the terrible past has been overcome, the future promises happy prospects. But the notion of the 'happy survivor', the person relishing in his 'success', is deceptive at best. Survival reveals a darker side, a dialectics which renders all idyllic imaginations of a comfortable 'afterlife' absurd.
>
> (17–18)

Echoing this, it takes decades for Fiona, Richard and Nora to find physical and material ways to vent out their grief. However, what remains in the end are only serene memories. This is best exemplified in the final chapter, where Fiona observes a short video of Yale, Nico and the others, captured during a random but joyous *rendezvous* sometime before the beginning of the epidemic. The video is played in loop at Richard's exhibition, its protagonists forever smiling and forever alive: "There they all stood. Boys with hands in pockets, waiting for everything to begin" (418).

Conclusion

Late in the novel, at the Strata exhibition, Fiona and Julian reminisce about the past as they observe Richard's work. Julian recalls his acting career, and how he was never able to play Horatio in *Hamlet* in any of the three different stagings in which he took part.

He said:

> The whole play is about Hamlet trying to avenge his father's death, trying to tell the truth, right? And then when he dies, he hands it all to Horatio. *In this harsh world draw thy breath in pain, to tell my story*. See, I'd have made a great Hamlet! But what a burden. To be Horatio. To be the one with the memory. And what's Horatio supposed to do with it? What the hell does Horatio do in act six?
>
> (Makkai 2019, 415; original emphasis)

180   Giulio Milone

Fiona smiles out of pure nostalgia at Julian's penchant for autoreferentiality, but his fascination for the character of Horatio is significant in that it serves as a key to the understanding of Makkai's intents. *The Great Believers* is a novel that focuses on all the Horatios who survived traumatic events such as epidemics and global conflicts, and who are now tasked with painful acts of remembrance in a socio-political context that fails or merely refuses to recognise their upheaval. More specifically, the events of the narrative aptly render, in fictional terms, the observations of those theorists who reflected on how the AIDS epidemic was perceived, experienced and reported differently—both by those actually at risk, and by the members of a majority characterised by contempt and denial. In this light, when reading of Yale's or Teddy's frustration over the government's negligent control of the epidemic, it is easy to hear echoes of Sontag's description of AIDS as a happenstance perceived as an inflicted and punishing calamity, or Bersani's resentful suggestion that things would have been handled differently if "white nondrug-using heterosexual[s]" (8) could also contract HIV. Several characters in the novel are, in Schulman's words, "survivor[s] of devastation" (45) as they carry with them scars that are either physical (like Julian's) or psychological (like Fiona's and Richard's), or both. The fact that almost none of the deaths from AIDS were publicly grievable losses—mentioned by Butler as the most apparent historical precedent of the socially constructed and conditioned ungrievability of those killed during the global war on terror—becomes the driving force of Makkai's novel.

Through the complex narrative structure, the outbreak and carnage of the AIDS epidemic is handled as chronological starting point, its echoes and effects sending ripples both towards the past and the future. Just as Nora holds on to her paintings as mementos of Ranko and all the other artists she befriended in Paris, so Fiona and Richard clutch at their memories of their friends, relatives and lovers. These different stories share a fundamental trait, which stresses the important role played by material belongings and memory pieces as tangible objects loaded with ambivalent meanings of a grief that has struggled to be properly expressed—or displayed, in the case of the paintings and photographs—in public. Seen in this light, then, the interconnection of the three distinct stories and the articulation of different perspectives may be said to prevent Makkai from using the AIDS narrative in a sensationalised, pity-inducing and patronising fashion, thus moving away from the risk, lamented by some critics, of partaking in the overabundance of simplistic trauma narratives in contemporary fiction.

As the analysis has attempted to demonstrate, *The Great Believers* is a novel that shows what happens when the socio-cultural construction of ungrievability condemns entire groups of people to senseless violence and progressive erasure. Makkai may not be as explicit in defining the political value of her fictional characters as Butler, Bersani or Sontag are

Overcoming Grief and Salvaging Memory 181

in their respective writings, but nonetheless their stories are a convincing and respectful representation of the aporias of ungrievability in a society dominated by heterosexual preconceptions, where members of the LGBTQ+ minorities are forced into what Jean Baudrillard called in *The Perfect Crime* (1996) a "phobic relationship with the other, idealized by hatred" (132). Nora, Fiona and Richard have all suffered considerable losses, and they were left to collect the wreckage without any form of psychological, emotional and social assistance: only they and all the other survivors are unacknowledged members of the same web of support. As Freiburg and Bayer observe:

> The survival of groups is a complex issue, fusing elements of emotion and rationality together, using psychological stratagems of encouraging each other in the common attempt to survive. This feeling of an intense solidarity is probably the cornerstone of a well-functioning group; its identity rests on complex processes of social practices to intensify the felling of 'belonging together', cherishing common notions and pursuing the same goals.
>
> (11–12)

Throughout the years, these characters attempt to overcome their grief while keeping their friends' memory alive through complex and often contradictory acts of remembrance, as their traumatic memories of ungrievable loved ones are now turned into narrative memories through the agency of art.

This transformative process can be easily described through historian Dominick LaCapra's famous twofold process (inspired from his reading of Freud) to be undertaken by survivors in order to overcome the trauma that haunts them. In the first phase, termed "acting out," the patient is "haunted or possessed by the past and performatively caught up in the compulsive repetition of traumatic scenes" (21). The most common examples of acting out are nightmares and flashbacks, such as Fiona's vivid lucid dreams. The second phase, denominated "working through," indicates the actual work of overcoming trauma: patients have become more cognisant of the causes of their own upheavals and can begin a course of actions that may lead to their own self-healing. In this respect, becoming conscious of one's own trauma and willing to share one's experience is crucial in order to overcome the phase of acting out and begin that of working through. However, in the preface to the updated edition of his book, LaCapra encourages us to see working through as "an open, self questioning process that never attains closure and counteracts acting out (or the repetition compulsion) without entirely transcending it, especially with respect to trauma and its aftermath" (xxiii). What LaCapra suggests is that working through does not necessarily entail full recovery. He writes: "it is deceptive to see it in terms of a

182   *Giulio Milone*

notion of cure, consolation, uplift, or closure and normalization" (xxiii). Most importantly, the moments of acting out should not be discredited, or dreaded: the two phases are quintessentially inseparable, one building up from the work of the other before.

Seen in this light, the title of Richard's exhibition could not be more relevant: the name "Strata" denotes the levelling of past and present, as well as the conflation and mutual reinforcing of the personal and the public meeting. However, by being attributed a narrative pattern, the traumatic event is placed in the past where it belongs, and so, in the healing temporality of working through. In other words, Richard's exhibition shows how much work has been done in terms of overcoming grief but, at the same time, it also suggests how much of it still lies ahead.

Works Cited

Baudrillard, Jean. *The Perfect Crime.* 1995. Trans. Chris Turner. London and New York: Verso, 2002.

Bersani, Leo. *Is the Rectum a Grave? and Other Essays.* Chicago, IL and London: The U of Chicago P, 2010.

Butler, Judith. *Precarious Life. The Powers of Mourning and Violence.* London and New York: Verso, 2004.

———. *Frames of War. When Is Life Grievable?* London and New York: Verso, 2009.

Caruth, Cathy. ed. *Trauma: Explorations in Memory.* Baltimore, MD: Johns Hopkins UP, 1995.

Castiglia, Christopher, and Christopher Reed. *If Memory Serves: Gay Men, AIDS, and the Promise of the Queer Past.* Minneapolis and London: U of Minnesota P, 2012.

Fitzgerald, Francis Scott. "My Generation." *A Short Autobiography.* Ed. James L.W. West, III. New York, London, Toronto and Sydney: Scribner, 2011. 154–62.

Freiburg, Rudolf, and Gerd Bayer. "Survival: An Introductory Essay." *The Ethics of Survival in Contemporary Literature and Culture.* Eds Rudolf Freiburg and Gerd Bayer. Basingstoke: Palgrave Macmillan, 2021. 1–45.

Kramer, Larry. *The Normal Heart.* New York: New American Library, 1985.

Kurtz, J. Roger. "Conclusion: After Trauma Studies?" *Trauma and Literature.* Ed. J. Roger Kurtz. Cambridge: Cambridge UP, 2018. 334–36.

Kushner, Tony. *Angels in America: A Gay Fantasia on National Themes.* 1991. New York: Theatre Communications Group, 2013.

LaCapra, Dominic. *Writing History, Writing Trauma.* Baltimore, MD: Johns Hopkins UP, 2014.

Makkai, Rebecca. "How to Write Across Difference." *Literary Hub.* 19 June 2018. Accessed on 05/01/2022 at: http://lithub.com/how-to-write-across-difference/.

———. *The Great Believers: A Novel.* 2018. New York: Penguin, 2019.

Parsons, Alexandra. "Queer." *The Routledge Companion to Twenty-First Century Literary Fiction.* Eds Daniel O'Gorman and Robert Eaglestone. London and New York: Routledge, 2019. 136–45.

Schulman, Sarah. *The Gentrification of the Mind: Witness to a Lost Imagination*. Berkeley, Los Angeles and London: U of California P, 2012.

Sehgal, Parul. "The Case Against the Trauma Plot." *The New Yorker*. 27 December 2021. Accessed on 05/01/2022 at: http://newyorker.com/magazine/2022/01/03/the-case-against-the-trauma-plot/

Self, Will. "A Posthumous Shock." *Harper's Magazine*. 15 November 2021. Accessed on 05/01/2022 at: http://harpers.org/archive/2021/12/a-posthumous-shock-trauma-studies-modernity-how-everything-became-trauma/

Sontag, Susan. *Illness as Metaphor*. 1978. New York: Vintage, 1979.

———. *Illness as Metaphor & AIDS and Its Metaphors*. 1989. London: Penguin, 2002.

Yanagihara, Hanya. *A Little Life: A Novel*. New York: Doubleday, 2015.

Part V

After the Subject

10 Grieving for the Subhuman in *Never Let Me Go* by Kazuo Ishiguro

Sylvie Maurel

Introduction

In *Precarious Life: The Powers of Mourning and Violence* (2004), Judith Butler posits vulnerability and loss as a common condition of the human subject and as the possible foundations of a fairer, more inclusive and less violent community. Establishing the fundamental relationality and interdependence of human beings, she also exposes in her work on war "the radically inequitable ways that corporeal vulnerability is distributed globally" (Butler 2004, 30), bringing to light the "hierarchy of grief" (32) on which war-waging thrives. In *Frames of War: When Is Life Grievable?*, she revisits these issues, placing the emphasis on grievability as the defining feature of a life that counts as a life: "Precisely because a human being may die, it is necessary to care for that being so that it may live. Only under conditions in which the loss would matter does the value of the life appear. Thus, grievability is a presupposition for the life that matters" (Butler 2009, 14). All bodies are finite, depend on others for sustenance and are therefore exposed to others. In this sense, all lives are equally precarious and should be equally grievable but "frames of war," that is to say, the discourse and the images that are circulated in wartime with an eye to making war both inevitable and legitimate, tamper with this ideal of equality. These discursive and visual frames of intelligibility organise a "differential distribution of grievability" (Butler 2009, 24), according to which certain lives matter less than others and certain deaths are more grievable than others.

Such inequities lie at the heart of *Never Let Me Go*, published in 2005. In Ishiguro's alternative England, human clones are bred and killed in their prime in order to save the lives of terminally ill, ordinary humans who depend on the clones' organs for higher life expectancy. The novel's bodies, cloned or non-cloned, are all precarious and interdependent: they are subject to untimely death or incurable illnesses; the two classes of humans represented in the book depend on each other, either for existence—the clones are brought into the world thanks to someone else's genetic code—or for survival to lethal diseases. However, in the

DOI: 10.4324/9781003347811-16

188 *Sylvie Maurel*

ghastly system of exploitation imagined by Ishiguro, the clones' lives do not really count as lives and do not qualify as grievable.

The chapter will argue that, if the clones can be used in this way by their non-cloned counterparts—"normals" as the novel calls them—it is because the frame of the subhuman is forced upon them, a conception of the cloned subject that legitimises the commodification of their body parts and preserves the status quo. Their subjugation is also secured by a general derealisation of loss, a whole set of compensatory fictions that not only facilitate their quiet observance of spoken or unspoken rules but also preclude grieving, for if there is no loss, there is no grief. Yet, Kathy H.'s elegiac narrative, a chronicle of loss, returns the clones to the position of the dispossessed human, and transforms their unmourned lives into grievable ones through a singularising drive that moves the clones from the realm of substitutable commodities to another form of substitutability that constructs them as human.

Framing the Subhuman

In *Frames of War: When Is Life Grievable?*, Judith Butler writes that, in the context of contemporary war, "the shared condition of precariousness leads not to reciprocal recognition, but to a specific exploitation of targeted populations, of lives that are not quite lives, cast as 'destructible' and 'ungrievable'" (2009, 31). Although there is no war in Ishiguro's dystopian world, this statement may be applied to *Never Let Me Go*, where this common precariousness—exposure to disease, violence, loss and untimely death—shades into exploitation of beings who are regarded as subhuman and whose lives are deemed "destructible and ungrievable" as a result.

Discussing the genre of *Never Let Me Go*, whose protagonists are genetically engineered clones, John Mullan notes that the novel is neither science fiction nor dystopia as it takes no interest in the science of cloning, does not imagine a future world—the story is set in England in the late 1990s—and is removed from any historical reality that we can recognise (104). The novel is more generally preoccupied with the creation of an underclass, one that is kept under the domination of other humans and that is gradually eviscerated "for a greater good." The word "clone" is only used twice in the narrative (Ishiguro 164, 256), and the readers discover that the narrator, Kathy H., is herself a clone only one-third into the novel. As John David Schwetman underlines, there is indeed no visual difference between clones and "normals," apart from markers which could be defined as social ones (423): the clones are identified as underprivileged by their second-hand clothes or the derelict places where they are made to live, whether the Cottages—a former farmhouse that is falling apart—or sinister recovery centres like The Kingfield, a former holiday camp hastily converted into a care home (Ishiguro 214).

Schwetman aptly claims that the clones' status is "a literary variation on social class and its function in negotiating states of grievance" (431), a social interpretation also put forward by Shameem Black. *Never Let Me Go*, she argues, offers

> a metaphor for the inequalities and predations of national and global economic systems. [...] On the national level, the creation of a service class for organ donation extends the principles of the British class system to its most horrifying extreme [...]. As a global metaphor, the condition of the students also speaks to the fate of postcolonial and migrant laborers who sustain the privileges of First World economies, the fortune of soldiers called on to serve in Afghanistan or Iraq, or the collateral damage of civilians killed in war so that other nations might maintain their power.
>
> (796)

As this description suggests, the novel reads as a dystopian exploration of precarity as Butler understands the word, that is, as "that politically induced condition in which certain populations suffer from failing social and economic networks of support and become differentially exposed to injury, violence, and death" (2009, 25). Precarity maximises precariousness, which is, by contrast, the condition common to all bodily beings. *Never Let Me Go* engages in a dystopian exacerbation of social inequities not only between clones and non-clones but also among the clones themselves. Some, like the novel's protagonists, are reared in humane, elitist institutions like Hailsham; others are bred in battery-farm conditions.

One way of sustaining this system of exploitation is to transform the clones into less than human creatures, as Miss Emily, the former head of Hailsham, makes clear at the end of the narrative:

> However uncomfortable people were about your existence, their overwhelming concern was that their own children, their spouses, their parents, their friends, did not die from cancer, motor neurone disease, heart disease. So for a long time you were kept in the shadows, and people did their best not to think about you. And if they did, they tried to convince themselves you weren't really like us. That you were less than human, so it didn't matter.
>
> (Ishiguro 258)

In the same passage, Kathy and Tommy are told that Hailsham ran out of funds when the Morningdale scandal erupted, a eugenic programme that meant to use the cloning technology for people to be able to adopt children with enhanced capacities. The reason for public outrage, as Miss Emily sees it, is that manufactured, *more* than human children, would "take their place in society" (259). As long as clones continued to

190   *Sylvie Maurel*

appear as "less than human," people had no fundamental objection to them, but when a new programme threatened to shatter the frame of the subhuman, then there was a public outcry.

Miss Emily's insightful comments are a perfect illustration of Butler's account of the frames that regulate perception and organise the unequal distribution of grievability. In Butler's own words:

> The epistemological capacity to apprehend a life is partially dependent on that life being produced according to norms that qualify it as a life or, indeed, as part of life. [...] The 'frames' that work to differentiate the lives we can apprehend from those we cannot [...] not only organize visual experience but also generate specific ontologies of the subject.
>
> (2009, 3–4)

In *Never Let Me Go*, the emphasis is less on the manufacturing of clones than on the links between frames of recognition and the production of ontology. The clones are in fact victims of a double violence, forced organ donation and defacement through the frame of the subhuman, an identification that makes their exploitation more acceptable by the rest of the population.

In this respect, the Hailsham project has ambivalent effects. Fighting for a more humane treatment of clones—but not going as far as raising the more fundamental question of their existence—Hailsham was created to challenge the frame of the subhuman. The "students" who, in the past, had been regarded as "[s]hadowy objects in test tubes" (Ishiguro 256) were to be recognised as humans, complete with "souls" (255). However, this philanthropic venture has the paradoxical consequence of making the clones even more monstrous in the eyes of non-clones, including those social activists who promoted the programme. Kathy H. remembers how the enigmatic Madame can hardly suppress her dread of the cloned children when she visits Hailsham; she responds to them as if they were spiders (35)—possibly an intertextual echo of H.G. Wells's "human spider[s]" in *The Time Machine* [47]. The system becomes much more uncomfortable when the victims are no longer considered as expendable matter.

In her discussion of the novel, where she asks "whether, within a radically materialistic society that reduces humans to collections of organs or body parts, a language of care can still be articulated" (Whitehead 63), Anne Whitehead demonstrates that the system is even more questionable when the socially sanctioned murder of the clones is founded on relations of care:

> By its very nature, care entails a risk that we privilege the needs of those who are closest to us, that in a 'selfless' devotion to our family

and friends, we paradoxically enact a 'selfish' inability to see beyond them and to recognize that their well-being often comes at another's (or others') cost.

(77)

This "social myopia" (Whitehead 77) is of course encouraged when those who suffer at the hands of the system are framed as less than human, substitutable commodities. In its concern with the welfare of clones, Hailsham fails to claim the equal value of lives and to produce more egalitarian grievability. In fact, Hailsham may be said to be complicit in exploitation. So is Kathy to some extent: as an outstanding carer who manages to make her donors stay calm (Ishiguro 3), she may be deemed to be an essential cog in the smooth running of the machine. In the first pages of the narrative, she explains that her reward for being such a good professional is that she gets to choose her donors, which suggests that she has developed the same social myopia since, as a rule now, she would rather take care of her own kind, that is to say, former Hailsham students like her (4). This exemplifies "the key moral dangers of basing a society or politics on empathy," as Whitehead observes: "it [empathy] is often governed by identity and similarity, and hence is prone to exclusion and ethnocentrism. Empathy, in other words, is not unambiguously beneficial, and it can lead as readily to exploitation and suffering as to more altruistic behaviors" (57). Incidentally, the name of Hailsham itself resonates with sinister echoes which undermine the professed altruistic agenda. The Dickensian ring of "Hailsham" brings to mind the Victorian workhouses which, after the new Poor Law of 1834, were also run by "guardians." Through the Victorian intertext, Hailsham appears as a latter-day workhouse, at best complicit in the exploitation of cloned and underprivileged orphans, while masquerading as an exclusive boarding-school. It is exposed as a sham.

Ungrievability as the Derealisation of Loss

Examining the "schemes of intelligibility" which determine what is human, what is not, what is a liveable life and what is a grievable death, Butler distinguishes between "two distinct forms of normative power":

> one operates through producing a symbolic identification of the face with the inhuman, foreclosing our apprehension of the human in the scene; the other works through radical effacement, so that there never was a human, there never was a life, and no murder has, therefore, ever taken place.

(2004, 147)

192   *Sylvie Maurel*

As well as producing the frame of the subhuman, the novel's society and its norms perpetrate their lawful violence through effacement. The clones are made to live in a parallel world on the edge of that of the normals. They are removed from the sphere of visibility, kept behind actual or imaginary fences, and they drive spectrally along dark, deserted roads which seem to have been made for their use alone (Ishiguro 267). They have little to no interaction with normals to the point that, at Hailsham for example, they take Culture Briefing classes in which, through role-play, they learn about situations and codes of behaviour to be found in the world of ordinary humans (108). Committed to invisibility, the clones' lives matter even less and their murders remain outside the scope of perception. For Shameem Black they are evocative of Giorgio Agamben's *homo sacer*:

> Like *homo sacer*, Ishiguro's students can be killed but not sacrificed; their deaths by organ removal create no source of transcendent meaning for them or for their community. Agamben identifies a central locus of such 'bare life' in the modern concentration camp, a paradoxical space included in political life only by means of its radical exclusion. Hailsham, the English boarding school-like institution where Ishiguro's characters grow up, provides precisely such a shadowy territory beyond the admissible political life of the realm it inhabits and enables.
>
> (789)

There are indeed echoes of the Holocaust and of the Nazi concentration camp as the locus of Agamben's bare life in *Never Let Me Go*— the donation system was born after World War II; the function of carers bears affinity with that of *Kapos*; a eugenic programme caused Hailsham to close down, etc.—but the clones may also embody, albeit in a nightmarish way, the condition of precarious beings as Guillaume Le Blanc defines them, a version which articulates a social critique of capitalism:

> For there is indeed a social status of precariousness: non-existence. Precarious people do not live outside society. They are not excluded but they are dispossessed of themselves by the society that produces them and keeps them afloat, one foot in, one foot out, thus creating the army of reserves that capitalism needs to prosper in an unlimited way. The dispossession of the precarious culminates in their being deprived of voice and face.
>
> (Le Blanc 19–20; my translation)[1]

Both inside and outside, the precarious clones are derealised in order for the society which created them to maintain its sovereign power. To go back to the Morningdale scandal evoked earlier, the main objection to it was that it would make the clones leave the shadowy territory of society's margins, earn them visibility and access to a place in society, a simply unacceptable option given the frames of recognition available at the time.

Derealisation is also an inherent effect of frames in Butler's account of the device. Because it selects the discursive or visual material that it disseminates, "the frame is always throwing something away, always keeping something out, always de-realizing and de-legitimating alternative versions of reality" (Butler 2009, xiii). A particular memory that Kathy relates in Chapter 8 gives a graphic representation of the editing process at work in frames. Sometimes, at Hailsham, when she feels oppressed by the crowds of children, Kathy will seek a view with no people in it, which implies focussing for long periods of time on one part of whatever she is looking at out of a window or through a doorway, until there is nobody in the frame (Ishiguro 88). Kathy's view keeps plenty out of the frame, thus creating a deceptive vision of reality, a welcome and ephemeral illusion from her perspective, but a laying bare of the invisibilising or derealising operation of official frames. In a way, the purpose of Kathy's narrative is to make visible what is invisible in society's frames of recognition; it constructs an alternative version of reality, at least an alternative frame.

For all her nostalgia of Hailsham, the place is itself presented as a derealising machine, a world of illusion that numbs the senses and participates in the general "derealization of loss" which Butler identifies as one of the mechanisms of dehumanisation that acts as a prohibition on mourning (2004, 148). Through this derealisation, Hailsham and the larger community make sure that the clones' lives remain ungrievable, and they secure their compliance with the donation system. At Hailsham, where the subhuman is meant to be humanised, effacement prevails. Hailsham implements strategies of effacement regarding what the students are and what their fate will be. In the lingo of the system, reality is consistently toned down by a set of deceitful euphemisms like "students," "donors" and "carers" instead of "clones" or, more tellingly, "completion" instead of "death." The staff is careful not to say too much, with the exception of one of the guardians, Miss Lucy, who makes it her duty to speak plainly to her students about what awaits them: "You'll become adults, then before you're old, before you're even middle-aged, you'll start to donate your vital organs" (Ishiguro 79–80). This key moment of plain talk, which causes Miss Lucy to be dismissed and which enlightens the reader about the nature of the donations, contrasts with the more common evasions or half-lies or tacit rules internalised by the students that things like the donations are not to be discussed openly (83). The realities of death and loss are never addressed except in the haziest of ways.

194 *Sylvie Maurel*

On the other hand, Hailsham produces or encourages sugarcoating, compensatory fictions thanks to which the clones' lives are deceptively made to seem liveable in their own eyes. Through the myth of "possibles," for example, they are allowed to indulge in an illusory and twisted quest for origins. The students believe that if they can find their model, they will have a clearer idea of *who* they are and, strangely enough, of the future that lies ahead of them, while in fact *what* they are, their ghastly function as organ providers, is the only thing that matters, and their future is of an unwavering nature. Another opiate is the possibility of "deferral," that is to say, of putting off the start of the donations by a couple of years, which, rumour has it, only Hailsham students can apply for if they can prove that they are truly in love. This fiction, in which Kathy and Tommy believe to the end, is part of the myth of privilege that is associated with Hailsham. The Hailsham children are made to think they are "special" (Ishiguro 43), a privileged set, which of course is a misleading representation of their precarity, even though they are slightly better-off than other clones reared in less comfortable circumstances. According to Mark Currie, this "privileged deprivation" explains "why we sometimes not only accept but actually beseech our own confinement: because relative deprivation causes us to misapprehend social injustice as privilege" (103). The combination of dispossession and privilege forecloses resistance or rebellion, and accounts for the subservience of the clones which has intrigued and frustrated so many readers.

The derealisation of loss culminates in the story that is circulated about Norfolk which, described as "a lost corner" in one of Miss Emily's classes, becomes, in the students' imagination, the place "where all the lost property found in the country ended up" (Ishiguro 65). At first a misinterpretation of Miss Emily's phrase, then a private joke running among former Hailsham clones, the story fuels the illusion that something that has been lost will always be retrieved somehow. The fantasy dies hard for, in their twenties, Kathy, Tommy and Ruth take a trip to Norfolk with high hopes of finding Ruth's possible. The woman turns out to be very different from Ruth and cannot have been her model, but Tommy and Kathy engage in a quest for a tape which Kathy loved as a child and which was inexplicably lost. Providentially enough, Kathy lands on a copy of the tape in a second-hand shop (169). Finally, in the last pages, after Tommy's death, Kathy cannot help going back to Norfolk, as if Tommy was likely to be in the lost-and-found (282). Thanks to the Norfolk fiction, loss comes to be perceived as reversible, therefore ungrievable. The tape found in the second-hand shop is an inscription of the economy of the substitutable and a metaphor for the duplicated beings whom society regards as disposable and replaceable. Like the tape, clones are serialised artefacts, as Jean Baudrillard reminds us (148), copies of genetic codes deprived of grievable singularity. Kathy's elegiac narrative, however, works towards a restoration of their grievability.

Kathy's Grieving Narrative

In the dystopian world of the novel, there is of course no public grieving for the ungrievable lives of the invisible clones. There is no obituary, "the instrument by which grievability is publicly distributed [...], the means by which a life becomes, or fails to become, a publicly grievable life" (Butler 2004, 34). There is no public mourning but Kathy's narrative, a narrative of loss, of grief, of mourning, constructs the lives of her peers as grievable lives, in response to the derealisation of loss. This is her one act of resistance: her grieving narrative flouts the tacit prohibition on mourning. Kathy's account reasserts the reality of irreversible loss which Sigmund Freud in *Deuil et mélancolie*, Paul Ricœur in *La mémoire, l'histoire, l'oubli* or Vincent Delecroix and Philippe Forest in *Le deuil* define precisely as the ultimate experience of reality, an "experience of the real as real" (Delecroix and Forest 91), reality as that over which we have no control:

> It remains that, for me, the experience of loss is, par excellence, the experience of the real. Paradoxical as it may seem, the real is not given in the positivity of what is there, but in the negation of loss, that is to say, in the unreachable and the irreversible: there it opposes a radical 'no' to our desires and our imagination, it is what escapes us, what we can do nothing about.
> (Delecroix and Forest 91; my translation)[2]

Kathy's narrative is predicated on loss. It borrows from elegy, a genre which, according to Jean-Michel Ganteau, dramatises "vulnerable object relationships and separate[s] the better to underline the need for relation" (69). The elegiac mode, he argues, "does not postulate that the object is reachable but, quite on the contrary, that it has been lost forever" (69). Part of the ethical dimension of elegy lies in this acknowledgement of irredeemable loss in that it "help[s] circumscribe the essentials of humanity as dependence on the lost other" (69) or the fundamental vulnerability and relationality of humans. In *Never Let Me Go*, the elegiac mode is, therefore, a humanising form that implicitly responds to and resists the frame of the subhuman that serves to invisibilise and to exploit the clones' bodies.

The inescapable, indomitable reality of loss informs the whole of Kathy's narrative, which elegiacally registers losses of all kinds. Cherished objects go missing, such as a calendar drawn by one of the Hailsham students (Ishiguro 90–91) or Kathy's tape and, with it, her favourite track, which she plays over and over, and whose title provides that of the novel (69). For Kathy, then an eleven-year-old child, "never let me go" is what a mother says to her newborn, "partly because she's so happy, but also because she's so afraid something will happen, that the baby will

196 *Sylvie Maurel*

get ill or be taken away from her" (70). The figure of the baby is a representation of the fragility of life, dependent on and exposed to others, to love, illness, danger and death. In Kathy's imagination, the baby's life is one that matters; it is a grievable life precisely because the loss of this life would matter. Although, even then, Kathy knows that this is a misreading of the words because they simply do not fit with the rest of the lyrics, she continues reading her own "fears and longings" (73) into the song: she laments the ungrievability of her own life, driven by the more or less conscious knowledge that she is a clone, that, as a clone, she matters to no mother; has been deprived of primary relations; of the possibility of procreating; and will die an early death that will go unmourned. In its desperate plea for unbreakable bonds, the song is a melancholic, repetitive and humanising inscription of attachment to what is lost, of dependence on others and of the risk of losing attachments. Eventually, the tape itself disappears, resurfacing many years later in Norfolk, as we saw, but only as an illusion of replaceability. Hailsham also vanishes, closing down after drastic cuts. Gradually the ties binding all those who grew up there fray, a loosening that haunts Kathy's sleepless nights: one day she sees a clown holding a bunch of helium balloons in his hand which she likens to a "little tribe" (208), worrying that one of them will drift up into the sky and away from the group. This is a foreshadowing of the more painful losses to come, the loss of Kathy's close friends with the demises of Ruth and Tommy.

Kathy's elegiac account also chronicles the loss of illusions and of consoling fictions. In the last lines, after Tommy's death, Kathy returns to Norfolk the better to dismiss the myth of the lost-and-found:

> I half-closed my eyes and imagined this was the spot where everything I'd ever lost since my childhood had washed up, and I was now standing here in front of it, and if I waited long enough, a tiny figure would appear on the horizon across the field, and gradually get larger until I'd see it was Tommy, and he'd wave, maybe even call. The fantasy never got beyond that—I didn't let it—and though the tears rolled down my face, I wasn't sobbing or out of control. I just waited a bit, then turned back to the car, to drive off to wherever it was I was supposed to be.
>
> (282)

This is a moment of recognition. Kathy is staring loss in the face and refuses, at the close of the novel, the solace of fantasy ("I didn't let it"). She merely acknowledges the presence of irreversible absence. She lets go of Tommy—moving perhaps from melancholy to mourning—grieving for her loss as indicated by her tears, which performatively establish his death as grievable. To a certain extent, Kathy also grieves for the loss of consolation here, which is a characteristic feature of contemporary elegy according to Ganteau, "a mode without consolation or resolution" (70) that resists final "apotheosis and remain[s] content with the more humble phases of acceptance or plunge into melancholia" (95). As the last sentence of the quotation and of the book shows, the loss of relation leaves the bereaved narrator in a poignant state of utter solitude which, at the same time, signposts the vulnerability and relationality of this all-too-human clone.

The Norfolk field in which the story ends is littered with rubbish caught in the barbed wire (Ishiguro 282), the refuse of this materialistic society and a metaphor for the wasted lives and disposable bodies of the clones who, Ruth says, are "modelled from *trash*" (164; original emphasis). This definition of the clones' status is earlier metaphorised by the piles of discarded objects that are periodically brought to Hailsham for "the Sales," one of the highlights of the children's lives. Watching the men unload the boxes filled with the refuse of normals, one of the children asks them if it is "a *bumper crop*" (41; original emphasis), a phrase that brings to mind another one: organ harvesting. Body parts are implicitly equated with disposable objects, thriftily upcycled into—often disappointing—treats for commodified children. In contrast to those repeated references to rubbish or unwanted odds and ends, Kathy's reminiscing fashions those butchered, expendable and interchangeable bodies into grievable lives by asserting their singularity. Mourning, Delecroix and Forest argue, has to do with "the absolute singularity of the lost being who remains irreplaceable" (22; my translation).[3] Through her grieving narrative, Kathy asserts the singularity of those she has lost, and challenges the dystopian substitutability that underpins the creation of clones. Founded on "the absolute singularity of the lost being," the experience of grieving is at odds with what can be copied, duplicated, manufactured, substituted; in other words, with the principle of cloning and the commodification of bodies:

> Singular is really the key word. What it implies is a vision of the human being as singular, that is to say not susceptible to being reproduced, manufactured, exchanged, etc. This is the horizon towards which we are heading when we talk about posthumanity, whether this posthumanity is produced by biotechnological means or simply through the commercialisation of the living or of individuals. To speak *for* mourning, in the sense that we are trying to give to this word, is to speak *for* singularity, which must be the lot of the individual, in a society that tends more and more to deny it.
>
> (Delecroix and Forest 31; original emphasis; my translation)[4]

This is perhaps the main function of Kathy's elegiac narrative: it reinstates the singularity or uniqueness of those framed as reproducible, subhuman creatures, as "serialized doubles" (Machinal 121). Giving an

198 *Sylvie Maurel*

account of her losses, Kathy works against this substitutability by singularising the lost ones.

The fear of effacement through memory loss is one of the mourners' most painful anxieties (Delecroix and Forest 35), as well as the driving force of Kathy's narrative, which stems from an "urge to order all these old memories" (Ishiguro 37) after the completions of Ruth and Tommy, and before she is caught in the process of her own slow death. Kathy's anamnesis re-members her butchered friends, and fashions their scattered body parts into human shape. In doing so, she erects a tentative memorial marking the publicly unmarkable losses and gives narrative sepulchre to those who have no graves, whose lives were not lives but instruments in the preservation of other lives, and whose deaths leave no trace at all. Interestingly, two important scenes take place in literal or figurative graveyards—not to mention the Norfolk field. In the first, set in an old churchyard, the three friends have a decisive argument over Tommy's drawings, after which they break off relations and Kathy leaves the Cottages to start her training as a carer (190). The old graveyard marks separation, the death of friendship, the end of the age of innocence and their entry into a dark adulthood marred by the prospect of their own deaths. Years later, the trio is reunited in a metaphorical graveyard: they drive to an area of marshland strewn with ghostly dead trees which are the remains of a defunct forest and where an old crumbling boat is stranded (220). The wreck and the dead trees stand for the wrecked bodies of Tommy and Ruth, who have started their donations at this stage and are in the last leg of their lethal journey. The whole episode almost reads as a death-bed scene. Ruth, who dies shortly after the trip, is very frail and has to be supported by her friends. On the ride back, she makes a confession and begs forgiveness for having deliberately kept Tommy and Kathy apart (227). Such scenes memorialise the dead and return singular beings to visibility in order to counter "the irreversible effacement of the image" that gives the grieving person such excruciating pain (Delecroix and Forest 35). Kathy's reconstruction of the clones' lives, however uncertain, limited and fragmented, conjures *personae* or effigies in the Latin sense of the words, those images of the dead that were displayed in Roman funeral rites, as Delecroix and Forest remind us, suggesting that there may even be affinities between the Roman *personae*, novelistic character and portraiture, between funerary effigies and representation: "in the end, perhaps this is what literature is all about: constructing *personae*, effigies, characters—portraying the absent. It is an art of mourning" (142; my translation).[5] I would not go so far as to say that all literature is "an art of mourning," but Kathy's elegy emerges as a singularising funeral rite that makes loss matter.

However, it could also be argued that by singularising the departed through storytelling, Kathy makes them substitutable in a different sense. In *Giving an Account of Oneself*, Judith Butler discusses Adriana

Grieving for the Subhuman   199

Cavarero's conception of the other as unique and nonsubstitutable, a singularity that is coextensive with corporeality: the other is "fundamentally exposed, visible, seen, existing in a bodily way and of necessity in a domain of appearance" (Butler 2005, 33). Our bodies make us different from one another but "we are bound to one another by what differentiates us, namely, our singularity" (34). Insofar as singularity is "a collective condition, characterizing us all equally," singularity is substitutable (35). In the last analysis, Kathy's narrative makes the clones recognisably human by rescuing them from a materialist conception of substitutability that results in the commodification of indiscriminate bodies, and by immersing them in an ethical form of substitutability that proclaims their singularity, within the common frame of the recognisably human. The shift places them on a par with non-clones. Their lives, it is implied, are as grievable as the lives of the non-clones for the sake of whom they are murdered, and their eviscerated bodies are but the quintessence of grievable human vulnerability.

Conclusion

In his dystopian novel and through the metaphor of cloning, Ishiguro investigates precarity in contemporary, market-based society, and engages with the issue of "the differential allocation of grievability" (Butler 2004, 37) that is produced and legitimised in order to exploit certain lives for the benefit of others. In *Never Let Me Go*, the frame of the subhuman and other derealising devices, such as strategies of effacement or myth-making, generate ungrievable lives. However, as Butler notes, frames have an inbuilt tendency to leak, a leakage that happens not just when they are called into question but in the reproduction and dissemination that are necessary to their hegemony:

> The frame that seeks to contain, convey, and determine what is seen [...] depends upon the conditions of reproducibility in order to succeed. And yet, this very reproducibility entails a constant breaking from context, a constant delimitation of new context, which means that the 'frame' does not quite contain what it conveys, but breaks apart every time it seeks to give definitive organization to its content.
> (2009, 10)

Kathy's narrative, which does not openly or consciously challenge the frame of the subhuman, nevertheless cracks it: where derealisation prevails, she articulates an elegy in which loss is irredeemable and no consolation will be found. In her story, she replaces substitutable bodies, framed as less than human, with singular, recognisably human ones, affirming the equal worth of all human lives. After reading the book, however, one may wonder whether some of the briefly evoked

200 *Sylvie Maurel*

lives, those of the clones outside the circle of Hailsham's happy few or even those of the non-clones in the background, are not less grievable than those closer to Kathy. The hierarchy of grief persists, but awareness of this persisting hierarchy may at least lead to a more ethical apprehension of how and why, in the readers' world, certain lives matter more than others and certain deaths are more grievable than others.

Notes

1 "Car il existe bien un statut social de la précarité : l'inexistence. Les précaires ne vivent pas hors de la société. Ils ne sont pas exclus, mais ils sont dépossédés d'eux-mêmes par la société qui les fabrique en les maintenant à flot, un pied dedans, un pied dehors, et en créant ainsi l'armée de réserve dont a besoin le capitalisme pour prospérer de manière illimitée. La dépossession de soi culmine dans la privation de voix et de visage du précaire." (Le Blanc 19–20).

2 "Il reste que, pour moi, l'expérience de la perte est, par excellence, l'expérience du réel. Aussi paradoxal que cela puisse paraître, le réel ne se donne pas dans la positivité de ce qui est là, mais dans la négation de la perte, c'est-à-dire dans l'inaccessibilité et dans l'irréversible : là, il oppose un 'non' radical à nos désirs et à notre imagination, il est ce qui nous échappe, ce sur quoi nous ne pouvons rien" (Delecroix and Forest 91).

3 "la singularité absolue de l'être perdu, qui reste insubstituable" (Delecroix and Forest 22).

4 "'Singulier' est vraiment le mot essentiel. Il en va d'une vision de l'humain, en tant qu'il est singulier, c'est-à-dire en tant qu'il n'est pas susceptible d'être reproduit, manufacturé, échangé, etc. Or tel est bien l'horizon vers lequel on se dirige lorsqu'il est question de posthumanité, que cette posthumanité soit assurée par des moyens biotechnologiques ou simplement sous l'effet de la commercialisation du vivant ou des individus. Parler *pour* le deuil, au sens que nous essayons de donner à ce mot, c'est parler *pour* la singularité, qui doit être le lot de l'individu, dans une société qui tend de plus en plus à la dénier" (Delecroix and Forest 31; original emphasis).

5 "Finalement, c'est peut-être cela la littérature: fabriquer des *personas*, des effigies, des personnages—faire le portrait des absents. C'est un art du deuil" (Delecroix and Forest 142).

Works Cited

Agamben, Giorgio. *Homo sacer: Le pouvoir souverain et la vie nue*. 1995. Trans. Marilène Raiola. Paris: Seuil, 1997.

Baudrillard, Jean. *Simulacres et simulations*. Paris: Galilée, 1981.

Black, Shameem. "Ishiguro's Inhuman Aesthetics." *Modern Fiction Studies* 55.4 (Winter 2009): 785–807.

Butler, Judith. *Precarious Life: The Powers of Mourning and Violence*. London and New York: Verso, 2004.

———. *Giving an Account of Oneself*. New York: Fordham UP, 2005.

———. *Frames of War: When Is Life Grievable?* 2009. London and New York: Verso, 2016.

Currie, Mark. "Controlling Time: *Never Let Me Go.*" *Kazuo Ishiguro: Contemporary Critical Perspectives.* Eds Sean Matthews and Sebastian Groes. London: Continuum, 2009. 91–103.

Delecroix, Vincent, and Philippe Forest. *Le deuil: Entre le chagrin et le néant.* 2015. Paris: Gallimard, 2017.

Freud, Sigmund. *Deuil et mélancolie.* 1917. Paris: Payot, 2011.

Ganteau, Jean-Michel. *The Ethics and Aesthetics of Vulnerability in Contemporary British Fiction.* London: Routledge, 2015.

Ishiguro, Kazuo. *Never Let Me Go.* 2005. London: Faber and Faber, 2010.

Le Blanc, Guillaume. *Vies ordinaires, vies précaires.* Paris: Seuil, 2007.

Machinal, Hélène. "From Behind the Looking-Glass: Kazuo Ishiguro's *Never Let Me Go* and Beyond." *Études britanniques contemporaines* 37 (2009): 115–27.

Mullan, John. "Afterword: On First Reading *Never Let Me Go.*" *Kazuo Ishiguro: Contemporary Critical Perspectives.* Eds Sean Matthews and Sebastian Groes. London: Continuum, 2009. 104–113.

Ricœur, Paul. *La mémoire, l'histoire, l'oubli.* Paris: Seuil, 2000.

Schwetman, John David. "'Shadowy Objects in Test Tubes': The Ethics of Grievance in Kazuo Ishiguro's *Never Let Me Go.*" *Interdisciplinary Literary Studies* 19.4 (2017): 421–40.

Wells, H.G. *The Time Machine.* Ed. Michael Moorcock. 1895. London: Everyman, 1993.

Whitehead, Anne. "Writing with Care: Kazuo Ishiguro's *Never Let Me Go.*" *Contemporary Literature* 52.1 (Spring 2011): 54–83.

11 The Grievability of the Non-Human

Ian McEwan's *Machines Like Me*

Jean-Michel Ganteau

Introduction

Ian McEwan's 2019 novel, *Machines Like Me. And People Like You*, may have come as a surprise to some readers in relation to its main theme, that is, artificial intelligence as embodied in sentient machines. Still, it evinces a high degree of continuity with some of his previous novels. As in *Saturday* (2005), that concentrated on the issue of consciousness in a very systematic way, both thematically and aesthetically, *Machines Like Me* presents the reader with a thoroughly researched, largely realistic narrative—at least in most of its aspects—nodding towards the *roman à thèse*, since it explores a cultural and ontological conundrum by tackling the issue of what philosophers call "the problem of other minds" (Kopka and Schaffeld 59). In line with *Saturday*, the tone does not hesitate to borrow from the essayistic as a welter of information concerning the specific topic that has to be imparted to the reader, a trait that a certain number of reviewers have found fault with (Giles; Patterson; Saleem; Theroux). I have argued elsewhere that this characteristic has to be envisaged in relation to the plausible evocation of an inexperienced first-person narrator whose ontological condition and status as a subject remain a moot point (Ganteau, 116). Echoes from *The Children Act* (McEwan 2014) may also ring in the narrative strand that deals with the complications due to the adoption of a child, little Mark, the contemporary picture of the Dickensian orphan landed into late-twentieth-century London. Besides, this first-person narrative harks back to *Atonement* (McEwan 2001), with its retrospective focus on a period of the narrator and protagonist's life, taking place some thirty years after the events of the story, and distilling a compound of self-justification, nostalgia and regret.

Among the tutelary references that were most often spotted by reviewers come essentially Mary Shelley and Shakespeare. In fact, the novel has been envisaged through the generic angle of SF tainted with dystopia, which underlines its kinship with the mythical Romantic predecessor. The first pages, which narrate how Charlie Friend, the narrator and protagonist, came to buy a highly sophisticated intelligent humanoid

DOI: 10.4324/9781003347811-17

The Grievability of the Non-Human 203

robot, ring with references to the founding Romantic myth of creation. After being unpacked, Adam, stark naked in a perfect imitation of the human body, has to be plugged to the electric socket so that he may charge up. This makes Miranda, Charlie's prospective girlfriend, wish the teenage Mary Shelley were sitting with them, observing this technological wonder, to which Charley retorts that what the original creature and this critter share is "a hunger for the animating force of electricity" (McEwan 2019, 4). Of course, the story will focus on how the creature becomes autonomous, and how, at the same time, it is the seat of deep feelings of attachment and vulnerability to the sense of loss, among other similarities to Shelley's monster. Another hypertext in which the utopian and dystopian impulses meet is Shakespeare's *The Tempest*, whose all-embracing modal configuration, the romance, allows for a great deal of latitude as to the realistic evocation of external events and is more concerned with the "truth of the human heart," to take up Nathaniel Hawthorne's famous phrase (xi). As indicated above, the female protagonist's name, Miranda, typecasts her as a descendant from the Shakespearean heroine whose words gave the title to one of the most celebrated of Modernist dystopias, Aldous Huxley's *Brave New World* (1932). Indeed, McEwan's Miranda shares a great deal of honesty and innocence with her Renaissance prototype—although its manifestations are distinct. Above all, Adam qualifies as a technological avatar of Caliban, both human and not quite human (Beck n.p.), whose monstrosity is not physical but is still very much present and displaced, even while problematising the idea of what it is to be human and a subject. Yet, the most structural and lingering tutelary presence may well be that of Rudyard Kipling, whose poem, "The Secret of the Machines" (1911), provides the novel's epigraph. Its last two stanzas encapsulate the conflicting tone of the poem that starts by glorifying the power of the machines before asserting human supremacy, in what looks like an italicised afterthought and coda to the fascinated vision of technological progress:

> But remember, please, the Law by which we live,
> We are not built to comprehend a lie,
> We can neither love nor pity nor forgive.
> If you make a slip in handling us you die!
> We are greater than the Peoples or the Kings—
> Be humble, as you crawl beneath our rods!—
> Our touch can alter all created things,
> We are everything on earth—except The Gods!
> *It will vanish and the stars will shine again,*
> *Because, for all our power and weight and size,*
> *We are nothing more than children of your brain!*
>
> (Kipling 759; original emphasis)

204   *Jean-Michel Ganteau*

The poem clearly sets off an anti-humanist vision against a more traditionally humanist one that is allowed to triumph *in extremis*. Still, a great deal of ambivalence accrues from this text which, I shall argue, McEwan's novel captures in its turn, even while importing the themes of the impossibility to lie and of the machine as a child of the human subject.

When Charlie, who is in his thirties, buys Adam, he decides that he is going to set his basic personality parameters in collaboration with Miranda, his neighbour, whom he is falling in love with, so that Adam will become their child. As the plot thickens, Adam, whose access to the internet is total and instantaneous and whose hacking powers seem to be fairly well developed, warns Charlie that perhaps he should not trust Miranda, whom he fears to be a first-rate liar, hence a menace to his owner. Following on such a warning, Adam becomes Miranda's lover for one night, while Charlie listens to the heated sexual concourse from his own bedroom, directly under Miranda's. At this point, Charlie starts hating Adam and asks him never to betray him again. The plot becomes even more complicated as it appears that Miranda is hiding a secret, in conformity to Adam's original disclosure: after the loss of her dear school friend Mariam, who was raped and chose to commit suicide rather than tell her family, Miranda was racked by pain and guilt and thought her friend's death should be avenged. This is why she had sex with the rapist, Gorringe, and then accused him of raping her, so that he was sentenced to serve some time in jail. In the early stages of the novel, she learns that Gorringe is about to be released and has vowed to find her so as to take his own revenge. Adam, ever the reliable adviser on account of his encyclopaedic knowledge that he manages to scientifically transform into the expression of probabilities, suggests that the three of them should confront the jailbird, which they do in a climactic scene in which Miranda gives vent to her anger, while Adam makes a recording of Gorringe's full confession. Through a fairly melodramatic sleight of hand, it so happens at that very moment that Gorringe is ready to accept her blame as he has converted to religion while in prison and considers Miranda an agent of God's grace. This implies that he is ready to let the truth come out and to face a trial again, which Miranda is very unwilling to let happen, as his revelations would imply the probable cancellation of the adoption process that she initiated with a view to adopting Mark. This leaves her with the following dilemma: should she reveal what she did so that she pays for her crime and starts with a clean slate or should she remain silent, a more comfortable option and one that would warrant that her adoption plans come to fruition? Adam, prompted by his programmed incapacity to lie, chooses in her place and proposes to send Gorringe's confession and a precise narrative of the situation to the police. This is when, with Miranda's complicity, Charley kills Adam by cracking his skull with a hammer, leaving

The Grievability of the Non-Human 205

just enough time for the humanoid to save his personal data and deliver a final speech.

The narrator's gesture, of course, raises the issue of the human subject's sovereignty, that is, of his/her capacity to decide who should be killed and, one step further, who should/can be mourned, a prerogative that, in the works of Michel Foucault, but also of Giorgio Agamben, Judith Butler and Achille Mbembe among others, is attributed to the State. In fact, the capacity to kill an intelligent, sentient critter—which Adam is shown to be throughout—without any judiciary consequence, ties in with situations when the law is suspended and replaced by a state of exception (Agamben 159; Butler 2006, 51; Mbembe 66). In the world of *Machines Like Me*, while some characters have the capacity to be grieved—as is the case with Mariam, Miranda's friend, who is not only mourned but also avenged—, some others, with a prominent narrative position, are not. From this point of view, the novel may be said to raise a series of questions which were formulated by Butler in *Precarious Life*: "Who counts as human? Whose lives count as lives, what makes for a grievable life?" (2006, 20). At the heart of the novel there lie interrogations on the limits of the human and on the opening of the human, on life, consciousness and subjectivity, as well as on the role of emotions in determining subjectivity (Colombino). In the following pages, I will show how *Machines Like Me* addresses Butler's triple question by concentrating first on ungrievability. My second part focuses on the permanence and power of grievability. I end up addressing the issue of literature's capacity to anticipate and shift the norms of grievability.

Ungrievability

Examples of grievability abound in *Machines Like Me*. As suggested above, Mariam is mourned, intensely so, by her friend Miranda and by her family. Several pages are devoted to the evocation of the devastation that her suicide provokes in those who love her, enhanced by religious and judicial rituals. This narrative strand, which is fairly well developed, is instrumental in fuelling the main plot in its *film noir* dimension (Theroux n.p.). It also contributes to making the narrative veer towards the melodramatic, with Mariam and Miranda's unconditional, intense childhood and teenage bond, and the survivor's plea that she would avenge her lost friend—some sort of a pact with herself. The feeling of loss is so intense, and made even more so by Miranda's guilt, that it translates into an image of radical faithfulness to the departed, a component of melancholia, so that it seems as if, for Miranda, being were to be strictly understood as being *for* the other. And it is not before the climactic confrontation between Miranda and Gorringe that melancholia starts transforming into mourning. In other terms, intense grieving is given the shape of a protracted incorporation of the lost object of love

206   *Jean-Michel Ganteau*

that, in extreme forms, is conducive to a loss of self, the characteristic of melancholia according to Freud, as opposed to mourning, which he defines as the loss of an object (Freud 53). The very long phase of arrested development and obsession with loss that Miranda has to go through before achieving some relief offers a paroxysmal testimony to the grievability of a dear friend, whose status, through grief's validation, is clearly that of a subject.

The private mourning occasioned by Mariam's death is also presented against a wider framework, which is that of national mourning. One of the most singular characteristics of the novel consists in its warped evocation of historical time, as the scene takes place in 1982, but a very special 1982. Indeed, among other genres, *Machines Like Me* also belongs to the category of speculative fiction as it retrospectively presents the reader with an alternative present in which some events correspond to our historical knowledge of what happened at the time, while others clearly depart from historical fact. As indicated by the narrator, "[t]he present is the frailest of improbable constructs" (McEwan 2019, 64), an axiom that the narrative transforms into a fictional experience. One of the main points of departure from our empirical knowledge of the period concerns the Falklands war which, in McEwan's alternative scenario, brings about the quick and absolute defeat of Britain, followed by the resignation of Margaret Thatcher and an enduring economic and social crisis with unemployment, strikes and a general unweaving of class relations. The Falklands disaster takes a heavy toll both on the British military and civilian citizens, as a part of the fleet is sunk: "The loss of life was in the low thousands. Sailors, troops, cooks, doctors and nurses, journalists" (42). Of course, this gives rise to an official period of national mourning, with ceremonies broadcast on national networks and other public manifestations. The official allocation of grievability to the victims of the conflict indicates that their worth as human subjects—and their lives' recognition as such—is beyond doubt: the perceptual parameters for the recognition of these lives are clearly established (Butler 2009, 25) thanks to official frames that seem to be shared by the whole nation, including citizens who, like Charlie, were originally against the war.

Such is emphatically not the case with Adam's demise. One could expect this to be normal as, after all, a robot is not expected to be mourned. Still, Adam is a special humanoid and, above all, it is a *literary* machine. In Kipling's poem, the eponymous machines are given the power of speech, and the prosopopoeia indicates a form of anthropomorphism of a limited type, as their assertiveness and aggressiveness, in the bulk of the poem, leave very little room for empathy and ultimately serve as a glorification of the human and as the upbeat confirmation of anthropocentrism. The situation is altogether different in McEwan's novel where, even if Adam is always seen from outside and even if he

The Grievability of the Non-Human   207

remains in many ways cryptic to the narrator and the readers till the end, some of his words and reactions generate a non-negligible degree of attachment. Granted, things are not pushed to the extremities presented in Kazuo Ishiguro's 2021 novel *Klara and the Sun*, whose protagonist *and* narrator is the eponymous humanoid robot so that her perceptions and thought-processes are intimately shared with the reader, granting her a great deal of consistency as a round character. Still, the mere phrase "humanoid character" indicates that Adam's treatment has much in common with that of the human protagonists. This is all the truer as Adam, being a learner and being programmed to garner experience and knowledge, is a round character and certainly not a stereotype. He is endowed with a fair degree of autonomy, as suggested above, which makes him make decisions that run counter to Charlie's will but never against his or Miranda's interests, as becomes clear in the end. Besides, he has feelings, and many positive ones at that, since he falls madly in love with Miranda, writes haikus in her honour and becomes extremely devoted to her while remaining loyal to Charley. His feelings are recognised by the other characters. Admittedly, there remains a great deal of rigidity in his reactions, which makes him at times ridiculous in a way reminiscent of Henri Bergson's analyses of the absence of plasticity in some subjects: such a characteristic reveals some sort of automatic, non-human reaction, thereby creating a comic effect that laughter is meant to correct (Bergson 21). Likewise, his haikus are generally fairly trite, triggering off some mocking reactions from the other characters. Still, such defects also count as frailties that may make the humanoid endearing, his social awkwardness being perceived at times as that of a child confronted with the complexity and hypocrisy posed by human situations. Besides, his frailties put him somehow on a par with the human protagonists who are themselves characterised by extreme vulnerability or "frailty" (Colombino 16). In other terms, the fact that Adam should be a character caught in a fictional narrative grants him an ontological status that is comparable to that of the other characters, and this is the main reason why, in the end, he is considered as a subject, with a life of his own, by the scientific and moral authority of the novel, Alan Turing, the computer scientist who, in the alternative experience of 1982, is still alive and has substantially contributed to the advance of knowledge in the field of AI.

On such an account, the scene of Adam's execution comes as a shock. As Charley slips behind his back and deals him a powerful blow on the head while Miranda is entertaining him, the narrator specifies: "The sound was not of hard plastic cracking or of metal, but *the* muffled thud, as of bone. Miranda let out a cry of horror and stood" (McEwan 2019, 278; emphasis added). The definite article "the," when the reader would have expected the indefinite form, testifies to the lingering effect of the episode in Charley's memory, making the scene—the prey of traumatic

208 *Jean-Michel Ganteau*

shock thirty years hence—present as if he were re-enacting it while he is recording it in writing. After this event and Adam's final confession and last orders, the body is hidden in a cupboard, only to be retrieved one year later and brought to Turing for scientific investigation. After creating a humanoid character that makes the protagonists and the reader opt for granting him human status at several stages of the narrative, and after securing a fair measure of empathy for Adam, the summary execution is deeply unsettling. When transposing to the individual sphere the categories that Agamben, Butler and others have applied to their analysis of states, it appears that Adam here is the representative of bare life as he embodies the "unconditional capacity to be killed" (Agamben 85). This is made possible by a state of exception that suspends the law—with the difference that, in *Machines Like Me*, the speculative, anticipatory nature of the narrative plunges the characters into a situation in which there is yet no law about the judicial status of intelligent, sentient humanoid robots. Therefore, there is no suspension of a law but a state of exception emerging from some sort of judicial limbo but otherwise corresponding to the situation described by Agamben as "life [that can be] killed without the commission of homicide" (159). This in turn refers to Charley's (and Miranda's) accession to sovereignty, a capacity that emerges when the law that can decide about the state of exception is suspended. Hence it is instrumental in determining who is the bearer of bare life (Butler 2006, 60). In his analysis of contemporary society as that of enmity, Mbembe takes examples from the field of colonial history to consider the origins of what he calls "necropolitics." He defines sovereignty as "the power and capacity to dictate who is able to live and who must die" (66) and, even more strikingly, as "exercising a power outside the law" (76). Like Butler's and a great deal of Agamben's, his analyses are inspired by reflections on the specific context of wars, but they also concentrate on some historical figures that are not necessarily associated with armed conflicts. He focuses on slavery and shows how the figure of the slave, whose life has a price and who is needed for his capacity to produce, is "kept alive, but in *a state of injury*, in a phantom-like world of horrors and intense cruelty and profanity" (75; original emphasis). He stipulates that the specific precarity of the slave's life lies in the fact that it may be curtailed at will, in a sacrilegious way and outside the law. He goes further in his analysis by insisting that sovereignty "means the capacity to define who matters and who does not, who is disposable" (80; original emphasis). This idea of disposability is at the heart of Judith Butler and Athena Athanasiou's reflections on dispossession, which they consider not only in a colonial context but also in relation with other issues like that of gender (27). Indeed, what we are presented with in McEwan's novel is the disposability of a body that is deprived of the status of the cadaver and of proper burial. This is confirmed by Charlie when, one year after the fact, he retrieves the body from the cupboard

The Grievability of the Non-Human   209

in which it had been smothered away: "It wasn't a murder, this wasn't a corpse" (McEwan 2019, 293). The narrative presents a character who escapes the frames that allow for the perception of grievability, let alone its recognition. From this point of view, it demonstrates that Adam does not qualify as a grievable subject and that, in Roberto Esposito's terms, he is *immune* from the qualities and capacities shared by the members of the community (n.p.), which confirms his double exceptionality in the context of a state of exception. Clearly, *Machines Like Me* addresses the issue of the differential allocation of grievability (Butler 2006, xiv) and answers Butler's triple question: "Who counts as human? Whose lives count as lives, what makes for a grievable life?" (2006, 20), detailing that Adam falls short of the three categories.

Grievability

And still. In the scene when Adam is retrieved from his year's long seclusion in the entry hall cupboard, his body appears in pieces, as if it were dismembered, which emphasises the character's objectification. During the episode, Charlie has to catch him "in an awkward embrace" (McEwan 2019, 294), which reminds the reader of his initial fascination for Adam's anatomy, in the early scene when the humanoid was charging up prior to what is presented as his awakening (25–27). He realises there and then that even if Adam's body is generally flexible, his legs remain bent—"[a] form of rigor mortis perhaps," the narrator pointedly adds (294). This is an example of how the novel regularly problematises the strict binaries opposing such categories as life/death, human/non-human, organic/artificial, allowing for a sense of doubt as to Adam's status to hover over the text.

This impression is buttressed by an evocation of his face: "He looked healthy. In repose, the face was thoughtful rather than cruel" (294). With these words, it seems as if Adam were granted human status, at least at a seemingly post-mortem stage. In fact, as Butler's reading of Levinas reminds us, the face of the other, exposed in its vulnerability and defencelessness, is what makes the subject responsible for the other and that which is at the root of the ethical and non-violent relation with the other, which, in Levinas's idealistic conception, defines the ethics of alterity (Butler 2006, 131). This face, which is described at the beginning of the novel as reminiscent of that of a "docker from the Bosphorus" (McEwan 2019, 4), is decidedly an emblem of alterity, as signposted by the ethnic allusion. With the extraction of the body from the cupboard where it had been invisibilised under a pile of coats, tennis rackets and other domestic items, what appears and is confirmed is Adam's humanity, or at least semblance of humanity, as if the non-human being were caught in a discreet yet unmistakable form of becoming-human. In other words, it seems as if the semblance of life mobilised enough power to

210   *Jean-Michel Ganteau*

become an animation, through the singular power of fiction. Interestingly, through the following scenes in which Charlie carries the body through the congested streets of London, on his way to Alan Turing's quarters, first with his car, and then with an improvised cart, it seems as if the relationships between Adam and Charlie were reversed: "I imagined myself as a servant in pre-industrial times, transporting my impassive lord to his leisured appointment" (296). In this passage, as in sundry others, the theme of the double that hovers over the narrative finds a precise incarnation in the figure of the see-saw or theme of exchange, which implies a commonality of status, somehow and to some degree, as I have argued elsewhere (Ganteau 114). This theme builds up into the last vision of Adam, lying on a stainless-steel table, in Turing's laboratory, when Charlie departs from the great scientist's house. He lays his hands on Adam's "stilled heart" and looks down into the "sightless cloudy green eyes" before catching himself doing something totally unpremeditated: "Sometimes, the body knows, ahead of the mind, what to do. [...] Hesitating several seconds, I lowered my face over his and kissed his soft, all-too-human lips" (McEwan 2019, 306). In death, and in this picture of repose, Charlie's gesture retrospectively grants Adam something not unlike human status, which is mediated by the body, this seat of vulnerability common to all living beings, human and non-human. Through the kiss, as if the body recognised the body and the face recognised the face, and through Charlie's dispossession and precariousness in front of what his body identifies as the face of otherness in its—or rather, his—vulnerability, the frames of perception and recognition of grievability are shifted. In death is Adam's existence retrospectively validated as a *life* and his status accepted as that of a *subject*.

In other terms, Charlie's precariousness, in the acceptation of the term used by Butler in *Frames of War*—that is, implying the subject's own exposure or vulnerability and his/her *dependency* on the other (2009, 14)—, is displayed and fully solicited, so that his grief may be expressed and sealed by the post-mortem kiss, the expression of his attachment to Adam. It complements and endorses his and Miranda's earlier regrets, after Adam's execution, emphasising their attachment to the lost friend-concubine-child figure, and underlining their own vulnerability as "orectic" subjects submitted to needs and appetites oriented towards the external world (Nussbaum 46). This is expressed in one of Charlie's confessional passages: "The truth was, we missed him [...]. But we missed him. We agreed that he loved us. Some nights the conversation was interrupted while Miranda quietly cried" (McEwan 2019, 283). In *Machines Like Me*, then, subjectivity is not validated by autonomy or sovereignty as the capacity to make independent decisions on account of powerful reckonings that emulate a hypertrophied or enhanced rationality. It is rather dependent on the capacity to feel and to generate emotions in others, negative and positive ones—overwhelmingly positive ones,

The Grievability of the Non-Human   211

ultimately. It is not because he is intelligent but because he is *sentient* that Adam enters the frame of visibility or rather allows it to shift so that he is taken into consideration. His belated recognition as a subject is encapsulated in a homage that Charlie tardily pays him, as he realises that he was right in insisting that Miranda be judged and sentenced so as to pay for her perjury and to be at one with herself. Protractedly, Adam's intellectual powers and understanding of the human heart are revealed, accepted and extolled. In the narrator's terms: "Adam's luminous love had triumphed" (287). Ultimately, the novel showcases a fascination for vulnerability, human or non-human, as a concretisation of the claim that "[t]he human is always the event of its multiple exposures" (Butler and Athanasiou 32). I would like to modify this slightly, replacing "the human" with "the subject" so as to extenuate the separation between human and non-human, which the novel invites us to do. I would like to add that this is accomplished by presenting readers with a series of singularities embodied by and embedded in the protagonists, these singularities being all composed by "the irreducibility of exposure, of being *this* body exposed to a publicity that is alternately intimate and anonymous" (Butler 2005, 34). In these terms resides a way of defining the subject (human or non-human or both) as essentially relational, that is, existing in a radical being *for* the other that at times may migrate into a becoming-other.

Adam's life, like those of Mariam and the Falkland victims (on the British side at least), is grievable, in the end, on account of a redefinition of the frames of perception and production of grievability indexed on a logic of emotion. The definition of subjectivity is thereby dependent on a conception of the individual as embedded, orectic, vulnerable. It is on account of such an unconditional relationality that Butler's triple question: "Who counts as human? Whose lives count as lives, what makes for a grievable life?" (2006, 20) can also be answered in a more positive way as regards Adam, who passes the test of being considered as human, as having a life and of being eminently grievable.

Moving Frames

In this final movement, I want to argue that *Machines Like Me* envisages the future conditions of grievability for the sentient, intelligent humanoid robot and prepares the ways for its advent. To do this, I need to return to the temporal organisation of the novel and more specifically to the alternative present that it offers the reader. As already mentioned, the scene takes place in an alternative 1982, when many things correspond to the reader's historical knowledge of that time, but with some oblique departures from historical fact. There are minor points of divergence, like the fact that The Beatles have just re-united and released two albums, which implies, among other things, that John Lennon was not

212 *Jean-Michel Ganteau*

assassinated in 1980. The fact that the story of The Beatles constitutes a stable enough element of knowledge for the new generations is the guarantee that they will identify the uncanniness of the mention, compounding the familiar with the unfamiliar and injecting a sense of awkwardness into our reading. Such micro-references multiply in the novel, but the main levers of chronological slippage rely on two items: Britain's defeat in the Falklands, which plunges the country into a political, economic and social crisis, as mentioned above; and the prodigious advance of research in and application of artificial intelligence, which leads to the early production of humanoid robots like Adam. The latter is due to a change in the history of British and world-science, namely, the facts that Alan Turing refused the medical treatment he was prescribed to "cure" him of his homosexuality; that he never committed suicide; and that he chose the imprisonment option offered to him as an alternative to the hormone therapy and took advantage of the time he spent in jail to set the mathematical groundwork for his research on AI. On account of his ground-breaking production and investment in this field, the whole area of AI is so advanced, at such a premature stage in world history, that it makes McEwan's 1982 a very strange, destabilising mixture of historical realism and fantasy that, as argued elsewhere, corresponds to the generic strategy of slipstream (Ganteau, 102–4).

This means that the technologically advanced world of 1982 anticipates by several decades key developments that are still to materialise in the twenty-first century. Now, the narrator rarely refers to the moment when he is writing the account of himself that the novel is supposed to be, and only once does he mention that it is produced at least thirty years after the events took place (McEwan 2019, 173). This situates the act of writing sometime after 2012, possibly at the time of the novel's publication, even though this fact is left unspecified. If this were the case, then the technological advances described in *Machines Like Me* are still to be concretised, but only just so as the thematic belatedness confers on them a higher sense of imminence. Such a situation brings in what Laura Colombino has called a "paradoxical foreseeing of the recent past" (15), and builds a permanent sense of delay or lack of chronological fit into the narrative, as if our idea of 1982 were already mired in lateness, as is the case with our present. This destabilising sensation of anticipation compounded with lateness is productive of an impression of untimeliness that the novel not only performs technically but also thematises. In fact, Alan Turing appears as *the* tutelary figure and moral hub of the narrative. His commitment to innovation and to public welfare is underlined several times, and he is the one who, in more ways than one, pronounces Adam's obituary. One year after the latter's demise, when Adam's torn body is taken to Turing's lab, Michael has a conversation with the great scientist that he deeply admires. He tells him about the reasons that led him and Miranda to "execute" Adam, and about their

The Grievability of the Non-Human   213

regrets, and Turing's reaction comes as a final judgement taking place in the very last pages of the novel:

> My hope is that one day, what you did to Adam with a hammer will constitute a serious crime. Was that because you paid for him? Was that your entitlement? [...] He was sentient. He had a self. How it's produced, wet neurons, microprocessors, DNA networks, it doesn't matter. Do you think we are alone with our special gift?
>
> (McEwan 2019, 303–304)

Such words state with authority the possibility of grievability thus anticipating a shift in frames of perception, recognisability, apprehension and intelligibility (Butler 2009, 4–6) that would make the mourning of Adam possible.

Such a situation would imply the impossibility of enjoying sovereignty and the right to decide on Adam's life and death, once laws are available as strict framing measures. More importantly, this would entail the recognition of Adam's status as a subject having a life that is grievable and worthy of obituaries. All this, the novel suggests, is a matter of time, and Adam's plight is that of being produced out of his time. What the narrative diagnoses is, then, an untimeliness, as if the advent of such humanoid robots as Adam was too huge an event to be apprehended synchronically, an occurrence of such magnitude that it defies a stable inscription in time and is provisionally granted a floating existence, like that of a ghost, coming from the past and from the future at the same time. Such an untimeliness is expressed in Adam's parting words: "It will happen. With improvements over time ... we'll surpass you ... and outlast you ... even as we love you. Believe me, these lines express no triumph ... Only regret" (McEwan 2019, 279). In these words, the fear of human obsolescence is addressed directly, and in a potentially scary way. But the theme is taken up later by the narrator, who rephrases it in more positive terms, concerning the intelligent, sentient humanoid robots as a different species from humans, thereby granting them more visibility and contributing to the shifting of frames: "wondrous machines like Adam and his kind, whose moment had not quite yet come" (297).

"Wondrous machines," indeed, and not to be feared too much, possibly, despite Adam's parting allusion to regret, as the novel takes care to build up a great deal of proximity between humanoid robots and humans, Adam and Charlie, they and us. This proximity is mediated through the figure of the double that crops up from the beginning as Charlie decides that he is, somehow, Adam's father, but also that the proximity of both protagonists is not merely inter-generational. As I have already indicated, one night Adam substitutes for Charlie, when he has sex with Miranda, an event that grants a strikingly concrete incarnation to the idea of the double. But the theme of the double is present

214 *Jean-Michel Ganteau*

throughout the novel. Very early on, when he wakes up after being charged up, Adam finds his own nakedness awkward, so Charlie gives him a set of clothes of his own (McEwan 2019, 27). Besides, Charlie is mistaken for Adam at least twice in the novel. When Miranda's father meets both of them on their visit to the family home in Salisbury, he has a private conversation with each of them and Charlie realises, torn between laughter and dismay, that the old man thought he was speaking to Adam even while he was speaking to him, Charlie. This is why he attributes to Charlie a non-human status, and thinks that Adam is a human being because of his encyclopaedic knowledge (225–27), thus putting the two on the same see-saw, and making their identities relate and blur in more ways than one.

In the end, even if *Machines Like Me* does not literally present the reader with a cyborg, it smudges the frontiers between the human and the non-human, at times in a fairly destabilising way. Therefore, Donna J. Haraway's comments about the function of the cyborg myth that produces "transgressed boundaries" may be applied here (154). More precisely, it seems as though "the human [were standing] on a line between the human and the non human" (Weil 84) and *vice versa*, of course, as the same precarious position is also associated with the non-human, so that the two seem to be compounded of each other, in some sort of an "embodied being with" that does not shy in front of a use of technology, even if this is not propounded in a militant way (Rutsky 184). In fact, the novel reminds us, in Rosi Braidotti's terms, that, "embedded and embodied, we are deeply steeped in the material world" (2019, 39), and that this material world is not always strictly organic or "natural," but made up of artificial compounds that make the hesitation between organic and non-organic, sentient and non-sentient, human and non-human reel. Because of the hesitation on grievability and on the final assertion of its possibility, the novel not only contributes to the shifting of its frames of perception, recognition and intelligibility but also to the displacement and the refashioning of the same frames. Despite some reviewers' opinion that *Machines Like Me* ultimately buttresses an undiluted humanistic message, I would argue that, even though it does not forsake humanism it also puts forward an anti-humanistic vision in which "subjectivity is associated with otherness" (Braidotti 2013, 15) and which promotes a relationality expressive of an "ethics of becoming" (Braidotti 2013, 49) that is at the heart of posthuman aspirations. By offering a complex, nuanced vision of grievability based on a specific practice of characterisation, the novel clearly ponders on human humility and recommends it even though it exposes the myth of exceptionalism and stands "against the arrogance of anthropocentrism" (Braidotti 2013, 66). Granted, the novel attends to the complexity of the human heart and to the "godawful messiness of being human" as most literary fictions do (Giles n.p.), with the difference that such a vision is allowed to enter in a dialogue with another one, namely with that of the messiness of what it is to be non-human, expressed here in terms of grievability and showcasing the vulnerability of both types of lives: human and non-human, considered separately or jointly. With *Machines Like Me*, McEwan clearly chooses to contribute to the debate around AI by yoking together intelligence and sentience in one and the same android robot. The implication is that, even if it predicts the inevitable advent of such machines in true transhumanist fashion, the novel favours a more distinctly posthumanist perspective: despite his superhuman powers, Adam is an icon of grievability and, above all, vulnerability, so that the stress is laid not so much on enhancement, unlimited cognitive capacities and exceptional longevity as on the in-built, programmed limits of a critter endowed with affects and emotions that make him human, all-too-human—hence dependent on and exposed to others.

Acknowledgements

Research for this chapter was funded by the Spanish Ministry of Science and Innovation (MICINN) (code PID2021-124841NB-I00).

Works Cited

Agamben, Giorgio. *Homo Sacer. Sovereign Power and Bare Life*. 1995. Trans. Daniel Heller-Roazen. Stanford, CA: Stanford UP, 1998.

Beck, Stefan. "Do we Want Dystopia? On Nightmare Tech as the Fulfilment of Warped Desire." *The New Atlantis* 61 (2020). Accessed on 12/08/2021 at: https://www.thenewatlantis.com/publications/do-we-want-dystopia/.

Bergson, Henri. *Laughter. An Essay on the Meaning of the Comic*. 1900. Trans. Cloudesley Brereton and Fred Rothwell. New York: Macmillan, 1913.

Braidotti, Rosi. *The Posthuman*. Cambridge and Malden: Polity, 2013.

———. *Posthuman Knowledge*. Cambridge: Polity, 2019.

Butler, Judith. *Giving an Account of Oneself*. New York: Fordham UP, 2005.

———. *Precarious Life. The Powers of Mourning and Violence*. 2004. London and New York: Verso, 2006.

———. *Frames of War. When Is Life Grievable?* London and New York: Verso, 2009.

Butler, Judith, and Athena Athanasiou. *Dispossession. The Performative in the Political*. Cambridge: Polity, 2013.

Colombino, Laura. "Consciousness and the Nonhuman: The Imaginary of the New Brain Sciences in Ian McEwan's *Nutshell* and *Machines Like Me*." *Textual Practice* 36.2 (February 2022): 1–22. Accessed on 05/02/22 at: https://www.tandfonline.com/doi/full/10.1080/0950236X.2022.2030116/.

Esposito, Roberto. *Immunitas. The Protection and Negation of Life*. Trans. Zahiya Hanafi. 2002. Cambridge: Polity, 2011. Ebook.

Freud, Sigmund. "Mourning and Melancholia." 1917. *The Standard Edition of the Complete Psychological Works of Sigmund Freud* Vol. XIV. Trans. Joan Riviere. Ed. James Strachey. London: The Hogarth P, 1971. 237–60.

Ganteau, Jean-Michel. *The Poetics and Ethics of Attention in Contemporary British Narrative*. London and New York: Routledge, 2023.

Giles, Jeff. "Love, Sex and Robots Collide in a New Ian McEwan Novel." *The New York Times* 1 May 2019. Accessed on 25/08/2021 at: https://www.nytimes.com/2019/05/01/books/review/ian-mcewan-machines-like-me.html/.

Haraway, Donna J. *When Species Meet*. Minneapolis and London: U of Minnesota P, 2008.

Hawthorne, Nathaniel. *The House of the Seven Gables*. 1851. London: Everyman, 1982.

Huxley, Aldous. *Brave New World*. 1932. London: Everyman, 2013.

Ishiguro, Kazuo. *Klara and the Sun*. London: Faber, 2021.

Kipling, Rudyard. "The Secret of the Machines." 1911. *The Collected Poems of Rudyard Kipling*. Introduction and Notes R.T. Jones. Ware: Wordsworth, 1994. 759.

Kopka, Katalina, and Norbert Schaffeld. "Turing's Missing Algorithm: The Brave New World of Ian McEwan's Android Novel *Machines Like Me*." *Journal of Literature and Science* 13.2 (2020): 52–74.

Mbembe, Achille. *Necropolitics*. 2016. Trans. Steven Corcoran. Durham and London: Duke UP, 2019.

McEwan, Ian. *Atonement*. London: Cape, 2001.

———. *Saturday*. London: Cape, 2005.

———. *The Children Act*. London: Cape, 2014.

———. *Machines Like Me. And People Like You*. London: Cape, 2019.

Nussbaum, Martha. *The Fragility of Goodness. Luck and Ethics in Greek Tragedy and Philosophy*. 1986. Cambridge: Cambridge UP, 2001.

Patterson, Ian. "Sexy Robots." *The London Review of Books* 41.9 (19 May 2019). Accessed on 25/08/ 2021 at: https://www.lrb.co.uk/the-paper/v41/n09/ian-patterson/sexy-robots.

Rossini, Manuela. "Bodies." *The Cambridge Companion to Literature and the Posthuman*. Eds Bruce Clarke and Manuela Rossini. Cambridge: Cambridge UP, 2017. 153–69.

Rutsky, R.L. "Technologies." *The Cambridge Companion to Literature and the Posthuman*. Eds Bruce Clarke and Manuela Rossini. Cambridge: Cambridge UP, 2017. 182–95.

Saleem, Rabeea. "Machines Like Me by Ian McEwan Review: A Baggy and Jumbled Narrative." *The Irish Times*. 20 April 2019. Accessed on 25/08/2021 at: https://www.irishtimes.com/culture/books/machines-like-me-by-ian-mcewan-review-a-baggy-and-jumbled-narrative-1.3849775/.

Theroux, Marcel. "Machines Like Me by Ian McEwan—Intelligent Mischief." *The Guardian*. 11 February 2019. Accessed on 25/08/2021 at: https://www.theguardian.com/books/2019/apr/11/machines-like-me-by-ian-mcewan-review/.

Weil, Kari. "Autobiography." *The Cambridge Companion to Literature and the Posthuman*. Eds Bruce Clarke and Manuela Rossini. Cambridge: Cambridge UP, 2017. 84–95.

Index

Note: Page numbers followed by "n" denote endnotes.

Aborigine(s) 83–85; -al and Torres Strait Islander(s) (culture) 76, 78, 86; -al children 85; -al culture 77; -al English 88; -al girl(s) 86, 92; -al epistemology and ontology 81; -al groups 79; -al identity 84; -al languages 81; -al modernism 90; -al people 75, 84, 86; -al (philosophy) (and) spirituality 9, 78, 86, 88, 93; -al realism 9, 88, 91, 93; -al reservation 82–83; *see also* Australia; Australian; dreaming
Abu Ghraib 3; pictures 70
acting out 67, 181–82; *see also* repetition compulsion
Adorno, Theodor 40
affect(s) 215, human 124; -ive bonds 131; theory of 68; value of 68; waning 52; *see also* Ahmed
Agamben, Giorgio 3, 5–8, 17, 19, 21, 37, 55–56, 58, 61, 76, 106, 113n3, 122, 129, 192, 205, 208; *Homo Sacer: Sovereign Power and Bare Life* 3, 192; *Infancy and History: The Destruction of Experience* 55; *see also* bare life; *bíos*; *homo sacer*; *zoē*
Ahmed, Sara 68
Andersen, Hans Christian 89
Artificial intelligence 202, 212, AI 202, 207, 212, 215
AIDS 3, 153–59, 161–63, 165–66, 169–71, 173–75, 177–78, 180; crisis 154, 156, 173, 178; dystopia 165; elegy 163; epidemic 10, 169–72, 180; fictions 9, 153; historicisation of 170; narrative 172, 180; pandemic 156, 162; spectacularisation of 153; stories

171; trauma(ta) (of) 157, 174; related to 173; victims (of) 3, 9, 154, 156, 164, 178
alterity 1–2, 5, 37, 60, 63, 69, 120, 129, 209; aesthetics of 132; ethics of 1–2, 5, 36, 79, 100, 131, 209; *see also* Levinas; otherness
Amis, Martin 39; *Time's Arrow* 39
Anthropocene 98, 111
anthropocentrism 206, 214
anthropophagy 25; *see also* cannibalism
Antigone 9, 127–29, 132, 147; -like figure 147; 's myth 129; *see also* Butler; Sophocles
apocalypse 9, 96, 108–12
Arendt, Hannah 2, 127, 129; *The Human Condition* 127
Aristotle 123–25; *De Anima* 123
Ashcroft, Bill, Frances Devlin-Glass, and Lyn McCredden 81–82
Astley, Thea 75
Atemporals 28; *see also* carnivores
Atkins, William 119
Atkinson, Meera 76
Atwood, Margaret 108; *The Year of the Flood* 108
Auerbach, Nina 148n10
Australia 75–76, 80, 82, 84–86; Aboriginal 92; coast of (Western) 87; Anglo-Celtic 93n1; government 86; Indigenous 85; *see also* Australian; dreaming
Australian(s), Indigenous 9, 76–82, 84, 87–88, 92; non-Indigenous 85; white 78; *see also* Aborigine

Baccolini, Raffaella, and Tom Moylan 111

218 Index

Badiou, Alain 2
Bakhtin, Mikhail 26, 44
Ballard, J.G. 96; *The Drowned World* 96
Barad, Karen 113n2, 121
barbarian(s), the 16–18, 22, 32; red-haired 18; *see also* heathen; -ism 16
bare life 6–7, 37, 76, 99, 104–108, 122, 192, 208; *see also* Agamben; *zoē*
Barnouw, Dagmar 39
Barras, Arnaud 89
Batavia 19–20, 32; born brides 20
Batavian Republic 16, 22; *see also* Holland
Baudrillard, Jean 39, 51, 181, 194; *The Perfect Crime* 39, 181
Bauman, Zygmunt 1, 38–39, 47–48, 83
Bayer, Gerd 20
Bell, Vikki 111; "From Performativity to Ecology" 111
Benhabib, Sheila 2
Benjamin, Walter 76, 106; "Critique of Violence" 106
Bennett, Jane 124, 113n2, 124; *Vibrant Matter: A Political Ecology of Things* 124; *see also* ecology
Berger, James 110–11
Bergson, Henri 207
Bersani, Leo 170, 173–4, 180
biopolitics 4, 7, 17, 130, 153; *see also* Agamben; biopower; Foucault
biopower 7–8; *see also* biopolitics; Foucault
bíos 7, 76, 86, 122; *see also* Agamben; *zoē*
Bjornerud, Marcia 125
body(-ies) the 27–28, 30, 42, 67, 85–86, 107–108, 120, 123–24, 144, 159, 162–64, 208–11; AIDS (-infected) 154, 161; deadly 162; diseased 154; disposability of 208; dying 165–66; gay 165; grievable 9, 133; grotesque 26; host 28; human 203; parts 188, 190, 197–98; rights over one's 21; social 147; torn 212; ungrievable 9
Bouson, J. Brooks 135, 140, 145, 148n12
Braidotti, Rosi 82, 93n2, 113n2, 124, 214
Brennan, Elliot 76

Bronfen, Elisabeth 148n14
Bronfen, Elizabeth, and Sarah Goodwin 144
Brontë, Charlotte 24
Brontë, Emily 24, 119–34; *Wuthering Heights* 119–34
Brooks Bouson, J. 140
Buddha 25, 29; -ist doctrine 31; -ist ethics 27; -ist Kannon deity 25; (-ist) *oni* (band) 28–29; -ist perspective 30; -ist sins 26; -ist stories 27; -ist symbolism 26; *see also* faith
Butler, Judith 2–6, 8, 10, 16–17, 19, 27, 36–38, 44, 51, 56, 58–59, 62–63, 65–66, 68, 70, 77, 79–82, 86, 98–100, 102, 106, 108, 111–12, 120–22, 127–30, 136–39, 144, 147, 153–54, 156–8, 163, 169, 173, 175, 177–78, 180, 187–88, 189–91, 193, 195, 198–99, 205–206, 208–11, 213; *Antigone's Claim. Kinship between Life and Death* 2, 127; *The Force of Non-Violence* 3–4, 82, 129, 136, 138, 157, 163; *Frames of War* 3–5, 58, 100, 144, 169, 187–88, 190, 210; *Giving an Account of Oneself* 198; *Precarious Life. The Powers of Mourning and Violence* 2–3, 5–6, 10, 36, 65, 70, 80–81, 100, 120–21, 144, 169, 175, 177–78, 180, 187, 199, 205; *The Psychic Life of Love* 138; *see also* frame
Butler, Judith and Athena Athanasiou 8, 105–108, 208, 211–12
Bush (George W.) administration 3, 169

camp(s) 20, 41, 159; concentration 38, 192; detention 76; holiday 188; Nazi death 7
cannibal(s) 20, 22, 25, 32, 130; narratives 20; -istic practises 25, 29; *see also* Carnivore
cannibalism 20, 23, 25, 31, 40, 130; consubstantial 23; trope of 17, 20; *see also* anthropophagy
capitalism 7, 200; critique of 192; global 36, 105; industrial 16
care 4, 30, 43, 48, 50, 88, 90, 175, 177–78, 188, 190–91; attention and 73; (and) empathy (and) 132, 177;

ethics of 30, 33, 36, 93, 164; home 188; for nature 123; health 36; language of 190; mutual 112
carnivores 28; *see also* Atemporals
Caruth, Cathy 173; *Trauma: Explorations in Memory* 173
Castiglia, Christopher and Christopher Reed 177
Catalan, Jose 153
Chapoutot, Johann 39
Chen, Mel 122–22, 126
climate: catastrophe 83; change 79, 87, 92, 96; crisis 79; fiction 9; human-induced 92; -induced disasters 77; migrants 83, 92; refugees 9, 82, 85, 90
clone(s) 10, 187–200
Colombino, Laura 212
colonialism 17–18; commercial or trading-post 17–18; settler (clichés) 18–19
colonisation 77, 88, 92
coloniser(s) 86, wives of 19; Western 25
commerce: international 20, 32; (peaceful) -al society 18
commodification 66, 188, 191, 197; norms of 140
community(ies) 3, 42–43, 47–51, 86, 136, 138–40, 144–47, 147n5, 192–93, 209; agricultural 27; of artists 176; concordant 121; consubstantial 25; decimated 171; Dutch 28; of friends 178; gay 10, 155; global 77, 81; immune 9; inoperative 51; marsh 50; tainted 170; violent 187; vulnerable 56; *see also* Nancy
Conrad, Joseph 24
Cornell, Drucilla 1
Crane, Nicholas 96, 112n1; *The Making of the British Landscape* 96, 112n1
cruelty 22, 27, 32, 208; gratuitous 32; institutionalised 8
Cunsolo, Ashlee, and Karen Landman 98
Currie, Mark 194

Daley, Linda 82, 90
Darwin, Charles 16; *see also* Social Darwinism
Davidson, Julia O'Connell 136, 138

Davoine, Francoise and Jean-Max Gaudillière 55
De Cristofaro, Diletta 110
De Waard, Marco 23
death 1, 5–7, 23–24, 28, 30, 33, 37, 47–48, 51, 62, 65–67, 69, 77, 82, 85, 97–98, 100, 103, 106–108, 111, 123, 127–29, 131, 135–37, 139, 143–47, 153–65, 170, 175–76, 178–79, 187, 189, 192–94, 196, 198, 200, 204, 206, 209–10, 213; from AIDS 169, 180; beautiful and novel 127; (of) the beloved(') other(s) 3, 158, 162; camps 7; -drive 132; gayness and 161; (as) grievable 121, 191, 196; -in-life 123; living 128–29, 133; lover(s)' 159, 176; mass 156; of Palestinian children 65; and rebirth 28; redemptive 163–64; social 21, 137–8, 147n5; of strangers 65; sacrificial 164; starved to 43; ungrievable 155; untimely 187–88; of war victims 61–62; *see also* Patterson
Defoe, Daniel 20; *Robinson Crusoe* 20
Delecroix, Vincent and Philippe Forest 195, 197–98, 200n2–n5; *Le deuil* 195
Deleuze, Gilles and Félix Guattari 11n7
dehumanisation 38–39, 123, 193
Dejima 15–16, 18, 21–24, 27–29, 31–32
denial 180; act of 48; of full humanness 38; of human rights 100
dependence 3, 105, 195–96, 187, 210, 215; (inter-) 7; *see also* interdependence
Desbois, Patrick 41; *see also* Holocaust
derealisation 4, 19, 32, 52, 193–95, 200
Derrida, Jacques 1, 59, 62; "Violence and Metaphysics" 1
Descartes, René 1
diachrony 61–62, 64; *see also* Levinas
discrimination 29; 39, 123, 131; epistemic 41; ideological 39; women's 24
disposability 7–8, 194, 197, 208
dispossession 8, 19, 32, 98–10, 105–106, 107–108, 112, 120, 192,

220 Index

194, 208, 210; *see also* Butler and Athanasiou
dissidence 154; sexual 154, 156
dissident(s) sexual 9, 153–54, 161, 166; religious 25
Doeff, Hendrik 28; *Recollections of Japan* 28
Dollimore, Jonathan 161
double(s), the 197, 210, 213
dreaming(s), the 75, 81–82, 87; dreamtime 81; narratives 82; stories of 89; *see also* Aborigine; Australia
Du Bois, W.E.B. 147n3; *The Souls of Black Folks* 147n3
Dutch, the 8, 15, 18–19
Dutch East India Company, the 15, 23; bankruptcy of 23; *see also* VOC
Dutch East Indies 18
Dutch Reformed Church, the 22
Dutch Republic, the 23
dystopia(s) 99, 106, 108–109, 111, 113n6, 158, 165–66, 188–89, 195, 197, 199, 202–203; AIDS- 165; eco- 9, 99; classical 109; critical 111; genre of 106; homophobic 153, 158; modern 113n6; modernist 203

Eaglestone, Robert 1
earth, the 8, 26, 31, 76, 78, 80, 82, 84, 86, 92, 103–104, 125–26, 132, 203; of their ancestors 86; crumbling 111; exploitation of 80; grieving 8, 73–115; healing of 78; health of 88; life on 79–80; materiality of 86; Mother 25; preservation of 92; populate 32; 's resources 79; water and 103
Eckersley, Richard M. 78
ecology 79, 82, 111, 119, 121–22; open 122; of practices 111, 113n7; of things 122; *see also* Bennett; Griffith and Kreisel; Stengers
Edo period 8, 10, 16; *see also* Tokugawa
Edwards, Caroline 89–90; "The Networked Novel" 89
elegy 9, 82, 96, 98–100, 105, 112, 156–57, 160–62, 165–66, 195, 198–99; AIDS 163–64; as counter-narrative 156; contemporary 197; ethics of 195; fake 161; homoerotic 156; melancholic 155; redemptive 161
Eliot, T.S. 176

emotion(s) 23, 131, 160, 181, 205, 210–11, 215; conflicting 177; -al wounds 103, 107
empire(s), the 21, 77, 80; ideology of 21–22, 32; Nazi 46; Roman 163
empathy 132, 177–78, 191, 206, 208; politics of 191; *see also* Whitehead
Eng, David L., and David Kazanjian 154
Enlightenment, the 16; ethics 22; Scottish 16, 22–23; philosophers 27; thinkers 16–18, 21, 31
environment, the 6, 36 ,85, 87–89, 91, 96–99, 101, 105, 111–12, 119; claustrophobic 96; marine 100; natural 126; urban 121; -al changes 102; -al degradation 98, 126; -al devastation 97, 108; -al disaster 113n6; -al literature 96; -al precariousness 103; -al precarity 104; -alism 122
erasure 58–59, 119, 127, 141, 171, 180; metaleptic 57, 61, 63, 66, 68; of the other 44; of the past 8, 63, 68; of young women 62
ethics 1, 9, 37, 39, 52, 77, 79–80, 87, 92–93, 121, 127; and aesthetics 40; of alterity 1–2, 5, 36, 79, 100, 131, 209; (and a politics) of attention 5, 101; of bare life and dispossession 106; of becoming 214; Buddhist 27; Butler's 17; of care 30, 33, 36, 93, 164; of compassion 27; Enlightenment 22; of grief 70; of hospitality 8, 17, 27; humanist 1; Levinas's (-ian) 2, 17, 36, 50, 79, 100; of life 121; of mourning 76–85; non-ontological 1; (of) non-violent(-ce) 17, 81, 130; postmodern; relational 91; of representation 51; temporal 55; (-al) turn (to) 2, 26; utilitarian 121; of vulnerability 36
exclusion 1, 3, 6–7, 22, 27, 39, 76, 80, 99, 106; 113n3; 120, 122, 125, 129, 133, 136–37, 139, 191–92
exception, state of 3, 7, 205, 208–209; *see also* Agamben
exploitation 16, 188, 190–91; of the earth 80; of Jewish labourers 46; neocolonial 78; system of 188–89
exposure 99, 178, 187, 196, 210–11; over- 178; to disease 188; to grief (-ability) 98–99, 112; to loss 3,

Index 221

101; to violence and death 6; to vulnerability 105

face, the 1, 24, 26, 30, 32, 47, 49, 60, 136, 142, 170, 191–92, 196, 209–10; encounter with 209; face to face (relationship) 2, 60, 62; Levinasian 49; of the other 1, 36, 50, 64; of otherness 210; scar(-) (-red-) (on her) 135–36, 141–42, 209
Falklands war 206
fate(s) 6, 31, 42–43, 48, 76, 82, 92, 129, 153, 189, 193
Ferguson, Adam 16
Fitzgerald, Francis Scott 176; "My Generation" 176
Foucault, Michel 5, 7, 205; *The Birth of Biopolitics* 7; *The Will to Knowledge* 7
frame(s) 5–7, 51, 56, 58–60, 62–65, 69–70, 100–101, 139–40, 187, 190, 192–93, 195, 199, 206, 209–14; cultural (Western) 169–70; epistemological 5, 38, 41, 44, 52, 158; narrative 99, of intelligibility 187; of (in-)visibility 22, 24, 211; of knowledge 102; of perception 6, 21, 206, 211, 213–14; temporal 110; of the subhuman 10, 188, 190, 192, 195, 199; of war 187; *see also* Butler
France 6, 23, 161; revolutionary 16
France, Louise 65
Franklin, Stella Miles 75
Freiburg, Rudolf and Gerd Bayer 179, 181
Freud, Sigmund 55, 90, 102, 160–61, 181, 195, 206; *Deuil et mélancolie* 195; *Unheimlich* 90, 102
Fricker, Miranda 6, 42, 142–43, 146; *see also* injustice

Ganteau, Jean-Michel 38, 101, 195, 197, 202, 210, 121
Ganteau, Jean-Michel and Susana Onega 1, 36; *Victimhood and Vulnerability in 21st-Century Fiction* 36; *see also* Onega and Ganteau
gender 8–9, 16–17, 22, 82, 119, 163–64, 208; (and) class (and) 9, 137, 139; discrimination 17; feminine 127; inferiors 8, 32; studies 36; wavering 128

German(s) 37–39, 42, 45–51; s' moral conscience 48
Germany 47; 96; Nazi 38
ghost(s) 86, 105, 146, 148n11, 213; embodied 146; -like landscape 105; -ly dead 198; place 87; ungrieved 9, 137, 143; *see also* spectre
Gibson, Andrew 1
Gilbert, Scott F., Jan Sapp, and Alfred I. Tauber 120
Gillan, Jennifer 138–39
Giles, Jeff 202, 214
Gilmartin, Sarah 96
Gioia, Ted 89; "The Rise of the Fragmented Novel" 89
Glaser, Brigitte 16, 24
Gleeson-White, Jane 91
global, the 80; capitalism 36, 105; community 77, 81; conflict(s) 169, 180; context of violence 3; economic systems 189; modernity 109; net 89; peace 17; unhomely 89; war 180; -isation 79–80; -ised commercial control 8; -ised free-wheeling liberalism 8; -ised world 17, 92
goddess(es) 24, 26, 28; God/- 28; Kami 25; Kannon 26; Mother 25; of Mercy 25; Sun 24
grief 4, 8, 55–58, 60, 62–64, 68–69, 81, 92, 97–98, 100, 102, 104, 106–107, 120, 153, 157, 165, 169, 175, 178–82, 188, 195, 206, 210; ecological 96–115; ethics of 70; hierarchy(-ies) of 4, 36–54, 175, 178, 187, 200; muted 171; overcoming 169–83; public 174; silent 176; traumatic 171; *see also* grievability; mourning
grievability 3–10, 21, 24, 30, 37–38, 40–41, 45, 51, 55, 58, 63–66, 69–70, 77, 85–86, 88, 91–92, 98–101, 103–105, 107–109, 111–12, 129–31, 136–37, 139, 145, 154, 156–57, 163–64, 166, 187, 191, 194–95, 205–206, 209–11, 213–15; (differential) (allocation of) 16, 121, 144, 199, 206; (differential) distribution of 4–5, 82, 100, 102, 105, 187, 190; equality of 4, 130; generational 157; hierarchy of 200; human 96–115; of the non-human 202–16; of the other 4; and race 147n3; representations of 98;

222 *Index*

socio-cultural construction of 9; *see also* grief; mourning; ungrievability

Grieves, Vicky 77–79, 81–82, 85–87, 92

Griffiths, Deving, and Deanna K. Kreisel 122; *see also* ecology

Guantánamo 3

Guy-Bray 156, 162

Hale, Dorothy J. 131

Hallam, Elizabeth, Jenny Hockney and Glennys Howarth 144

Hapke, Laura 140

Harack, Katrina 143

Haraway, Donna J. 214

Harris-Birtill, Rose 28

Hawthorne, Nathaniel 147–8n5, 203; *The Scarlet Letter* 147–8n5

heathen(s), the 16–17; *see also* barbarians

Hegel, Georg Wilhelm Friedrich 1, 127, 147

Heidegger, Martin 1

Hemingway, Ernest 176

Hicks, Heather J. 109

history 8, 13, 15, 23, 38–39, 61–62, 90, 173–74; of British and world-science 212; colonial 208; of detention camps 76; fabulous 22; family 75; geological 103; life 55; linear progression in 90; memory and 61; re-imagining 165; and trauma 40; world 8, 15–16, 212; of WW2 62

Hogarth, William 20, 159, 161

Holland 15–16, 31; Anglo-Russian invasion of 16; *see also* Batavian Republic

Hollinghurst, Alan 9, 154–61, 165–66; *The Line of Beauty* 9, 154, 160, 165–66; *The Swimming Pool Library* 165–66

Holocaust, the 37–38, 40–41, 44, 51; 178; 192; by Bullets 41, 45; fiction 40; literature 39–41; Memorial Museum 40; narratives 40; representation of 51; unrepresentability of 40; victim(s) 41, 155; *see also* Desbois; Vice

homo sacer 3, 76, 99, 106, 108, 113n3, 122, 129, 192; *see also* Agamben; bare life

hospitality 22, 50; ethics of 8, 17, 27; politics of 17, 21, 27, 33; universal 17

Howard, John 81; government 85

Hughes, Rowland, and Pat Wheeler 99

human(s), the 2, 9, 46, 48, 81, 92, 96, 99, 105–106, 108, 113n2, 123–24, 163, 187, 190, 192, 195, 213; and non-human(s) (things) 96–99, 102, 111–12, 113n4, 126, 211, 215; classes of 187; domination of other 188; hierarchy of 38; humanoid robots and 213; marginalised 100; wounded 112; *see also* humanoid; inhuman; non-human; subhuman

humanism 79, 214

humanoid 202, 205–209, 211–13

Husserl, Edmund 1

Huxley, Aldous 203; *Brave New World* 203

identity 42, 67–68, 79, 135, 144, 172, 181, 191; Aboriginal 84; complexity of 68; Jewish 48; political 19; self- 1

imperialism 16–17, 31

individual(s) 7–8, 36–38, 43–44, 51, 55, 68, 76, 80, 100, 112, 129, 147n5, 170, 197, 211; 's biopolitical position 122; death of 153; disabled 38; dominated 41; invisibility of 138; non-normative 3; other 45; right-bearing 2; uniqueness of 155, 161, 166; white 76

individualism 80, 82

individuality 120

infection 171, 174; HIV 153

inhuman, the 2, 191; *see also* humanoid; non-human; subhuman

injustice(s) 17, 44, 100, 173; epistemic 6, 41, 44; hermeneutic 6, 10; social 194; testimonial 6, 9, 142, 146–47; *see also* Fricker

interdependence(s) 3, 8, 26, 44, 79, 82, 93, 112, 120; (inter-) 7; textual 130; *see also* dependence

interrelationality 82, 120; *see also* relationality

invisibility 6, 138, 140, 192–93, 195; frames of 22; and inaudibility 6; social 6, 143; and ungrievability 9, 20; *see also* visibility

Iraq war 64–65, 69

Irr, Caren 90

Ishiguro, Kazuo 10, 187–200, 207; *Klara and the Sun* 207; *Never Let Me Go* 10

Index 223

James, Henry 148n12, 157–60; *The Turn of the Screw* 148n12
Janet, Pierre 55
Japan 8, 16–18, 22, 25, 89
Japanese, the 8, 18–19, 32; concubine 28; culture 18; economy 24; indigenous faith of 24; (normative) society 32, 26, 28; women 24
Jews, the 38, 40, 42–46, 48–49; and non-Jews 38; murder of 46

Kannon deity 25; goddesses 26; Lady 27; Maria 25; *see also* goddess
Kant, Emmanuel 1, 17; *Perpetual Peace: A Philosophical Essay* 17
Keene, Tom 22–23
Kennedy, David 98
Kenya, colonial 37
Kermode, Frank 110
kinship 2, 9, 82, 120–21, 126–30, 133, 202; normative 122, 129, 131, 133; patriarchal 121; symbolic-128; *see also* Lévi-Strauss
Kipling, Rudyard 24, 203, 206; "The Secret of the Machines" 203
Klein, Eileen 96
Kramer, Larry 170–71; *The Normal Heart* 171
Kurtz, Roger 173; *Trauma and Literature* 173
Kushner, Tony 171; *Angels in America: A Gay Fantasia on National Themes* 171

LaCapra, Dominick 181
Lacan, Jacques 127–28
Lang, Berel 40
Larsonneur, Claire 15, 28
Larsonneur, Claire and Hélène Machinal 27
Le Blanc, Gillaume 6, 8, 11, 17, 138, 143, 149, 192, 200–201; *L'invisibilité sociale* 6, 11, 138, 143, 149; *Vies ordinaires, vies précaires* 11
Le Blanc, Guillaume and Fabienne Brugère 17, 27
Leane, Jeanine 88, 91
Lévi-Strauss, Claude 127–28; *The Elementary Structures of Kinship* 128; *see also* kinship
Levinas, Emmanuel 1–2, 8, 17, 36–37, 45, 48, 61, 79, 81, 100, 209; "Judaism and the Feminine

Element" 17, 34; *Otherwise Than Being, or, Beyond Essence* 60–61, 64; *On Escape: De l'évasion* 50; *Totality and Infinity* 209; *see also* alterity; ethics
LGBTQ+ 171, 177, 181
liberalism 4, 8, 22, 70, 86, 130, 146, 197
living, the 4, 8, 22, 70, 84, 86, 100, 130, 146, 197
loss(es) 3–5, 8–9, 39–40, 47, 51, 55–56, 58, 68, 76–78, 81–83, 86–87, 90, 98, 100–101, 105–106, 109, 120, 131, 133, 136, 144, 147, 154, 157–62, 165–66, 174, 181, 187–88, 193–99, 203–206; caused by AIDS 159; of country and cultural heritage 77; death and habitat 77; deemed ungrievable 174; derealisation of 188, 191–95; exposure to 3, 101; grievable 169, 180; of home 21, 77; irredeemable 195; of life 77, 206; narrative of 194; negation 195; of memory 198; of political status 21; of rights 21; of self 206; stories of 83, 92; transformative effect of 70; traumatic 92; of the tribal lands 84; triple 21; ungrieved 10; unmourned 77; of value 8
Lucashenko, Melissa 75
Lyotard, Jean-François 41–42, 102, 113n5

Makkai, Rebecca 9, 169–82; *The Great Believers: A Novel* 9, 169–82
Malka, Shlomo 2
Mandel, Emily St. John 108; *Station Eleven* 108, 110
Marcellin, Katia 63
marginalisation 52, 106, 137, 142, 154
Martínez-Alfaro, María Jesús 39–41
Masih, Tara Lynn 41; *My Real Name Is Hanna* 41
Maugham, Somerset 24
materiality 86, 124, 145; vibrant 101
matter 31; inert 124; vibrant 124
Mbembe, Achille 7–8, 17, 20–21, 27, 76, 122, 147n3, 205, 208; *Necropolitics* 7, 147n3; "Necropolitics" 76; *see also* necropolitics
McCarthy, Cormac 108–109; *The Road* 108–109

224   *Index*

McEwan 10, 202–15; *Atonement* 202; *The Children Act* 202; *Machines Like Me. And People Like You* 10, 202–15; *Saturday* 202
melancholia 98, 105, 160–61, 165, 197, 205–206; *see also* mourning
melodrama 19, 204–205
memory(-ies) 9, 36, 55–56, 68, 77, 103–105, 108, 110–11, 131–32, 145, 148n6, 157–59, 166, 169–81, 193, 198, 207; collective 137; communicative 104; disconnected 110; narrative 55, 181; palimpsestic 104; public 39; traumatic 55, 176, 181; *see also* remembering
metalepsis 8, 20, 56–57, 61–64, 66–70; performative 56
Miller, John 16
Mills, Rebecca 100, 104
Mitchell, David 8, 15–35; *The One Thousand Autumns of Jacob de Zoet* 8, 15–35; *Utopia Avenue* 30
Miyoshi, Masao 79
Melville, Herman 20; *Moby Dick* 20
modernity 2, 5, 21, 79–80, 90; global 109; North American 80; *see also* transmodernity
Möller, Richard M. 17
Montesquieu, Baron de (Charles Louis de Secondat) 16, 22; *The Spirit of the Laws* 22
Moretti, Franco 148n8
Morrison, Toni 9, 131, 135–50; *Beloved* 142; *The Bluest Eye* 138, 142; *Jazz* 142; *Love* 9, 135–50; *Song of Solomon* 142
Mother Earth 26, 29, 37–38
mourning 55, 70, 75–77, 79–82, 85, 87–88, 90–93, 132, 146, 147n3, 160–62, 195, 197–98, 205; acts of 3; ethics of 80; of Indigenous Australians 82; losses 174; national 206; official 85; poetics of 88; political 81; public 85, 147n3; unresolved 98; *see also* melancholia
Mousoutzanis, Aris 89, 90; "The Networked Novel" 89
Mowaljarlai, David 77–78, 91
Mullan, John 188
Mulvey, Laura 147n4
myth(s) 25; Antigone's 129; cyborg 214; of creation 203; of exceptionalism 214; of the

lost-and-found 196; of "possibles" 194; Sophocles' 127; Western and Eastern 89

Nagasaki 15, 18, 24–25, 27, 29–30
Nancy, Jean-Luc 17, 27, 51, 145; *The Inoperative Community* 145; *see also* community
nation(s), the 18, 85, 93, 169, 175, 206; barbarous 17; civilised 32; Waanji 75; Western 32
Nayar, Pramod K. 98, 102, 105
Nazi(s), the 42–52; atrocities 52n1; auxiliary police force 42; crimes 39; concentration camp 192; death camps 7; discourse (of power) 39, 51; ideology 51; Germany 38; granddaughter of 37; ideology 51; monopoly on truth 44; officers 49; regime 40, 45; soldiers 42; state 39; violence 46; *see also* Ukraine
Nazism 38; *see also* (Third) Reich
necropolitics 17, 76, 208; *see also* Mbembe
Netherlands, the 18, 22–23, 33, 96
new materialism 123–24
9/11, 3, 76, 100; attacks 81; crisis 6; post-global conflict 169; *see also* War on Terror
non-human(s), the 96–99, 101–102, 104, 106–108, 111–13, 113n4, 120, 122–24, 126, 133, 202–15; actors 113n2; animals 123; bodies 124, 126; figure 120; form(s) (of bare life) 104, 106–107; *see also* human; humanoid; subhuman
Nishime, LeiLani, and Kim D. Hester Williams 121
Norman, Brian 146
norm(s) 9, 41, 44, 46, 109, 128–29, 133, 138, 140, 178, 190–92, 205; of grievability 5, 10, 205; of intelligibility 56; kinship 121, 130, 133; of recognition 5; patriarchal 143; social 32, 122, 133, 192
North Sea, the 9, 96–97, 101, 109–10, 112
novel(s): contemporary 89; dystopian 199; 's ethics 92; 's experimental form 90; fragmented 91; historical 15, 61; planetary 9, 76; polyphonic 44; ('s) poetics (of) 44, 88, 93; post-apocalyptic 109–10; 's structure

147n1; temporality (in) (of) 56, 112; temporal structure of 99, 106; Victorian 120; war 65; world 90; *see also* Edwards; Gioia; Irr

Obeyesekere, Gananath 20, 25, 30
obituary(-ies) 3, 5, 66, 169, 177, 195, 212–13
objectification 24, 60–61, 123, 209
O'Connell Davidson, Julia 136
O'Connor, Anne-Marie 137
O'Donnell, Patrick 19, 55, 60
Onega, Susana 8, 39
Onega, Susana and Jean-Michel Ganteau 36; "Introduction" 36; *see also* Ganteau and Onega
other(s), the 1–2, 4, 8, 37, 39, 41, 44, 81, 98, 100, 108, 111, 113, 131–32, 160, 162–63, 165, 199, 205, 209–11; encounter with 99; face (of) 1, 36, 54, 64, 209; time of 64, 69; vulnerability of 36, 108; *see also* kill; same; unjust
otherness 37, 41, 51, 60–61, 120–21, 131–32, 158, 164, 214; experience of 120; face of 120, intrusion of 64; recognition of 62; social 122; *see also* alterity

Page, Philip 145
Palladino, Mariangela 135, 145, 148n11
Patterson, Ian 202
Patterson, Orlando 138, 147n5; *Slavery and Social Death* 138
Pellicer-Ortín, Silvia 36–37
Perhamus, Lisa M and Clarence W. Joldersma 147n3
perpetrator(s) 36–37, 39, 41, 67, 153; *see also* trauma
plague 169–70; *see also* epidemic
poetics 51, 77, 88, 91, 93; of fragility 101; of fragmentation 89; Indigenous 88; of mourning 88; of ungrievability 164
politics 7, 37, 165–66; of attention 5; of hospitality 17, 21, 27, 33; homophobic 157, 165; neo-liberal 157; sexual 127
polygamy 19
poor, the 19, 32, 85, 87, 122–23
postcolonialism 36; *see also* colonialism

posthumanism 126; -ist perspective 215; -ist theory 82, 93n2; -ity 197
postmodern, critique 79–80; era 79; ethics 1; -ist deconstruction 42
power 17, 37, 62, 84, 91, 103, 122, 127, 203, 206; discourses of 37, 39–40, 44; economic 29; of fiction 209; of grievability 66, 205; performative 69; relations of 41, 98; social 6; sovereign 6–7, 76, 99, 192, 208; State 38, 156; structures 45; *see also* State
precarity 8, 37, 100, 108, 136, 189, 194, 199; eco- 98; environmental 104; of Jews 45; of the slaves' life 208
precariousness 5, 32–33, 36, 39, 49–51, 98–100, 103, 111–12, 188–89, 192, 210
prejudice(s) 6, 137; gender and class 9, 137; religious 137
prosopopoeia 146, 206
prostitute(s) 9, 23, 26–27, 40–42, 131, 135–38, 147n5

queer 156; ecologies 120; feminism 127; materialism 123; theory 123
Quilt of Names 154, 156

race(s) 16, 19, 20, 22, 77, 83, 93, 120, 123; ecologies of 122; inferior 16, 130; lesser 21; same- 32; superior 35
realism 24, 28, 90–91, 212; Aboriginal 9, 88, 93; magical 90–91
refugee(s) 39, 123; climate 9, 77, 82, 85, 90; crisis 36; policies 76
Reider, Noriko T. 24–25, 28
reincarnation 28, 30–31, 125
relationality 3, 60, 79, 86, 98, 100, 108, 111, 126, 130, 187, 195, 197, 211, 214; *see also* interrelationality
remains, the 154; animal 112–13n1; of beauty 159; of a defunct forest 198; geographical 158; loss and its 154, 158; spatial 154; types of 154–55; of (un-)grievability 166
remembering 55, 68, 103, 162, 165, 175–77, 179, 181; *see also* memory
repetition compulsion 67, 181; to repeat 56; *see also* acting out
responsibility 37, 49, 57, 60, 62, 78, 88, 98, 127; infinite 2; reader's 5, 36

226   Index

Ricœur, Paul 195; *La mémoire,
l'histoire, l'oubli* 195
Rigby, Kate 102, 104, 113n4
Rodríguez Magda, Rosa María 79–80;
see also transmodernity
Rose, Deborah Bird 82, 88
Rothberg, Michael 46, 77
Rotterdam 15, 23
Roynon, Tessa 139
Rutsky, R.L. 214

Salvan, Geneviève 56, 69
Samyn, Jeanette 120
Scott, Tim 75
Schulman, Sarah 170–71; *The
Gentrification of the Mind: Witness
to a Lost Imagination* 170
Schwetman, John David 188–89
Second World War 38–39, 41, 61; *see
also* World War II; WW2
secrecy 25, 136
secret 22, 44, 204; geological 96
Seiffert, Rachel 8, 36–54; *Afterwards*
37; *A Boy in Winter* 8, 36–54; *The
Dark Room* 37; *The Walk Home* 38
Sehgal, Parul 173–74
sentience 215; -ent and non- 214;
Country as -ent and sacred 81; -ent
being(s) 30, 87, 102; critter 205;
-ent (intelligent) humanoid robot(s)
208, 211, 213; -ent machines 202;
-ent status 90
Shakespeare, William 202–203; *The
Tempest* 203
Sharpe, Christina 147n3; *In the Wake*
147n3
Shelley, Mary 202–203
Shields, Rob 99, 104–105
Shintô 24; (spirit or) deity 24, 26;
dogma 26; Shrine 24–25; -ist
animal 26
singularity 51, 100, 197, 199;
collective 199; grievable 194; of the
lost 197
Silverman, Max 104–105
slave(s) 19–21, 32, 75, 130, 208;
master- dialectic 1; -prisoner of war
147n5; runaway 20; trade 18–19;
see also slavery; trader
slavery 19, 21, 130–31, 208; racism
and 7; *see also* slave
Smith, Adam 16, 22, 43; *The Wealth
of Nations* 22

Smith, Ali 8, 55–71; *The Accidental* 8,
55–71
Smith, Ben 9, 96–115; *Doggerland* 9,
96–115; *Sky Burials* 96
Stein, Gertrude 177
Social Darwinism 16, 21, 32; *see also*
Darwin
society(-ies), the 40, 50, 120–22,
133, 145, 170, 174, 176, 189,
191–94, 208; commercial 15–16,
18, 22, 24, 29; extra-European 16;
Indigenous 84; Irish 165; Japanese
26, 28, 32; materialistic 190,
197–98; normative 123, 178, 181;
technological 39, 51–52
Söderbäck, Fanny 129
Sontag, Susan 153, 167, 169–71,
174, 180; *Illness as Metaphor* 169;
*Illness as Metaphor & AIDS and Its
Metaphors* 169
Sophocles 130; *Antigone* 130;
Oedipus at Colonus 130; *Oedipus
the King* 130; *see also* Antigone
sovereignty 1, 3, 6–7, 17, 76, 83–84,
121, 127, 133, 138, 192, 205,
208, 210; of the Empire 21; post-
capitalist economic 7
spectrality 37, 59, 99, 100, 105,
169–70, 192; *see also* spectre
spectre(s) 70; Derridean 59, 62; of
incest 130, 133; *see also* ghost
Spinoza, Baruch 124
state(s) 6, 127, 129, 154, 205;
commercial 16; of emergency 3–4;
of exception 3, 7, 208–209; modern
3–4, 7, 19; Nazi 39; patriarchal 16;
(sovereign) power (of) 6, 38
Stengers, Isabelle 111, 113n7
stereotype 20, 24, 160, 172, 207
Stephenson, William 33
Stewart, Michael 9, 119–32; *Ill Will.
The Untold Story of Heathcliff* 9,
119–32
Stock, Adam 109, 113n6; *Modern
Dystopian Fiction and Political
Thought* 113n6
subhuman, the 187–201; frame of 10,
188, 190, 192, 195, 199; *see also*
humanoid; non-human
subject 55, 90, 144, 206–207, 210–11;
autonomous 1; dispossessed
107–108; grievable 16, 60, 209,
213; human 203–204, 211; invisible

143; positions 45, 50; ungrievable
127, 136; vulnerable 123
Sullivan, Jane 82, 87, 89
Surinam 20
survival 20, 30–31, 41, 96, 98, 107–
108, 111–12, 159, 179, 181, 187
Soviet(s), the 43; citizens 43; POWs
40; territory 40
Sweeney, Megan 139
symbiosis 106, 120

tale(s) 29, 96; ancient 25; apocalyptic
108; Dickensian 19; folk 48;
gothic 125; orally transmitted 25;
supernatural 25–26; truculent 21;
see also yarn
Tate, Andrew 108–109
temporality 56, 58, 60–61, 64, 69,
100, 103; apocalyptic 110; critical
110; diffuse 91; disarrayed 112;
mechanical 60; suspended 103;
timeless 64; truncated 56; uncertain
130; of working through 182; *see
also* time
terrorism 36, 169; -ist(s) 3; -ist attacks
3; *see also* 9/11; War on Terror
testament 75, 143–44
testimony (-ies) 143, 155–56, 166,
172, 177, 206; elegiac 154
Theroux, Marcel 202, 205
Third Battle of Ushant, the 20
(Third) Reich, the 38–42, 47, 52n1;
see also Nazi; Ukraine
Thomas, D.M. 41; *The White
Hotel* 41
Thorpe, Adam 41; *The Rules of
Perspective* 41
time(s), the 8–9, 40, 63–64, 66–69,
98, 104–105, 110, 125, 162–63,
213; ancient 104; and causality
68; circularity of 112; colonial 75,
92; contemporary 52, 77; dead
8, 55–71; Dream- 81; end of 66;
ethical approach to 56; feudal 7;
fixed 58; historical 206; human 61;
linear (-ity) (flow of) 100, 104, 110;
lived 58; lost 61; multiple 57; of
the other 64, 69; otherness of 64;
our 37, 83; passage (-ing) of 63, 87;
pre-gay 165; pre-industrial 210;
real 155; of socio political crisis 6;
(and) space(s) (and) (or) 63, 89, 91,
102, 104; tectonic 119; teleological

66; temporalised 61; transformative
power of 103; trauma 67; uchronic
62; of vulnerability 69; war- 187;
see also Agamben; temporality;
timeline; untimeliness
timeline(s) 57, 103, 171–72;
see also time
Tokugawa 16; *see also* Edo
Tóibín, Colm 9, 154, 161–66; *The
Blackwater Lightship* 9, 154,
161–66; "New Ways of Killing Your
Father" 165; *New Ways to Kill
Your Mother* 165
trader(s), VOC 19–21; -ing post 18;
see also slave
transmodernity 79–80, 93; -ern
critical trends 77; *see also*
Rodríguez Magda
trauma(s) (-ta) 10, 37, 40, 46, 55,
67, 69, 157, 173, 181, 207; (of)
AIDS 157, 174; cause by loss 55;
collective 153; criticism; and guilt
67; individual 52; limits of 173–74,
180; and loss 55; narratives 110,
173, 180; paradigm 36; perpetrator
67; personal 178; plot 173; post-
age 99; studies 36, 173; survivors
178; -ised by rape 89; -tic grief 171;
-tic loss 92; -ic memory(-ies) 55,
176, 181; -tic past 179; -tic shock
207; -tic weight 62; (-ic) (past)
event 153–54, 173, 179–80, 182;
time 67; unresolved 155; *see also*
memory
Troubles, the 37
Turing, Alan 207–208, 210, 212–13

Ukraine 41–43, 46–47; Nazi invasion
of 8, 41, 44; *see also* Nazi; Nazism;
Third Reich
Ukrainian(s), the 8, 38, 42–45, 48, 51;
auxiliary police 45; collaborators
45; Jewish and non-Jewish 44, 46;
names 49; plot 174; policemen 49;
soldiers 42; swamps 49; town 42;
village 44
uncanny, the 105; ecological 100, 102;
effect 105; parasite 33; supernatural
atmosphere 25; sublimity 102;
zone 100
ungrievability 3, 7–10, 15–27, 31–33,
105, 111–12, 131, 153–54, 157–58,
161, 163–64, 169, 173, 175,

228 *Index*

180–81, 190, 196, 205; essential 169; ethics of 17; gays' 166; *see also* grievability; (un-)grievability
(un-)grievability 7, 188, 191, 195–96, 205–209, 212; aporias of 181; construction of 173, 180; homophobic fantasy of 154, 156, 158, 164; poetics of 164; purifying 153, 161, 166; social construction of 180; *see also* grievability; ungrievability
Ungunmerr-Baumann, Miriam-Rose 89
untimeliness 212–13; *see also* time

Vernay, Jean-François 75–76
Vice, Sue 40–41; *Holocaust Fiction* 40
victim(s) 3, 19, 37, 41, 45, 83, 92, 106, 143, 153, 163; AIDS 3, 9, 154, 156, 164, 178, 190, 206, 211; Holocaust 41, 155; of testimonial injstice 146
violence 3–4, 6, 19, 32, 37, 39, 44–46, 49, 52, 70, 100, 109, 120, 122, 127, 129, 131–33, 153–54, 157, 178, 188–90; arbitrary 81; institutionalised 52; of law 106; legal 21, 192; of liberalism 7; military 68; normative 107, 192; perpetuation of 4; physical 122; social 6; structural 6
visibility 6, 24, 31, 140, 143, 192–93, 198, 211, 213; frame of 24; hyper-139; *see also* invisibility
VOC, the (Vereenigde Oost-Indische Compagnie) 15, 18, 20; officers 19, 22, 32; traders 19–21; *see also* Dutch East India Company
Vogt, Peter 16
voices(s) the 39, 45, 107, 143–44, 147, 148n13, 157; and agency 107; authorial 45; deprived of 193; different 39, 105; elegiac 156; external 88; human 101–102; Indigenous 75; -less 146; male 142; narrative 178; no 143; oppositional 51; plurality of 88; solitary 93; suppressed 172, 192; toneless 143; vindicatory 166
Voltaire (François-Marie Arouet) 16
vulnerability 1, 3, 5–7, 32–33, 36–38, 45–46, 48–49, 51, 58, 60, 62–64, 66, 68–70, 79–81, 86, 98–101, 105,

107, 111, 119–20, 123, 132–33, 157, 175, 187, 195, 197, 199, 203, 207, 209–11, 215; corporeal 187; ethics of 36; human (fragility and) 9–10, 17, 27, 36, 62; of kinship norms 9; to loss 3; ontological (and existential) 3, 36; of the other 36, 108; paradigm 36; physical 3, 175; relational 120; social 3

Waanji nation 75
Wagner, Richard 89; *Lohengrin* 89
Walker, Drew 100
Wallace, Cynthia 135, 148n13
Walshe, Eibhear 162, 164
war(s) 18, 21, 46, 62–65, 77, 175–77, 187–89, 206, 208; against terrorism 169; casualties 66; forces of 175; in colonial Kenya 37; Napoleonic 23, 29; novel 65; slave-prisoner of 147n5; the two World 51; US 169; victims 62, 65
War of the Second Coalition 16
War on Terror 3, 169, 180; see 9/11
warfare 3, 17, 36, 45
Warhol, Robyn R. 136, 143
Warner, Alan 96–97, 108
Watkin, Christopher 2
Watney, Simon 153, 165; *Practices of Freedom: Selected Writings on HIV/ AIDS* 153; *see also* AIDS
Weil, Kari 214
Wells, H.G. 190; *The Time Machine* 190
Wen-Ching, Ho 144
what matters 8, 106, 139, 187, 194, 196; *see also* who matters
White, Edmund 153–54
Whitehead, Anne 55, 190–91; *see also* empathy
who matters 7–8, 145, 196, 208; *see also* what matters
Winch, Tara June 75
Winterson, Jeanette 136; *Written on the Body* 136
Winton, Tim 93n1; *Island Home: A Landscape Memoir* 93n1
witness(es) 6, 9, 41, 45, 174; Jehovah's 40
Woloch, Alex 135, 147n1, 147n2
Wood, James 157, 159
world(s) 8, 16, 27–28, 31, 44, 78–79, 81, 83, 90–91, 93, 105–106, 165,

170, 174, 179, 187; banished people of 86; beauty in 87; changed 76; counterfeit 140; cultures 79; in decay 98; decayed 109; of the deceased 106; delusive 159; dystopian 108, 138, 188, 195; external 107, 210; First 65, 189; (pre-)gay under- 155–56; globalised 17, 92; of grief 99; history 8, 15–16, 212; (of ordinary) human(s) 30, 192; idealised 158; of illusion 193; Indigenous (Australian) thought- 80, 82; Japanese 24; of the living 8; material 99, 214; mattering of 124; modern 109; more-than-human 98; natural 9, 77, 86–87, 92, 105, 111; new 203; novels 90; Old 17; parallel 192; peaceful and prosperous 38; phantom-like 208; 's population 90; post-apocalyptic 97, 109; of resemblances 126; -science 212; self and 112; of the spirits and the ancestors 86; submerged 111; of swans 92; of unwanted people 83; texts and traditions 77; Third 178; vegetal and animal 85; Western 7

World War I 177
World War Two 8, 192; *see also* Second World War; WW2
working through 10, 181–82
wound(s) 21, 103, 107; bodily 146; emotional 107; exposed to 111; and grief 106
Wright, Alexis 8, 75–95; *Carpentaria* 75, 91–92; *Plains of Promise* 92; *The Swan Book* 8–9, 75–95
WW2 62, 65; *see also* Second World War; World War Two

Yanagihara, Hanya 171; *A Little Life: A Novel* 171
yarn(s) 20; reveries and 20; (traders' and) sailors' 20, 25; truculent 32; *see also* tale
Yates, Frances A. 31
Yebra, José Maria 157, 160–61, 164
Yep, Gust A. 154

zoē 7, 76, 86, 122, 126; *see also* Agamben; bare life; *bíos*
Žižek, Slavoj 2

Taylor & Francis eBooks

www.taylorfrancis.com

A single destination for eBooks from Taylor & Francis with increased functionality and an improved user experience to meet the needs of our customers.

90,000+ eBooks of award-winning academic content in Humanities, Social Science, Science, Technology, Engineering, and Medical written by a global network of editors and authors.

TAYLOR & FRANCIS EBOOKS OFFERS:

A streamlined experience for our library customers

A single point of discovery for all of our eBook content

Improved search and discovery of content at both book and chapter level

REQUEST A FREE TRIAL
support@taylorfrancis.com